Author
Wing Shing Ma

Translators
Peter Vlach
Duncan Cameron

Editor
Jeffrey Macey

Production Editor
Yuki Chung

Production Artists
Li-Cheng Yu
Hung-Ya Lin

US Cover Design
Yuki Chung

Lettering Fonts
Comicraft
www.comicbookfonts.com

President
Robin Kuo

S0-CFO-834

www.comicsworld.com

English translation by
ComicsOne Corporation 2002

Publisher
ComicsOne Corp.
48531 Warm Springs Blvd., Suite 408
Fremont, CA 94539
www.ComicsOne.com

First Edition: May 2002
ISBN 1-58899-145-8

The "chess form" head figure is mark of and used under
licence from Magnum Consultants Limited.

Preface to Storm Riders
About the Author

Wing Shing Ma, born in Hong Kong in 1961, showed a deep love for painting from a very young age. In 1976, at the age of 14 he read in a newspaper about positions available as an apprentice in comic book art. Determined, he sent in his submission. This step marked his official entrance into the Manga profession.

After entering the comics world, he spent his time moving around between different Manga companies, such as Ru Xi Bao, Jin Manga (Gold Manga) and Xin Lang Chao. In the beginning, Wing Shing Ma worked only as an assistant, but before long he had published some of his own work. His first creation was formally published in 1976 under the title, *Daydream* (Bai Ri Meng). However, it wasn't until the year of 1982, when Ma formally joined the Jade Group Publishing Company Ltd., that he began working on the famous Manga novel, *Chinese Hero*.

By the middle of 1983, he had already leaped into the highest levels of the Manga market. Apart from his market success, Wing Shing Ma had established a new and distinctive Manga style. This realistic style, painted with exquisite brush strokes and detail, allowed for a deeply expressive form of Manga. From that day forward, production of Manga comics would forever be changed due to the impact of Ma's original approach. In the beginning of 1989, Ma left Jade Publishing, and in July of the same year established Jonesky Limited, which began publishing *Storm Riders, Black Panther,* and *Heaven Sword and Dragon Sabre,* a Manga trilogy, as well as a fourth book, *Punishment from the Heavens.* By August 2000, Ma had released what to this day still stands as Hong Kong's most important and cutting-edge Manga comic. At present, *Storm Riders* has already been in publication for more than ten years. From the beginning, and throughout the entirety of those ten years, it has remained Hong Kong's foremost classic Manga novel. Apart from its success in Hong Kong, it is also a book that is in great demand throughout many countries of the world such as Taiwan, Malaysia, Singapore, Korea, Thailand, Mainland China, America and Canada.

Besides the *Storm Riders* Manga, *Storm Riders* has also given birth to a wide array of peripheral products that bear likenesses from the *Storm Riders* Manga, such as a line of letter openers based on Storm Riders' weapons, T-shirts, wrist watches, action figures, pens, paper fans, etc. Also, in 1998 a *Storm Riders* video game, as well as the *Storm Riders* movie was released. The *Storm Riders* movie achieved great box office success in Hong Kong, with box office sales exceeding 40 million Hong Kong dollars. Also in the works are a *Storm Riders* television series as well as a *Storm Riders* Net-based video game that will push the boundaries of the genre.

Wing Shing Ma has not been restricted to creating Mangas. He has also published many other books and periodicals, such as Manga novels, hardcover Manga novels and collections of individual artwork, as well as Chinese watercolor paintings. Also, in 1993 he began to import Japanese Mangas for translation into Chinese. His publication of a large number of high quality Japanese Mangas gave Hong Kong Manga readers the opportunity to come into contact with many different types of Manga genres, thus furthering diversification in the Manga market.

Apart from Hong Kong Manga, he has been invited many times to attend Manga exhibitions and conferences in Canada, Taiwan, Singapore and Macau, where he always receives an enthusiastic reception. Wing Shing Ma's success has shown the Hong Kong Manga world that a local product can most certainly reach the foreign marketplace and indeed achieve unprecedented success.

Relationship Chart

Wen Motley: Conquer's attendant. He discovers Conquer's scheme to divide Cloud and Wind and compiles a series of documents as evidence. To ensure Wen's silence, Conquer sends Frost to kill him and destroy the letters he has collected.
Technique: Flowing Sleeves, Swirling Sleeves, Dancing Sleeves

Conquer: Exceptionally powerful martial artist with plans of controlling the World Fighting Association. He takes on Wind and Cloud as his disciples in order to fulfill his destiny.
Technique: Chi of Triplication Returns to One, Triplication Fingers

Wen Motley ——————— # Conquer

Frost: Long-time disciple of Conquer. Married to Conquer's adopted daughter Kong-Chi. Leader of the Frost Corps: an elite fighting unit which is a part of the World Fighting Association.
Technique: Sky Frost Fist

Cloud: Son of Master Ho and disciple of Conquer. Leader of the Cloud Corps: an elite fighting unit which is part of the World Fighting Association.
Technique: Repelling Palm
Weapon: Ultimate Sword (briefly, Unrivaled Sword)

Wind: Disciple of Conquer and leader of the Wind Corps: an elite fighting unit which is part of the World Fighting Association. Son of Master Nie.
Techniques: Ice Heart Knack, Deity of Wind Kick
Weapon: Inherits the Snowy Saber

Kong-Chi

Kong-Chi: Adopted daughter of Conquer and wife of Frost, though her heart lies elsewhere.

Frost

Cloud
(Bu-Jing-Yun)

Wind
(Nie-Fong)

Duan-Lang

Sword Saint

DuGu Ming

Wu Buddha

Duan-Lang: Son of Master Duan. Rescued from death by Conquer as a child, he was ultimately forced to flee from Conquer for reasons not yet revealed. He teams up with Sword Saint, DuGu Ming, and Conquer's other enemies in order to seek revenge.
Weapon: Inherits the Flame Kylin Sword

Sword Saint: DuGu Ming's uncle and a Kung Fu master. He returns from retirement to help DuGu Ming defeat Conquer.
Technique: Sword Skill 21, Sword Skill 22, Sword Skill 23
Weapon: Unrivaled Sword

DuGu Ming: Son of the master of Peerless Castle, DuGu Yifang. He is the only survivor of Conquer's assault on Peerless Castle. He seeks revenge on Conquer for killing his father.
Technique: Dragon Kick

Wu Buddha: Friend of DuGu Yifang's family and a Kung Fu master. He aids DuGu Ming in his quest for revenge.
Technique: Buddha Palms

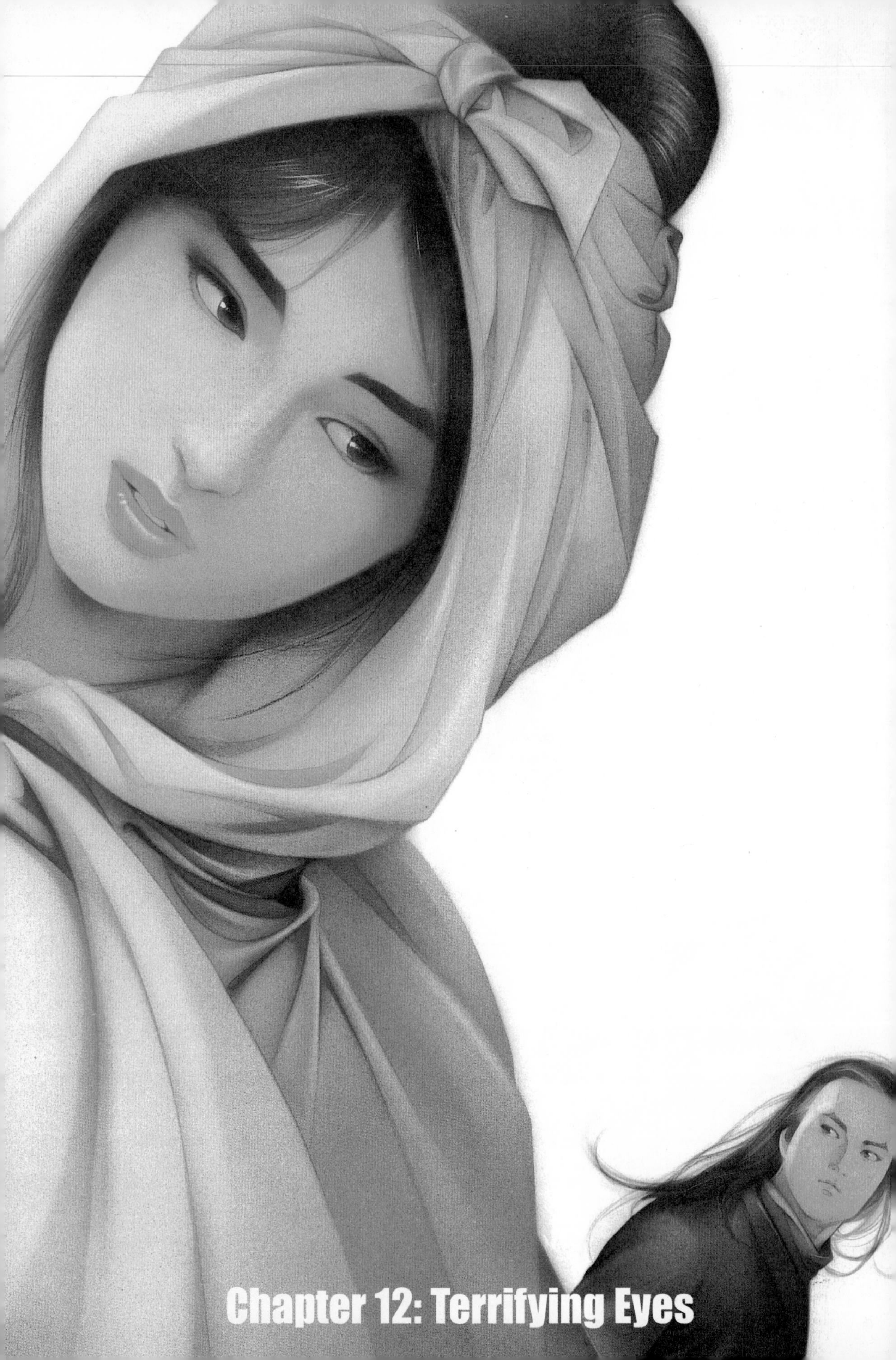

Chapter 12: Terrifying Eyes

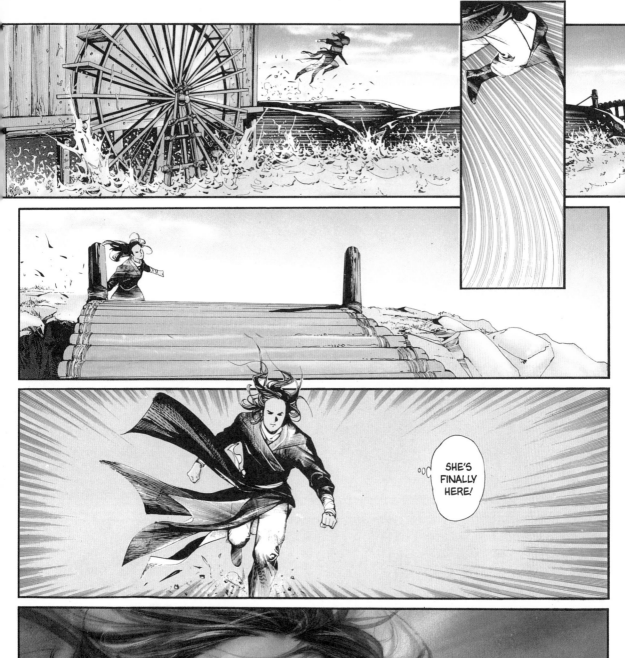

SHE'S FINALLY HERE!

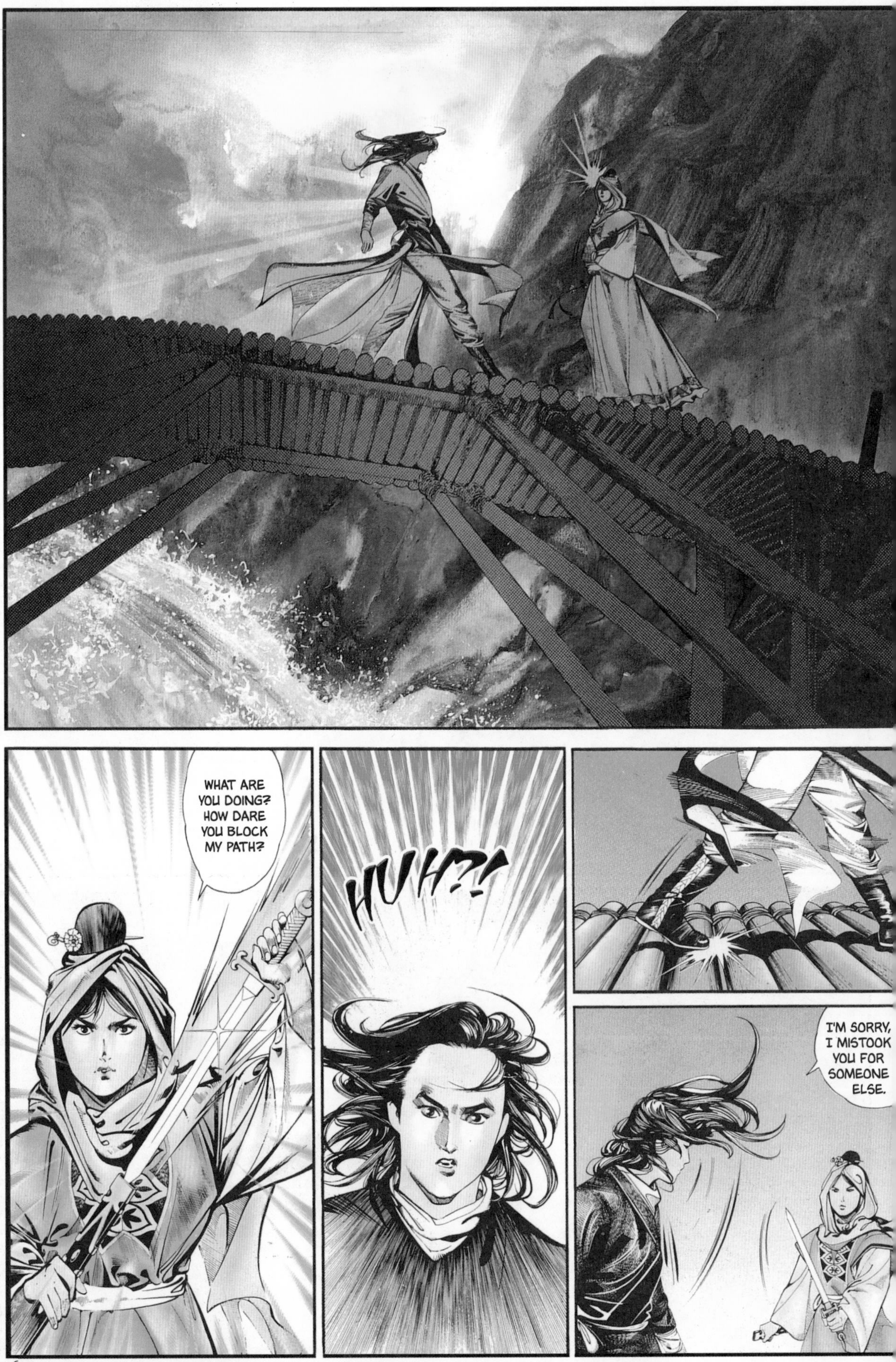
WHAT ARE YOU DOING? HOW DARE YOU BLOCK MY PATH?
HUH?!
I'M SORRY, I MISTOOK YOU FOR SOMEONE ELSE.

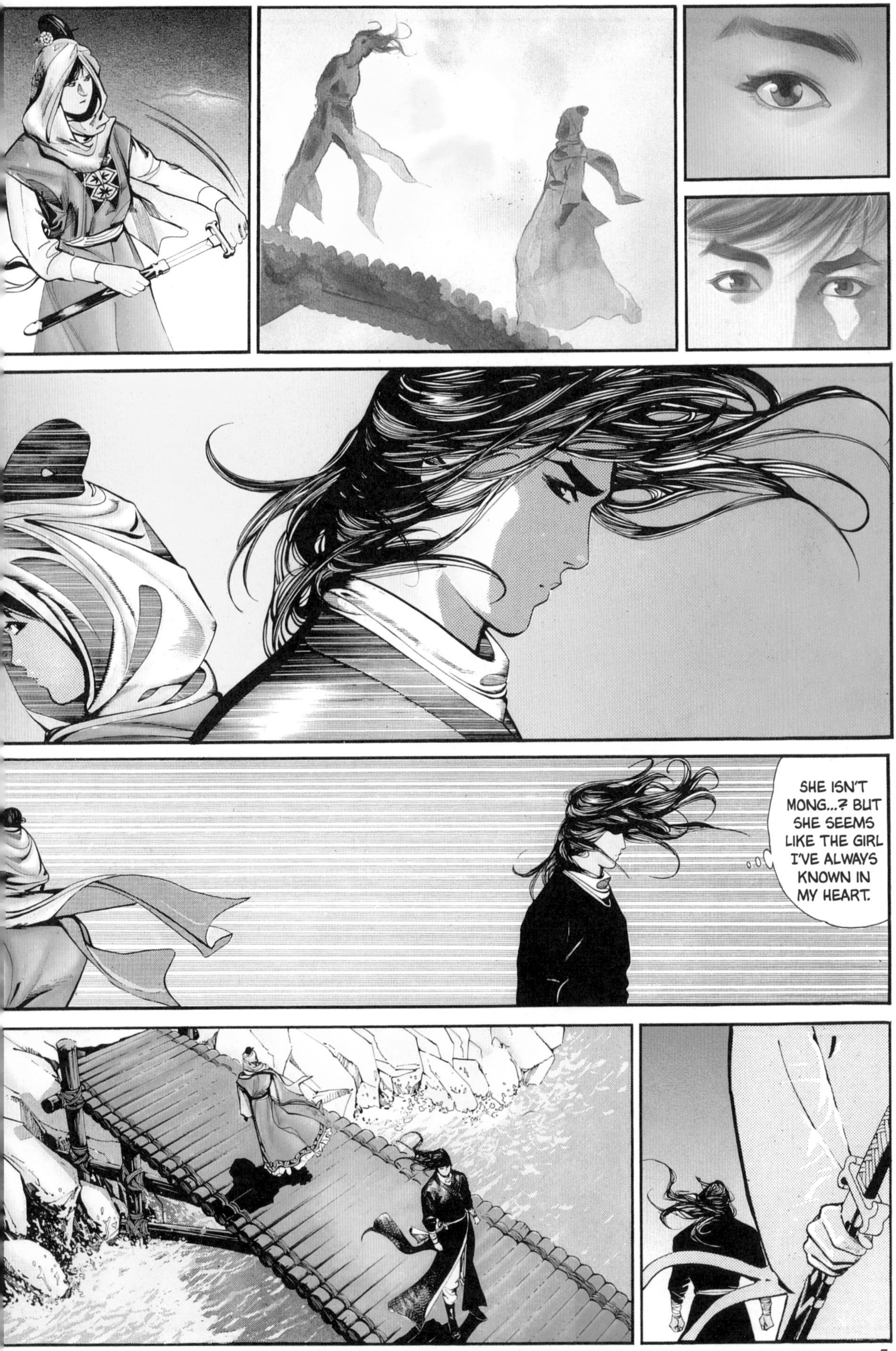
SHE ISN'T MONG...? BUT SHE SEEMS LIKE THE GIRL I'VE ALWAYS KNOWN IN MY HEART.

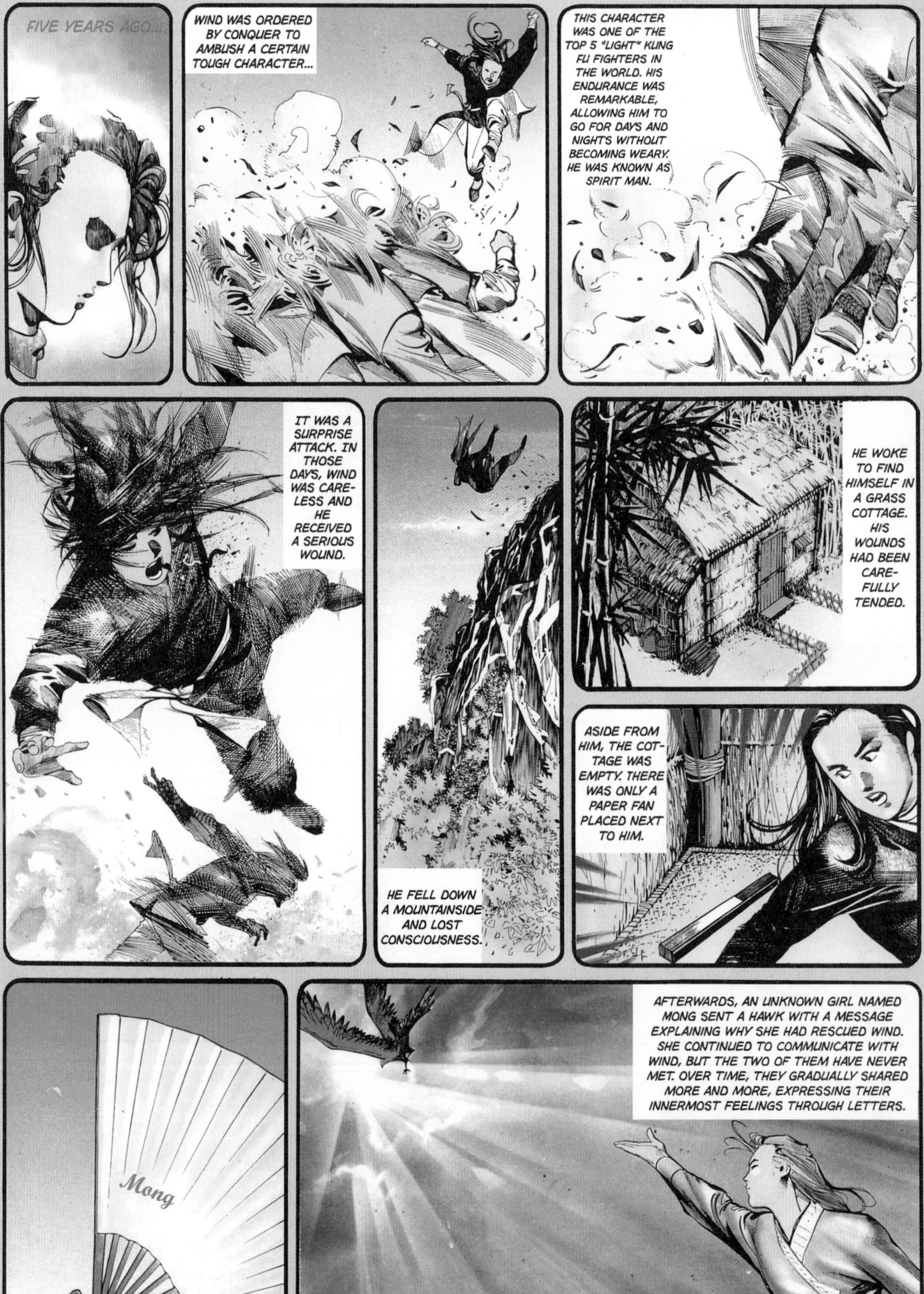
FIVE YEARS AGO...
WIND WAS ORDERED BY CONQUER TO AMBUSH A CERTAIN TOUGH CHARACTER...
THIS CHARACTER WAS ONE OF THE TOP 5 "LIGHT" KUNG FU FIGHTERS IN THE WORLD. HIS ENDURANCE WAS REMARKABLE, ALLOWING HIM TO GO FOR DAYS AND NIGHTS WITHOUT BECOMING WEARY. HE WAS KNOWN AS SPIRIT MAN.
IT WAS A SURPRISE ATTACK. IN THOSE DAYS, WIND WAS CARELESS AND HE RECEIVED A SERIOUS WOUND.
HE FELL DOWN A MOUNTAINSIDE AND LOST CONSCIOUSNESS.
HE WOKE TO FIND HIMSELF IN A GRASS COTTAGE. HIS WOUNDS HAD BEEN CAREFULLY TENDED.
ASIDE FROM HIM, THE COTTAGE WAS EMPTY. THERE WAS ONLY A PAPER FAN PLACED NEXT TO HIM.
Mong
AFTERWARDS, AN UNKNOWN GIRL NAMED MONG SENT A HAWK WITH A MESSAGE EXPLAINING WHY SHE HAD RESCUED WIND. SHE CONTINUED TO COMMUNICATE WITH WIND, BUT THE TWO OF THEM HAVE NEVER MET. OVER TIME, THEY GRADUALLY SHARED MORE AND MORE, EXPRESSING THEIR INNERMOST FEELINGS THROUGH LETTERS.

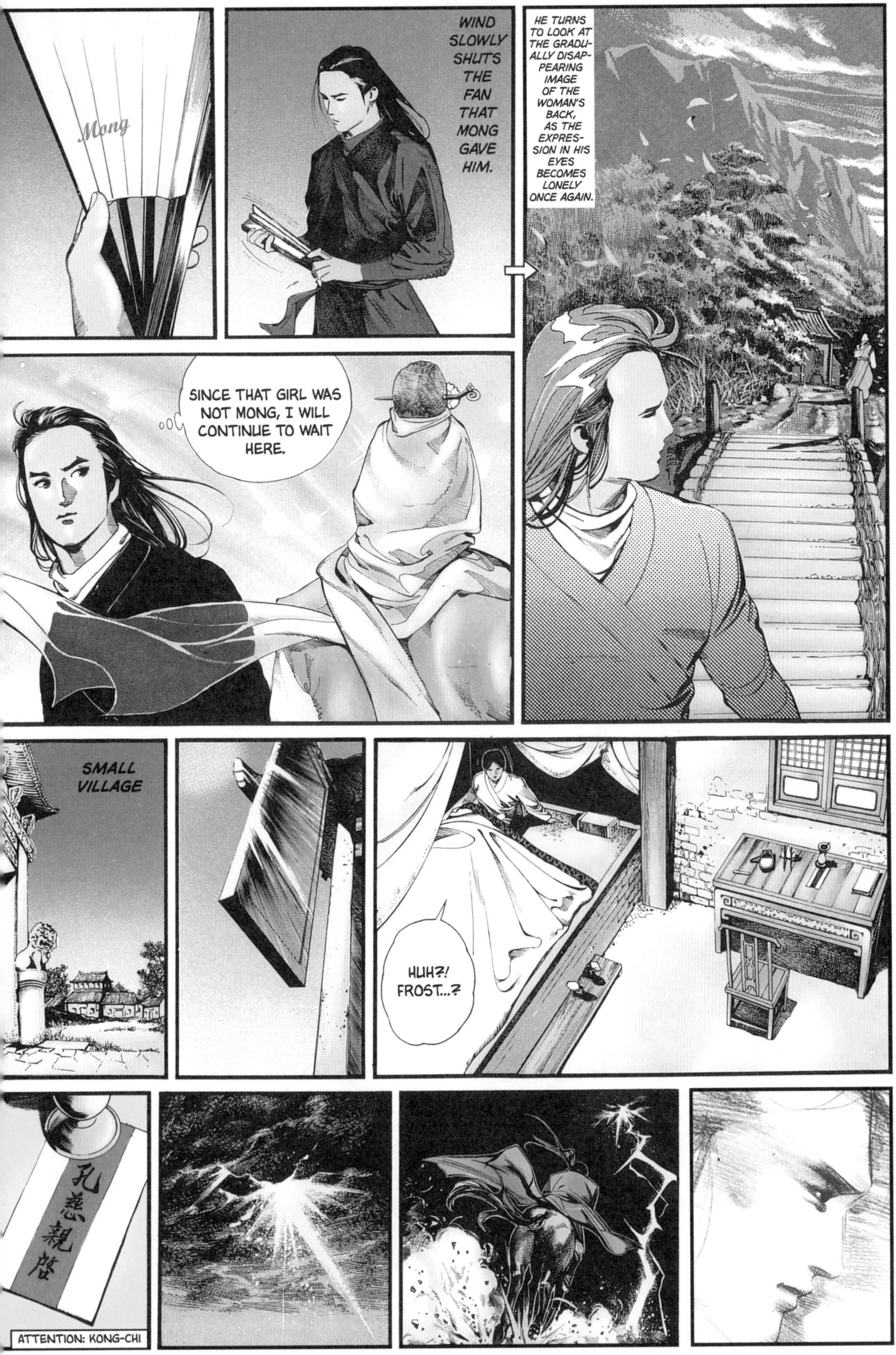

Mong
WIND SLOWLY SHUTS THE FAN THAT MONG GAVE HIM.
HE TURNS TO LOOK AT THE GRADUALLY DISAPPEARING IMAGE OF THE WOMAN'S BACK, AS THE EXPRESSION IN HIS EYES BECOMES LONELY ONCE AGAIN.
SINCE THAT GIRL WAS NOT MONG, I WILL CONTINUE TO WAIT HERE.
SMALL VILLAGE
HUH?! FROST...?
孔慈親啓
ATTENTION: KONG-CHI

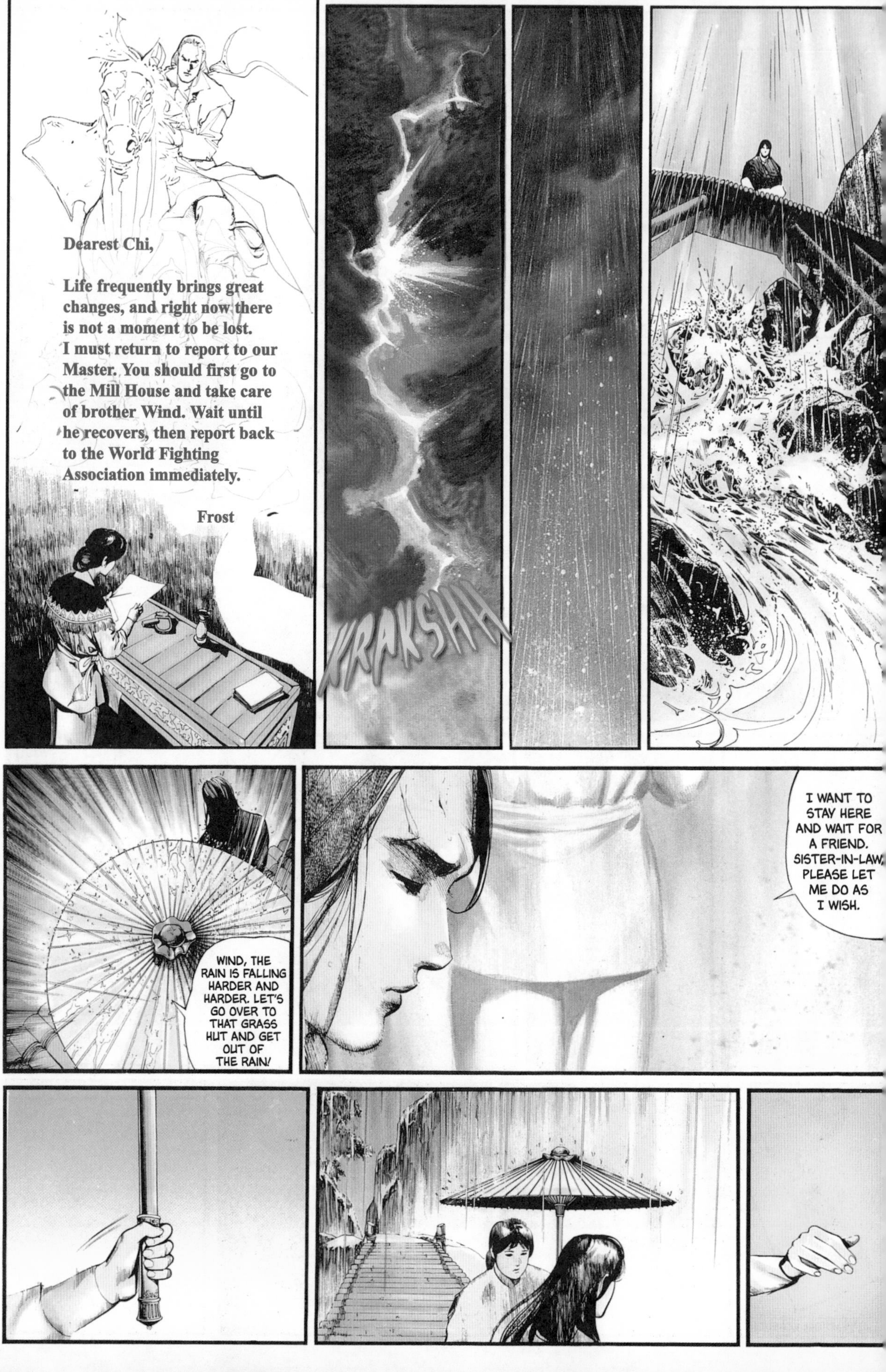
Dearest Chi,
Life frequently brings great changes, and right now there is not a moment to be lost. I must return to report to our Master. You should first go to the Mill House and take care of brother Wind. Wait until he recovers, then report back to the World Fighting Association immediately.
Frost
KRAKSHH
WIND, THE RAIN IS FALLING HARDER AND HARDER. LET'S GO OVER TO THAT GRASS HUT AND GET OUT OF THE RAIN!
I WANT TO STAY HERE AND WAIT FOR A FRIEND. SISTER-IN-LAW, PLEASE LET ME DO AS I WISH.

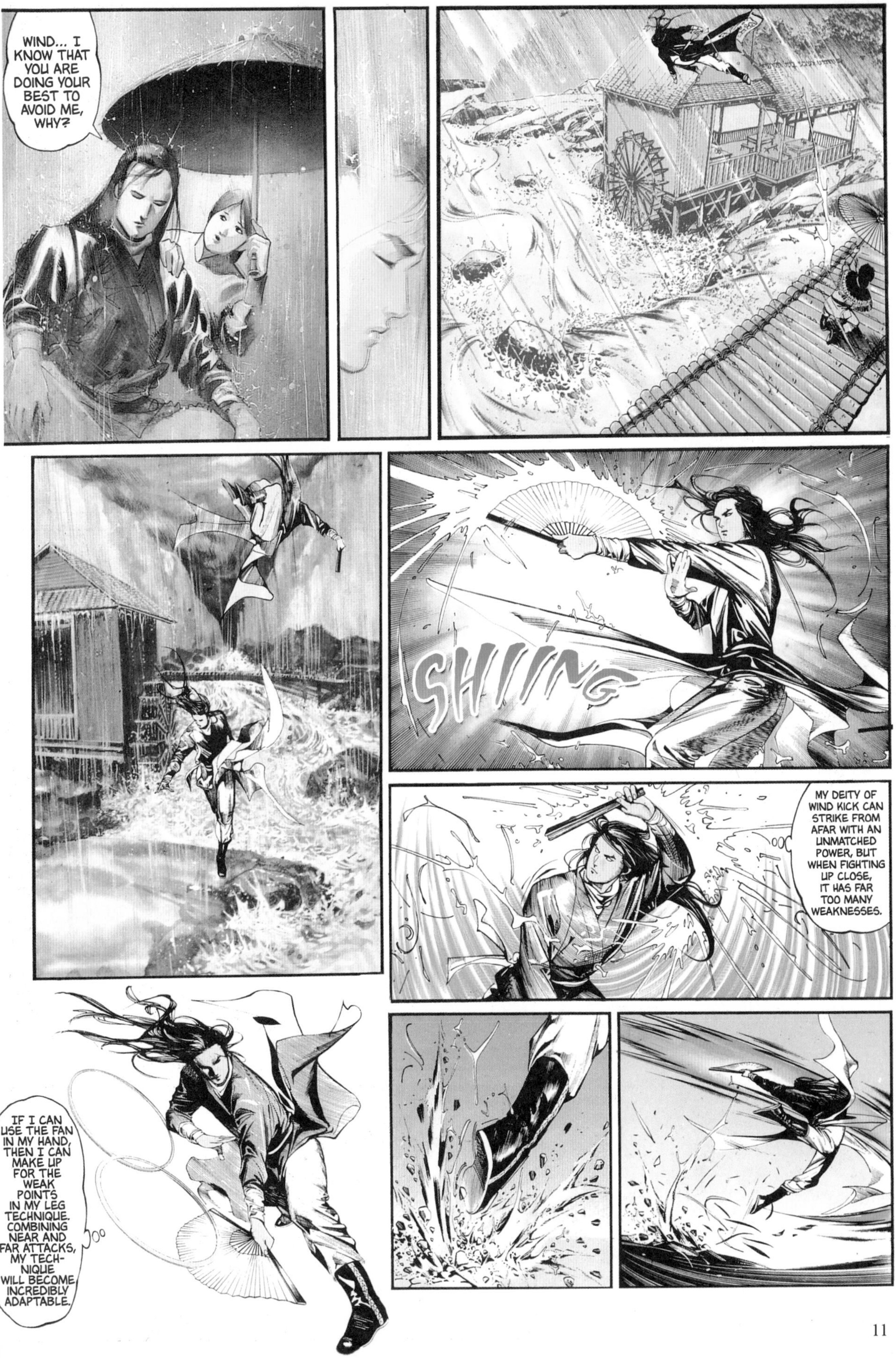
WIND... I KNOW THAT YOU ARE DOING YOUR BEST TO AVOID ME, WHY?
SHIING
MY DEITY OF WIND KICK CAN STRIKE FROM AFAR WITH AN UNMATCHED POWER, BUT WHEN FIGHTING UP CLOSE, IT HAS FAR TOO MANY WEAKNESSES.
IF I CAN USE THE FAN IN MY HAND, THEN I CAN MAKE UP FOR THE WEAK POINTS IN MY LEG TECHNIQUE. COMBINING NEAR AND FAR ATTACKS, MY TECHNIQUE WILL BECOME INCREDIBLY ADAPTABLE.

THAT GUY HAS ALREADY BEEN OUT THERE FOR A DAY AND A NIGHT WITHOUT EATING OR DRINKING. I WONDER WHAT'S GOT HIM SO WORKED UP.

HMM... IT'S STRANGE. HOLDING THAT FAN AND DANCING AROUND LIKE HE'S CRAZY... BUT HIS TECHNIQUE IS TRULY NOT BAD.

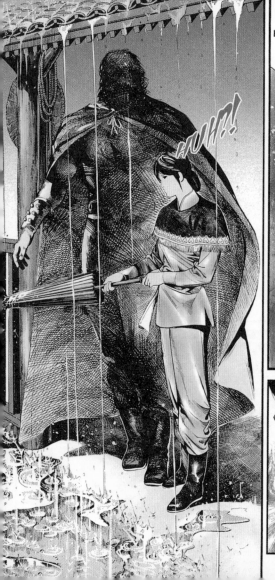

HUH!

YOU... HOW DID YOU KNOW THAT I WOULD COME HERE?

EVER SINCE I WAS SEPARATED FROM YOU I HAVE FOUND IT HARD TO BEAR. YOU ARE ALWAYS ON MY MIND.

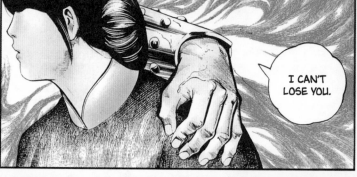

I CAN'T LOSE YOU.

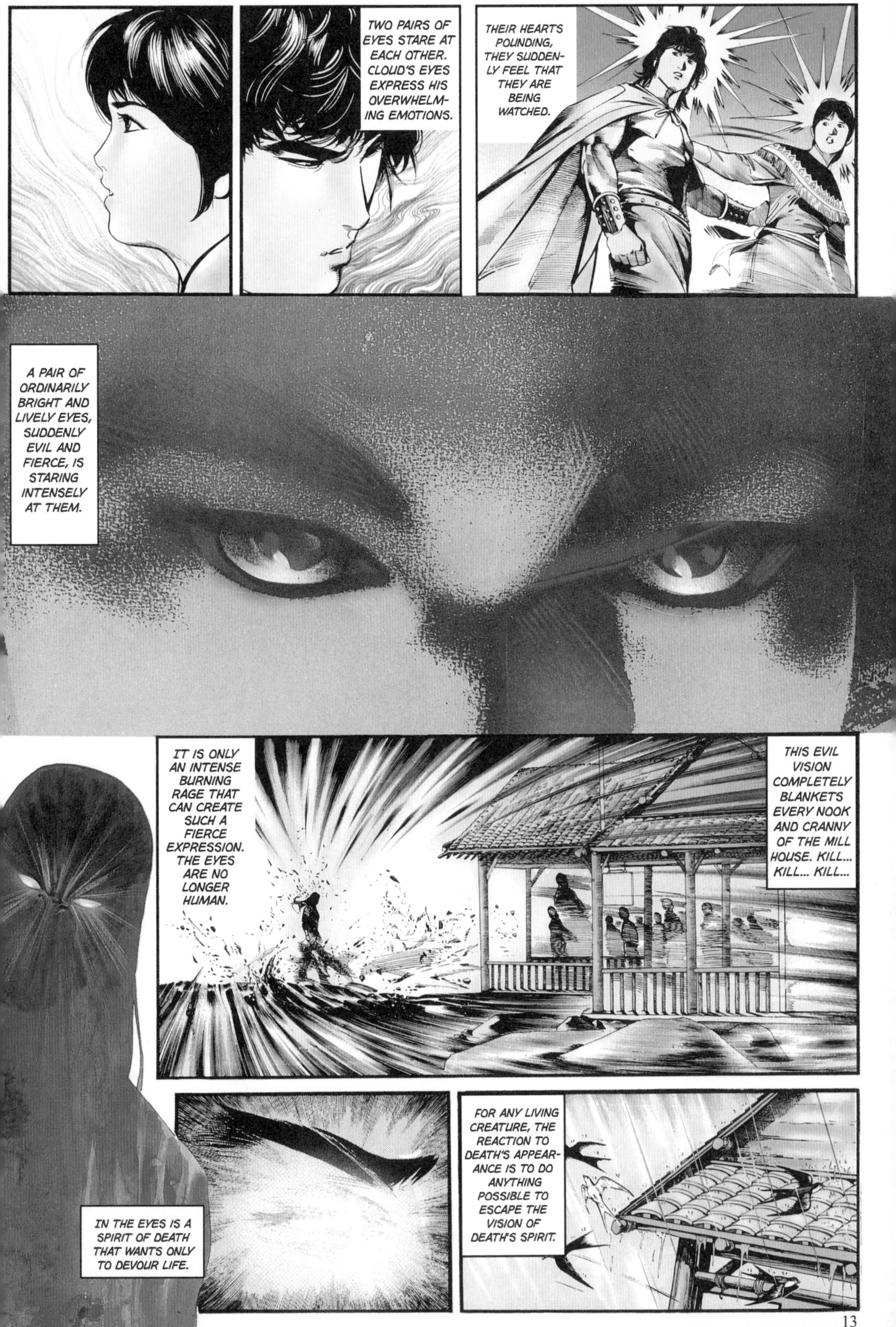
TWO PAIRS OF EYES STARE AT EACH OTHER. CLOUD'S EYES EXPRESS HIS OVERWHELMING EMOTIONS.
THEIR HEARTS POUNDING, THEY SUDDENLY FEEL THAT THEY ARE BEING WATCHED.
A PAIR OF ORDINARILY BRIGHT AND LIVELY EYES, SUDDENLY EVIL AND FIERCE, IS STARING INTENSELY AT THEM.
IT IS ONLY AN INTENSE BURNING RAGE THAT CAN CREATE SUCH A FIERCE EXPRESSION. THE EYES ARE NO LONGER HUMAN.
THIS EVIL VISION COMPLETELY BLANKETS EVERY NOOK AND CRANNY OF THE MILL HOUSE. KILL... KILL... KILL...
IN THE EYES IS A SPIRIT OF DEATH THAT WANTS ONLY TO DEVOUR LIFE.
FOR ANY LIVING CREATURE, THE REACTION TO DEATH'S APPEARANCE IS TO DO ANYTHING POSSIBLE TO ESCAPE THE VISION OF DEATH'S SPIRIT.

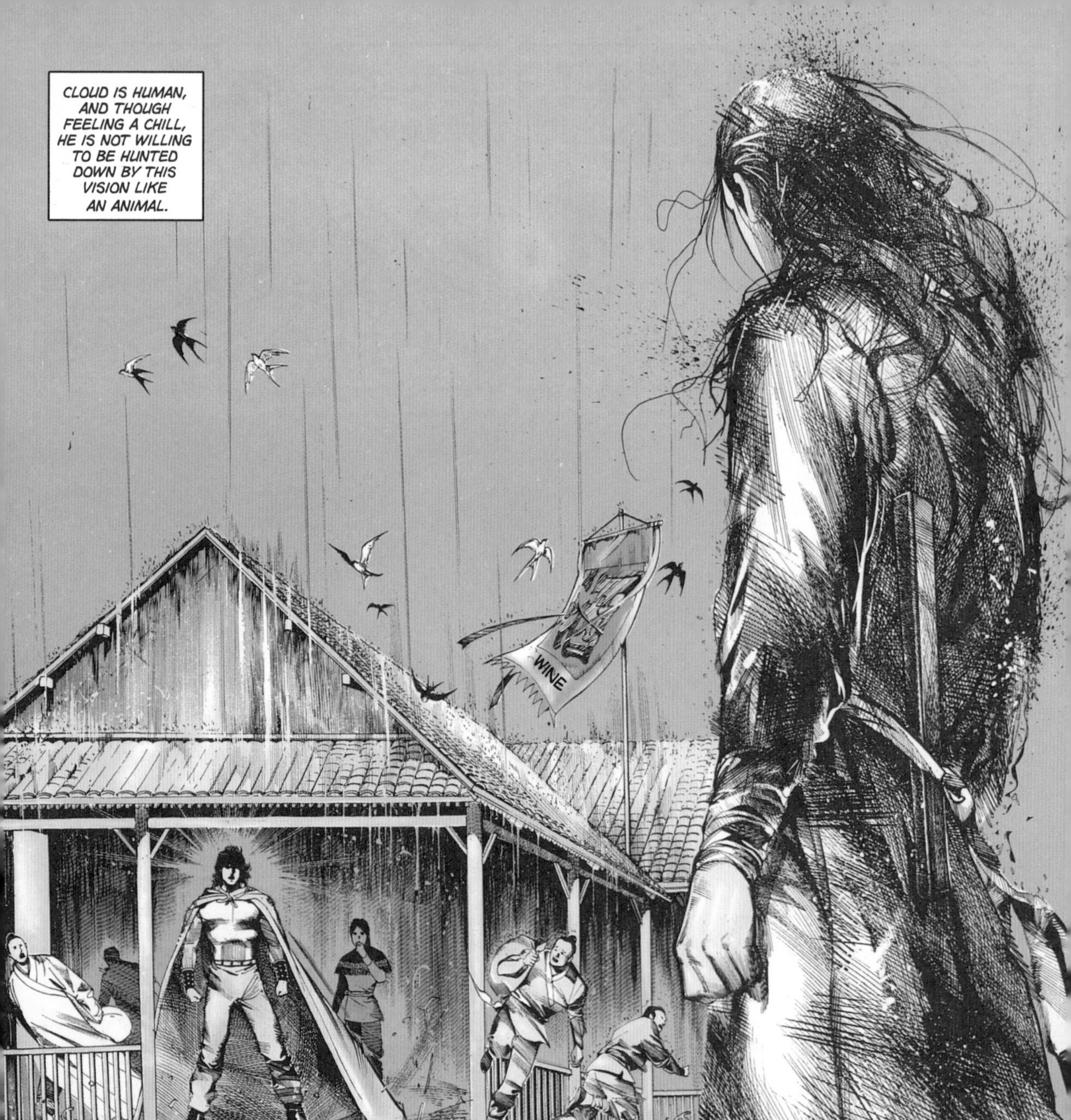
CLOUD IS HUMAN, AND THOUGH FEELING A CHILL, HE IS NOT WILLING TO BE HUNTED DOWN BY THIS VISION LIKE AN ANIMAL.
WINE

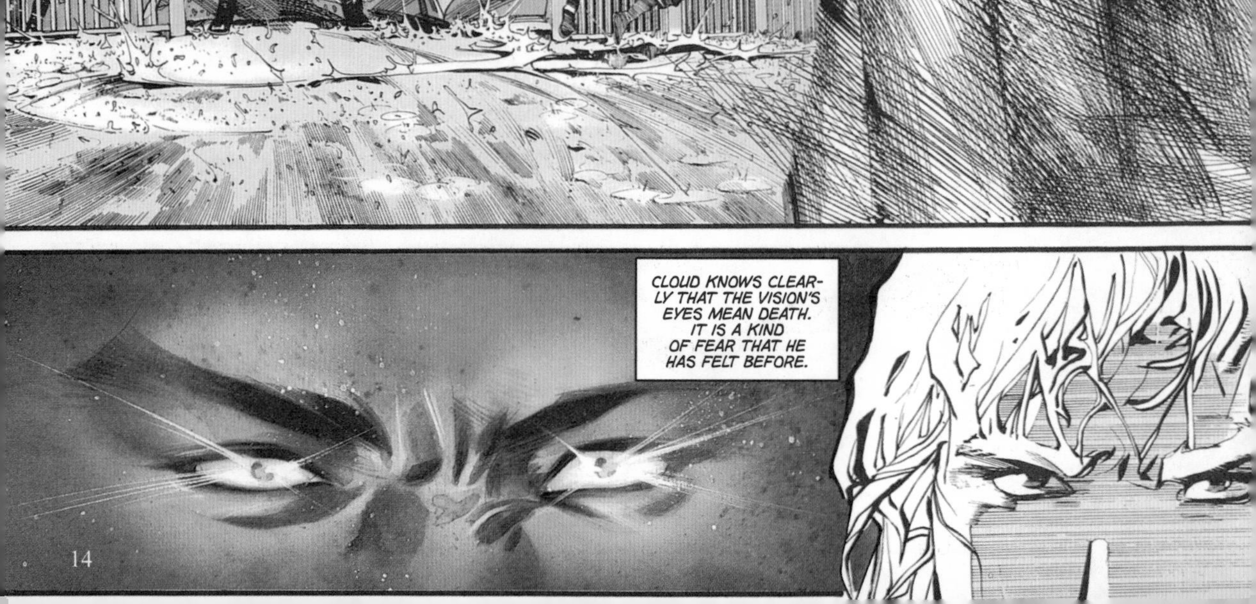
CLOUD KNOWS CLEARLY THAT THE VISION'S EYES MEAN DEATH. IT IS A KIND OF FEAR THAT HE HAS FELT BEFORE.

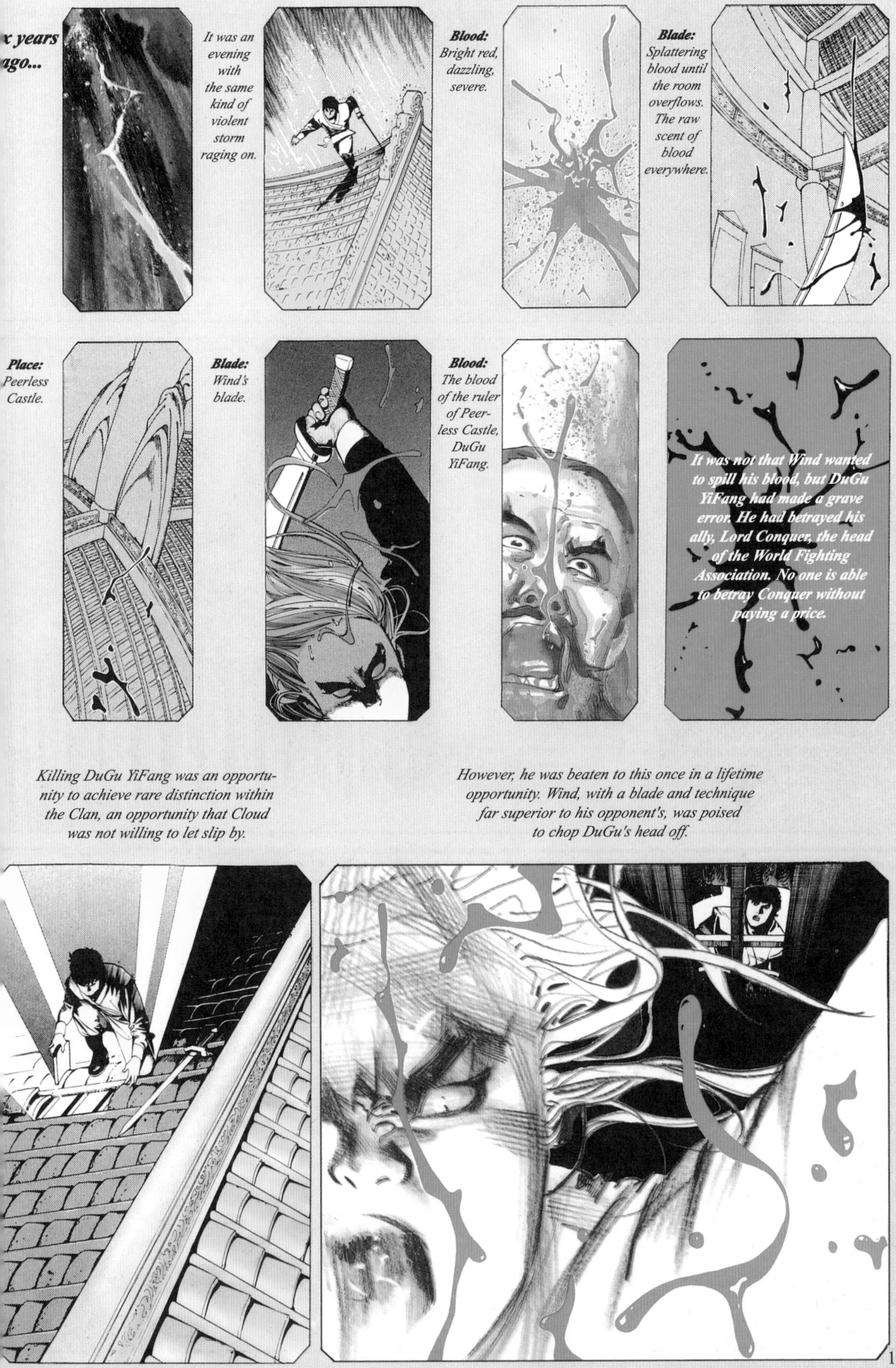
x years ago...
It was an evening with the same kind of violent storm raging on.
Blood: Bright red, dazzling, severe.
Blade: Splattering blood until the room overflows. The raw scent of blood everywhere.
Place: Peerless Castle.
Blade: Wind's blade.
Blood: The blood of the ruler of Peer-less Castle, DuGu YiFang.
It was not that Wind wanted to spill his blood, but DuGu YiFang had made a grave error. He had betrayed his ally, Lord Conquer, the head of the World Fighting Association. No one is able to betray Conquer without paying a price.
Killing DuGu YiFang was an opportunity to achieve rare distinction within the Clan, an opportunity that Cloud was not willing to let slip by.
However, he was beaten to this once in a lifetime opportunity. Wind, with a blade and technique far superior to his opponent's, was poised to chop DuGu's head off.

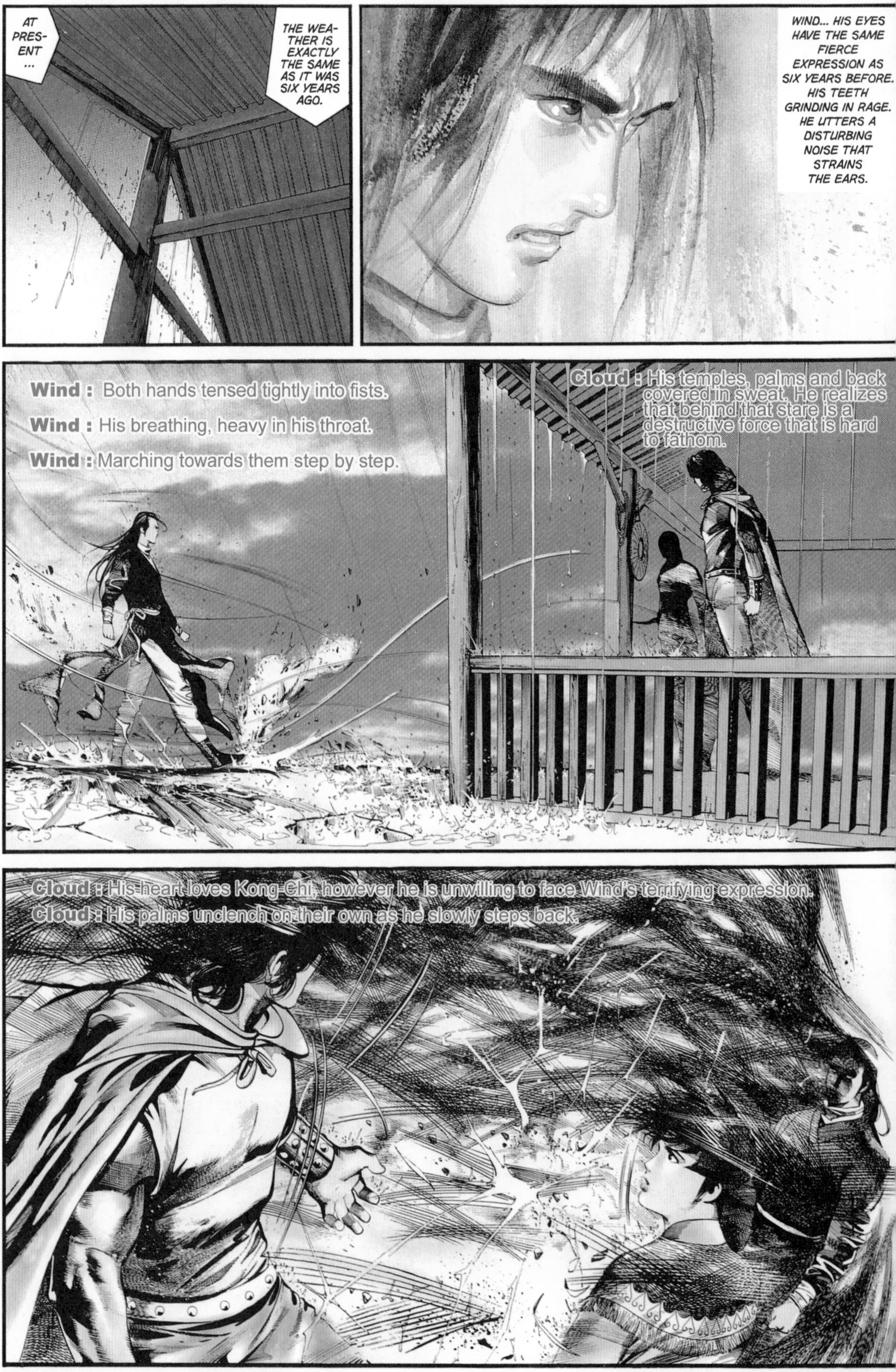
AT PRESENT ...
THE WEATHER IS EXACTLY THE SAME AS IT WAS SIX YEARS AGO.
WIND... HIS EYES HAVE THE SAME FIERCE EXPRESSION AS SIX YEARS BEFORE. HIS TEETH GRINDING IN RAGE. HE UTTERS A DISTURBING NOISE THAT STRAINS THE EARS.
Wind : Both hands tensed tightly into fists.
Wind : His breathing, heavy in his throat.
Wind : Marching towards them step by step.
Cloud : His temples, palms and back covered in sweat. He realizes that behind that stare is a destructive force that is hard to fathom.
Cloud : His heart loves Kong-Chi, however he is unwilling to face Wind's terrifying expression.
Cloud : His palms unclench on their own as he slowly steps back.

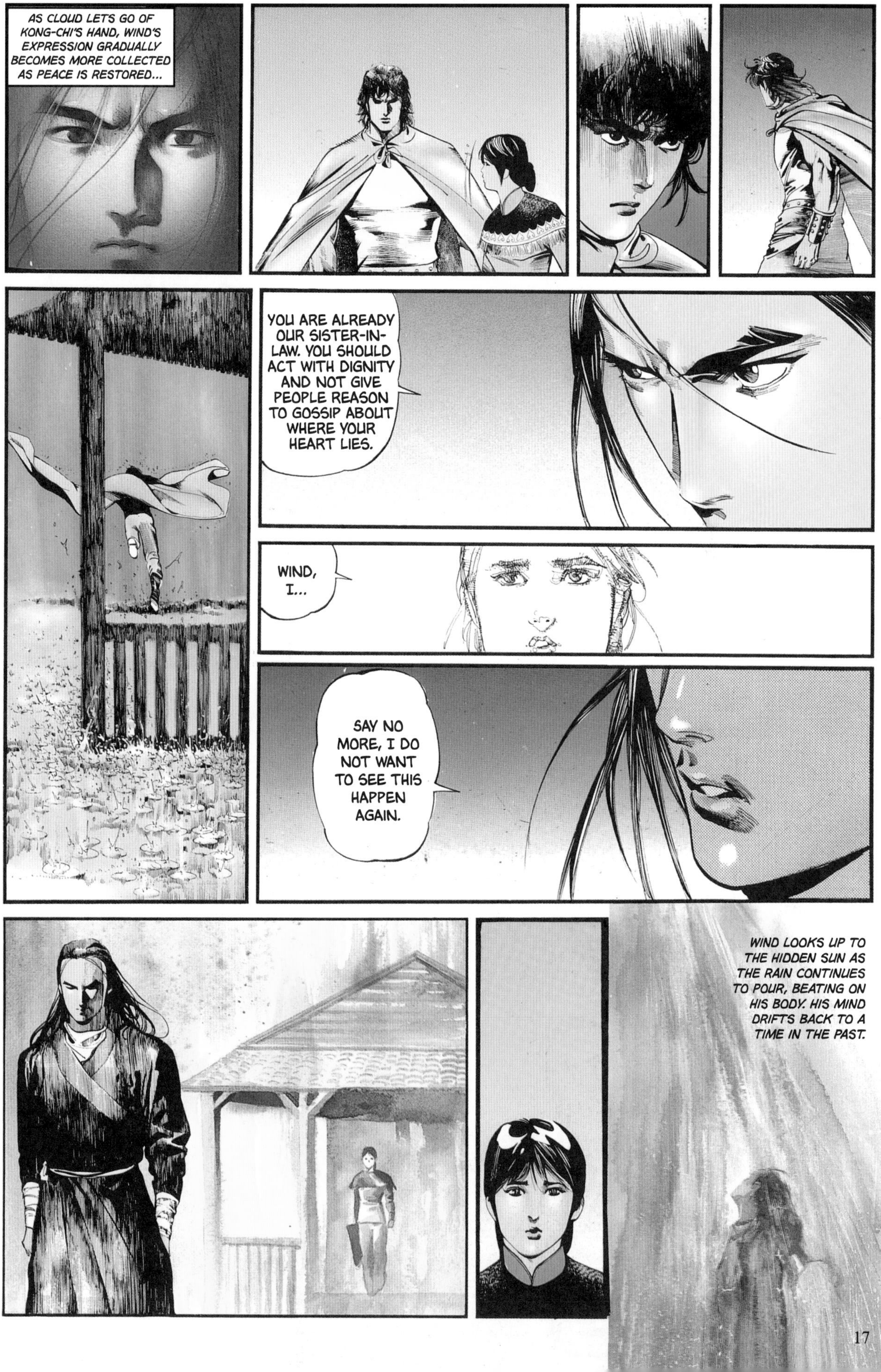
AS CLOUD LETS GO OF KONG-CHI'S HAND, WIND'S EXPRESSION GRADUALLY BECOMES MORE COLLECTED AS PEACE IS RESTORED...
YOU ARE ALREADY OUR SISTER-IN-LAW. YOU SHOULD ACT WITH DIGNITY AND NOT GIVE PEOPLE REASON TO GOSSIP ABOUT WHERE YOUR HEART LIES.
WIND, I...
SAY NO MORE, I DO NOT WANT TO SEE THIS HAPPEN AGAIN.
WIND LOOKS UP TO THE HIDDEN SUN AS THE RAIN CONTINUES TO POUR, BEATING ON HIS BODY. HIS MIND DRIFTS BACK TO A TIME IN THE PAST.

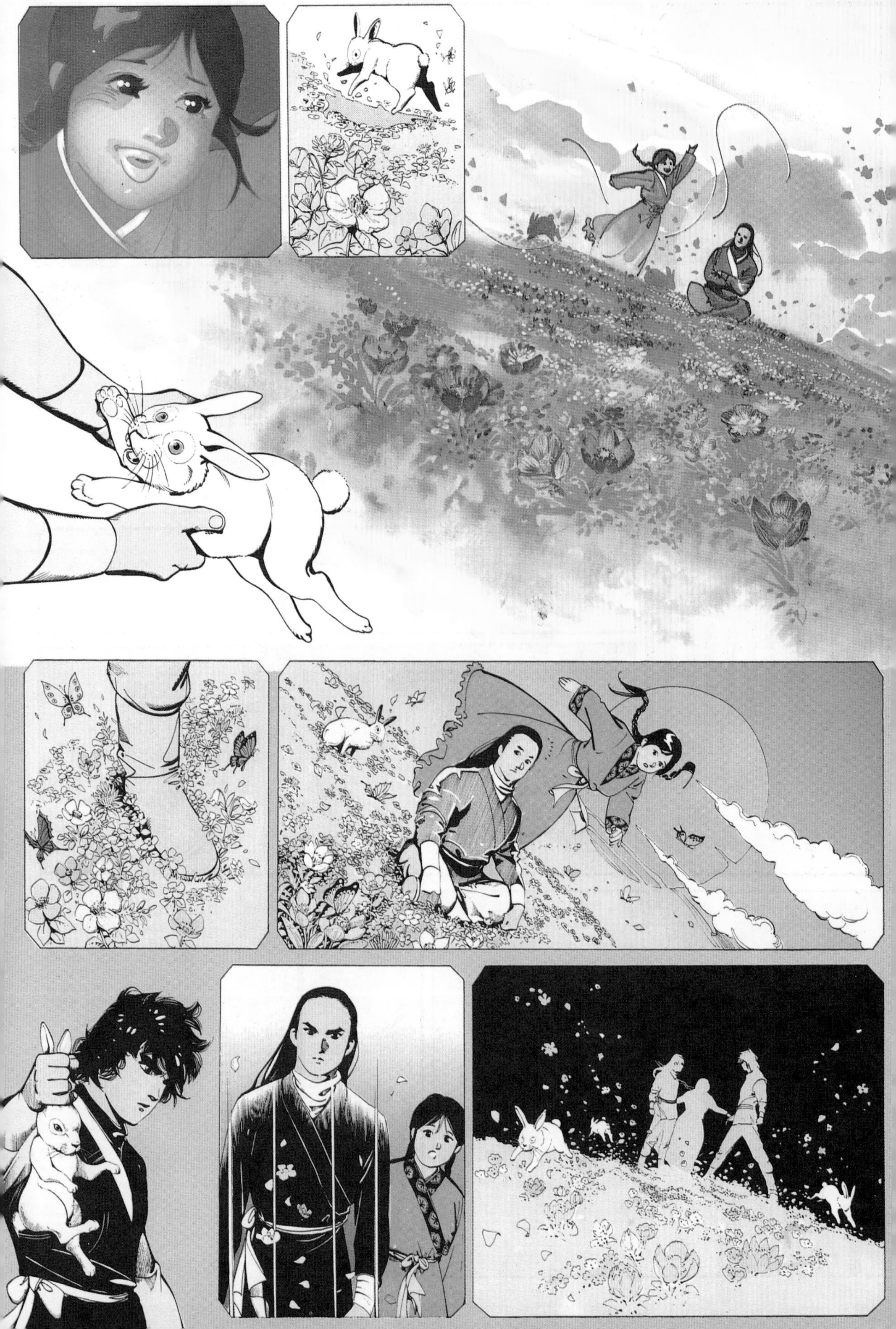

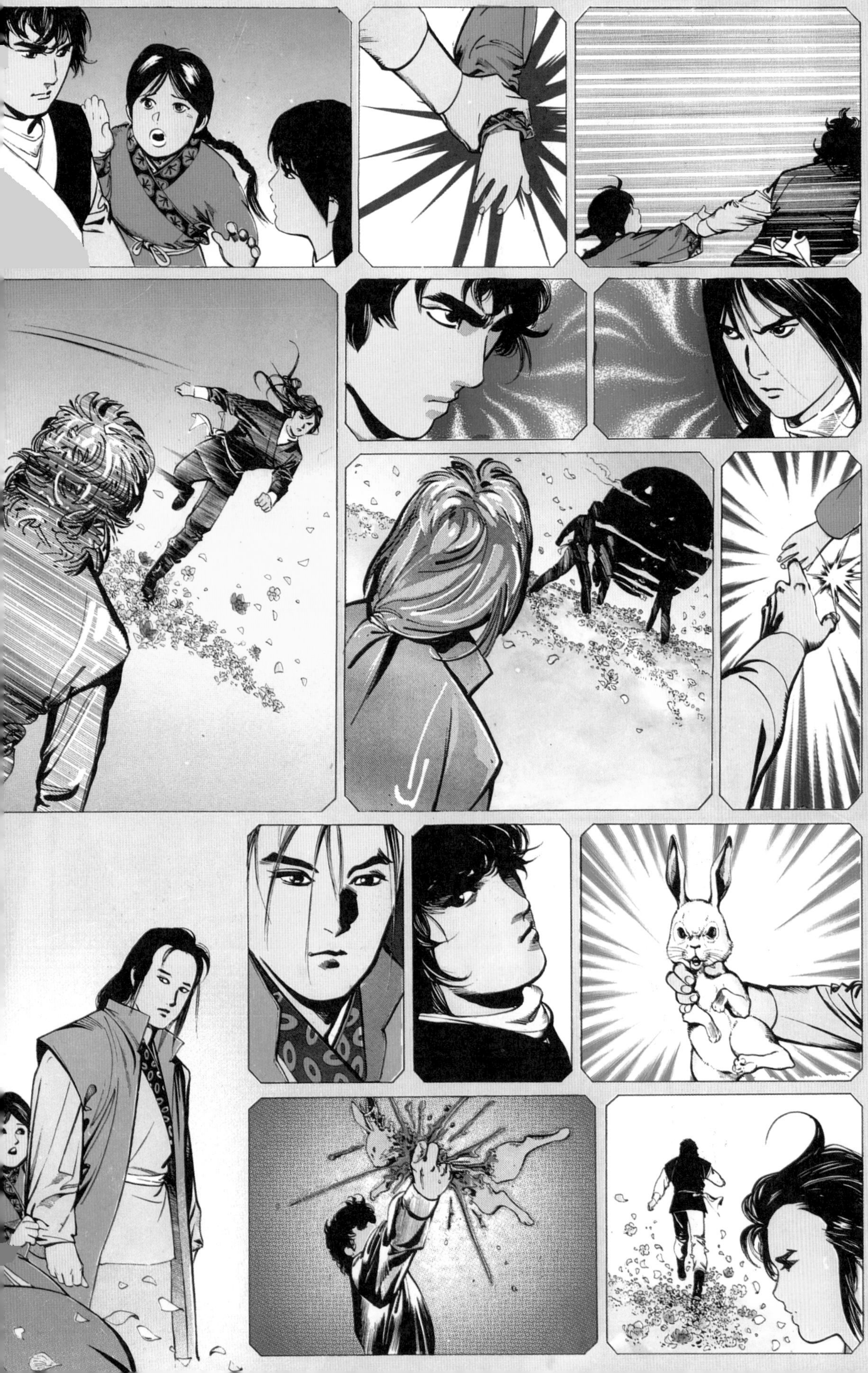

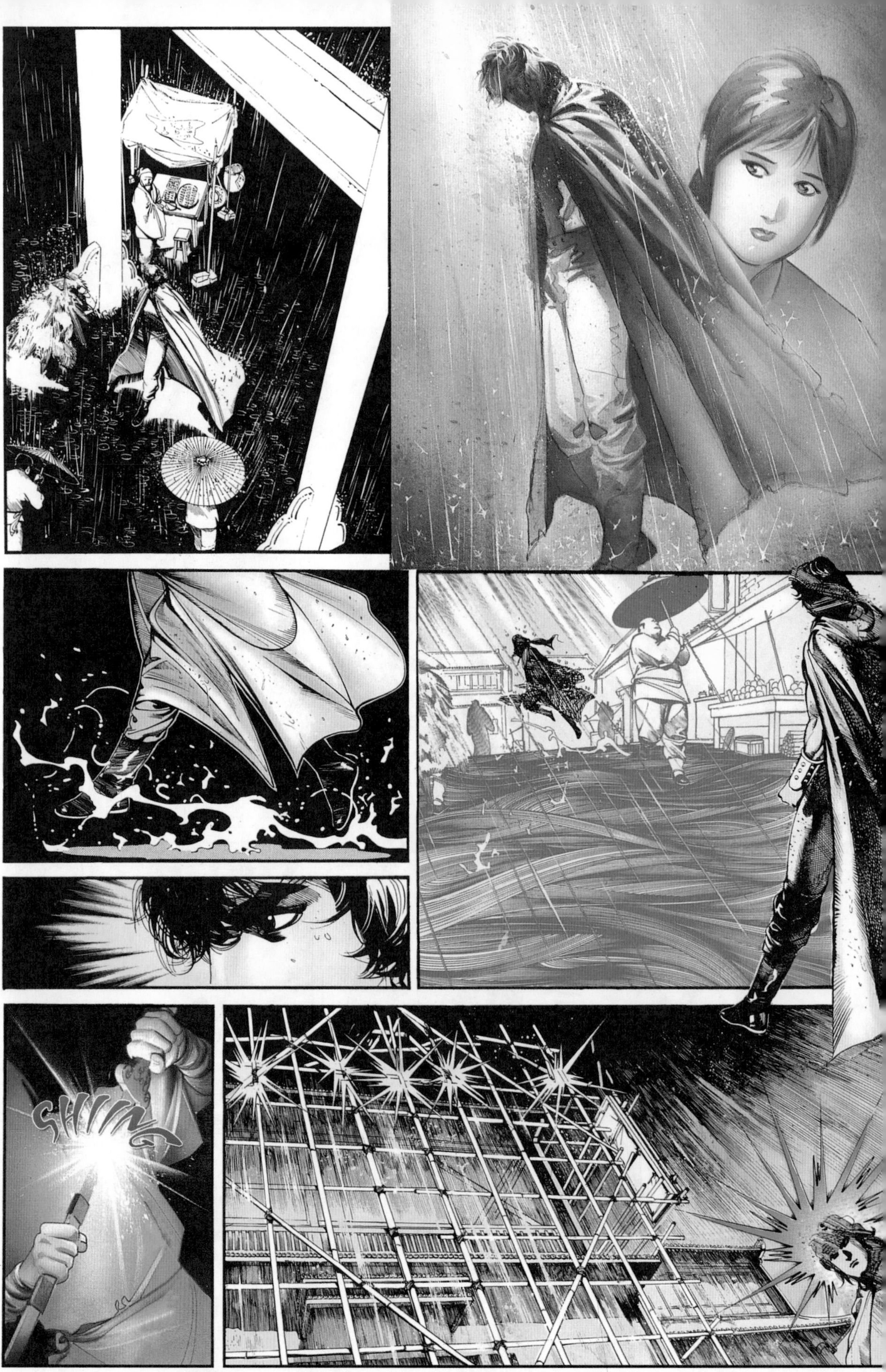
CHING

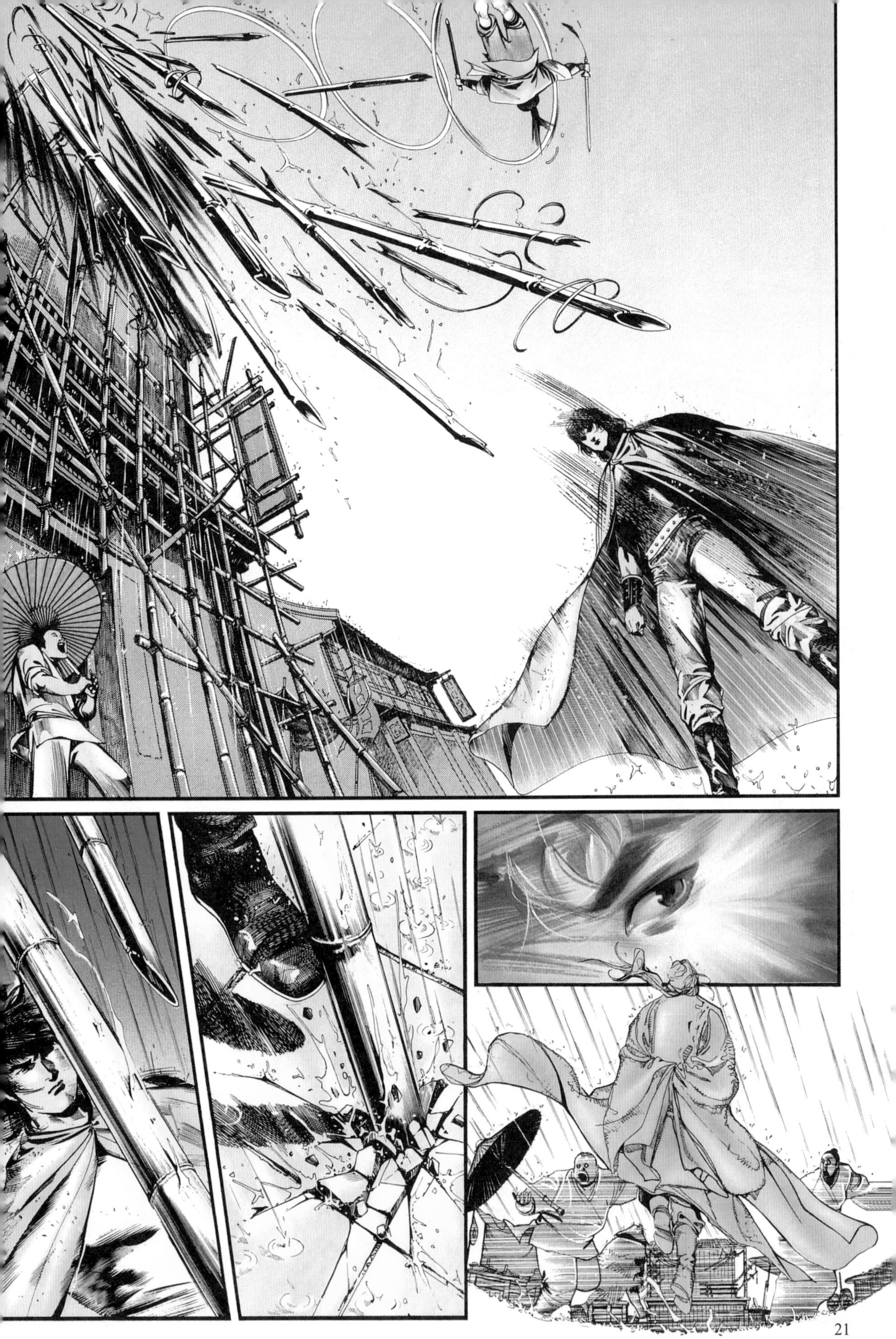

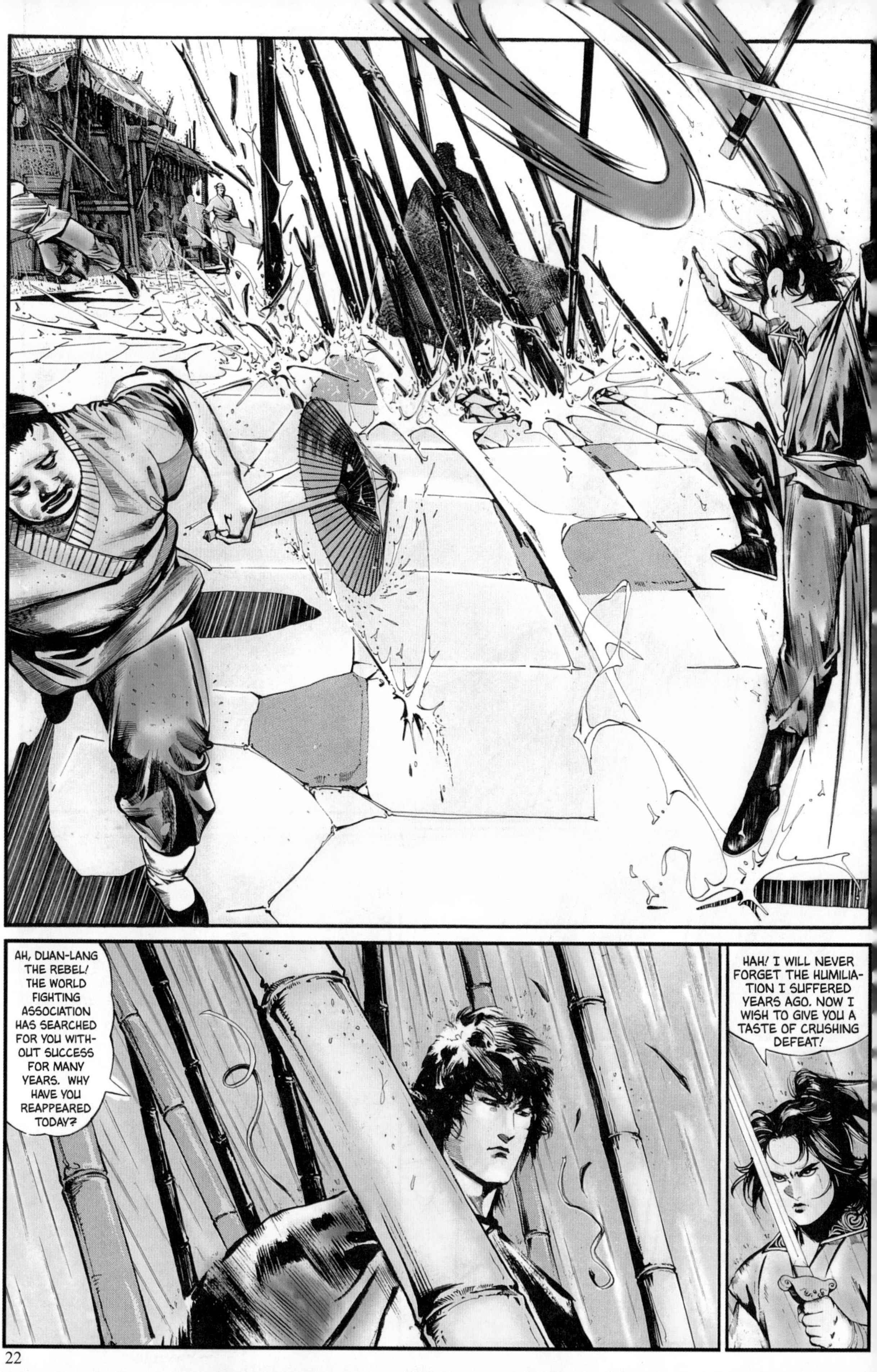
AH, DUAN-LANG THE REBEL! THE WORLD FIGHTING ASSOCIATION HAS SEARCHED FOR YOU WITH-OUT SUCCESS FOR MANY YEARS. WHY HAVE YOU REAPPEARED TODAY?
HAH! I WILL NEVER FORGET THE HUMILIA-TION I SUFFERED YEARS AGO. NOW I WISH TO GIVE YOU A TASTE OF CRUSHING DEFEAT!

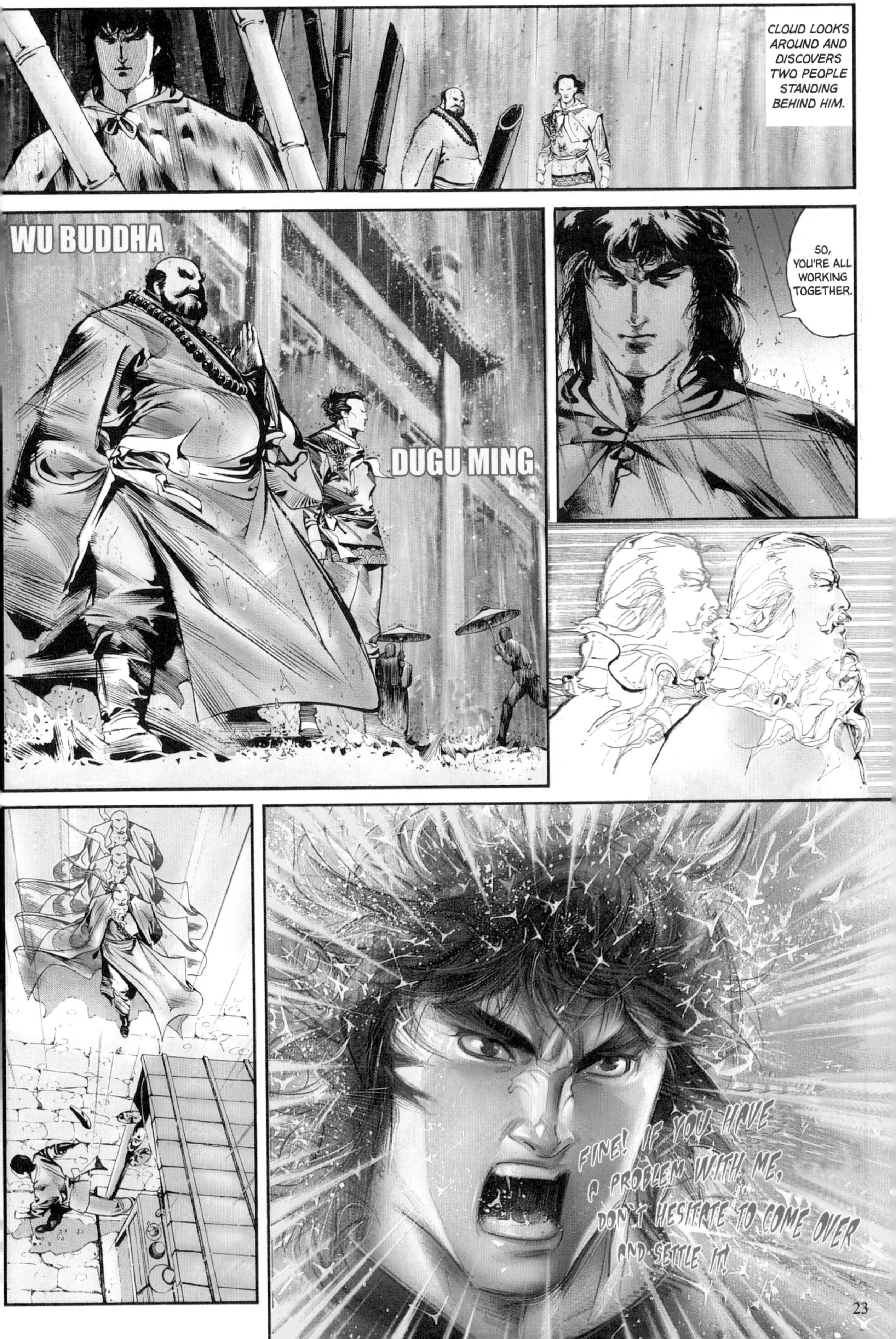
CLOUD LOOKS AROUND AND DISCOVERS TWO PEOPLE STANDING BEHIND HIM.
WU BUDDHA
DUGU MING
SO, YOU'RE ALL WORKING TOGETHER.
FINE! IF YOU HAVE A PROBLEM WITH ME, DON'T HESITATE TO COME OVER AND SETTLE IT!

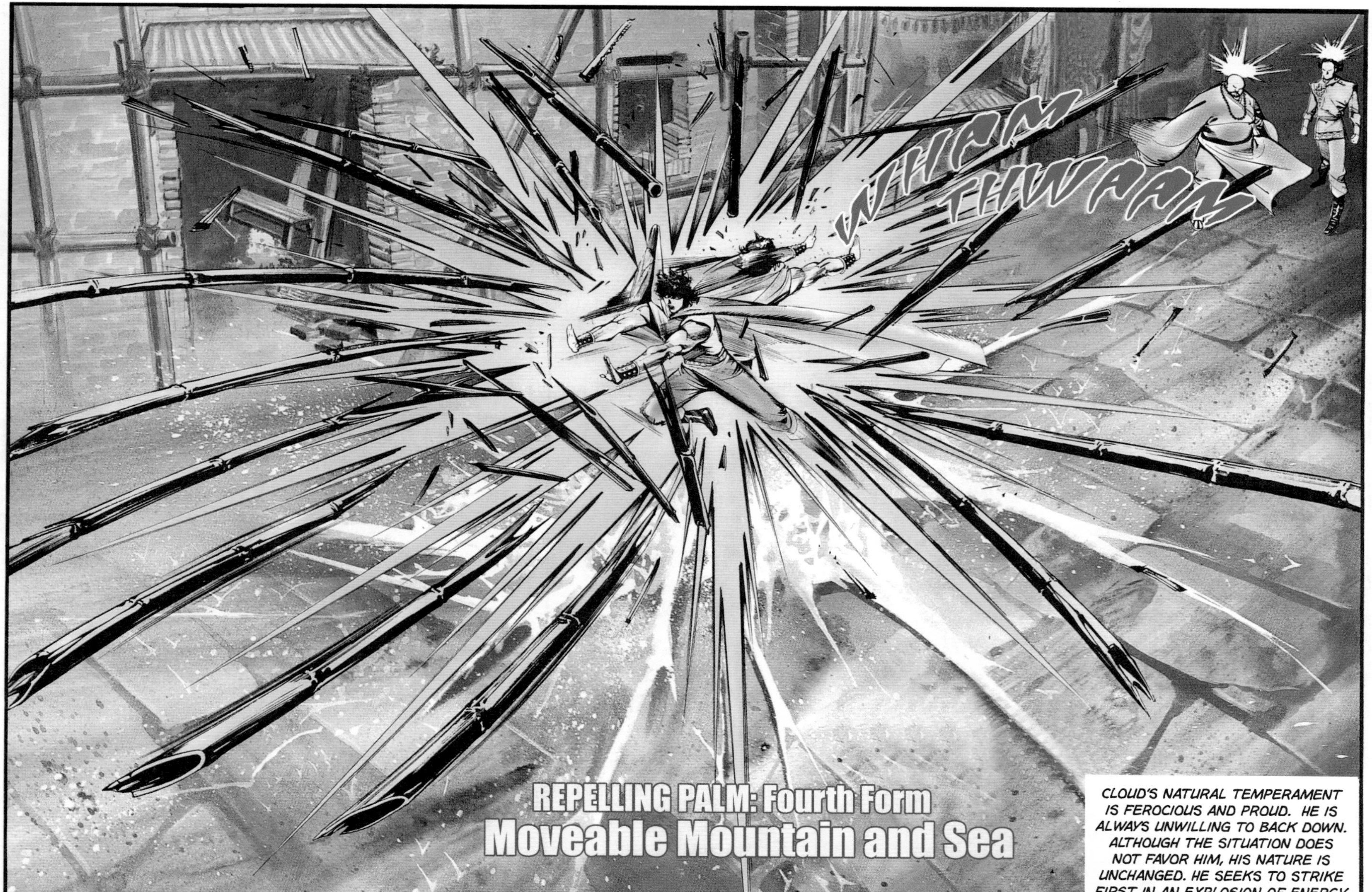
WHAM
THWAM
REPELLING PALM: Fourth Form
Moveable Mountain and Sea
CLOUD'S NATURAL TEMPERAMENT IS FEROCIOUS AND PROUD. HE IS ALWAYS UNWILLING TO BACK DOWN. ALTHOUGH THE SITUATION DOES NOT FAVOR HIM, HIS NATURE IS UNCHANGED. HE SEEKS TO STRIKE FIRST IN AN EXPLOSION OF ENERGY.

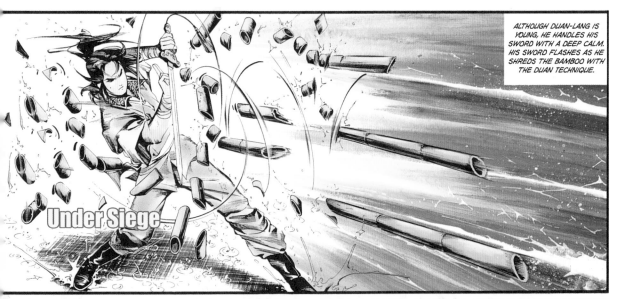

ALTHOUGH DUAN-LANG IS YOUNG, HE HANDLES HIS SWORD WITH A DEEP CALM. HIS SWORD FLASHES AS HE SHREDS THE BAMBOO WITH THE DUAN TECHNIQUE.

Under Siege

Glow of Buddhist Light

THE BUDDHA PALMS SIMPLY DOMINATE WHATEVER THEY ENCOUNTER. THEY DESTROY THE ONCOMING BAMBOO.

DUGU MING'S LEG BECOMES A BLUR, MOVING UP, DOWN AND SIDEWAYS. HE MANEUVERS WITH INCREDIBLE DEXTERITY.

DRAGON KICK
Leaping Dragon

CLOUD'S PREVIOUS ATTACK WAS TO TEST HOW GOOD HIS ENEMIES' KUNG FU STYLES ARE. HE REALIZES THAT THESE FOES WILL NOT BE EASY TO DEFEAT AND HE MUST RELY ON SPEED.

AMONG THE THREE, THEIR ABILITIES DIFFER LITTLE. BECAUSE DUAN-LANG STANDS ALONE, CLOUD RUSHES TOWARD HIM LIKE LIGHTNING, READY TO STRIKE.

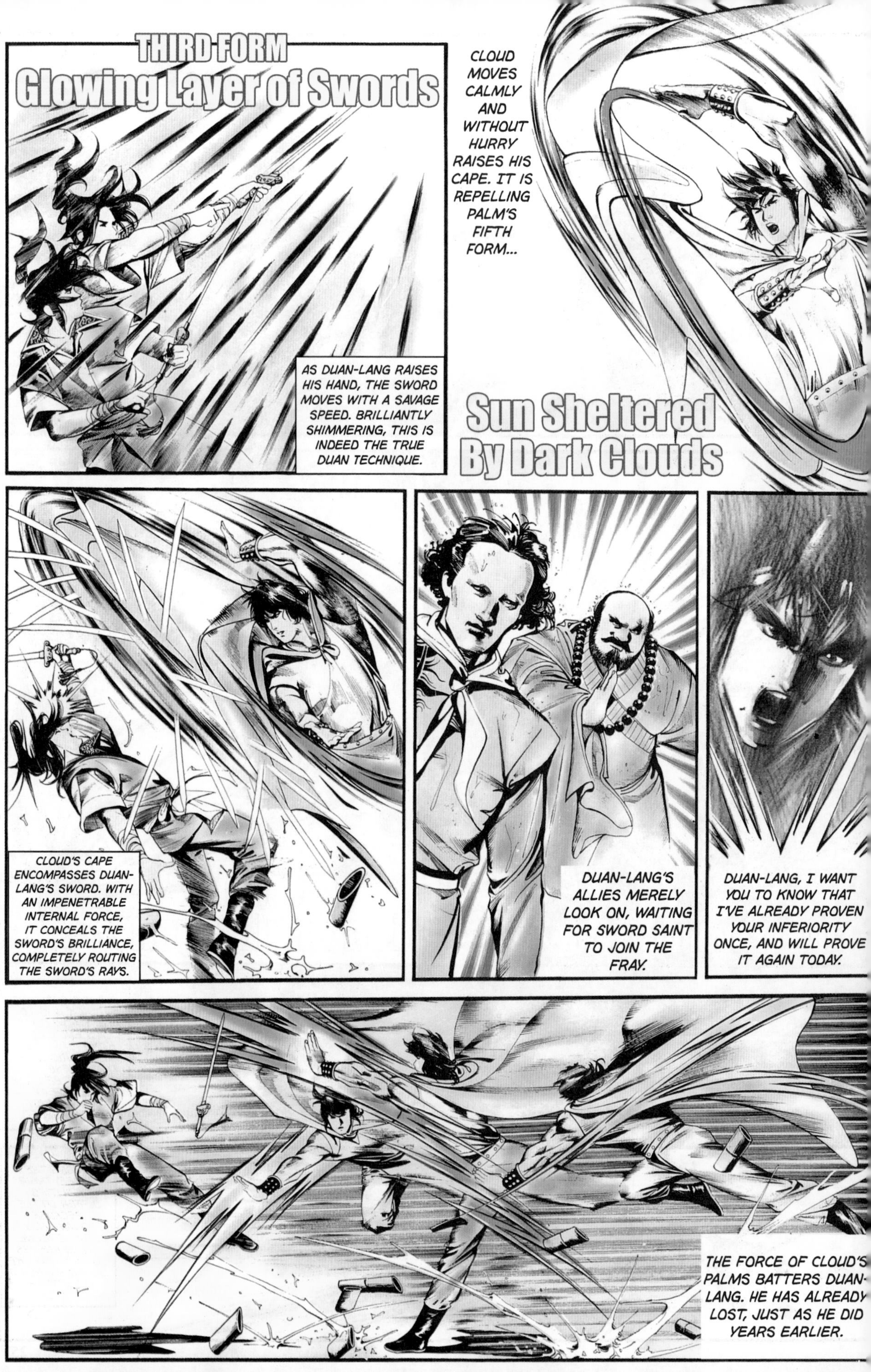
THIRD FORM
Glowing Layer of Swords
AS DUAN-LANG RAISES HIS HAND, THE SWORD MOVES WITH A SAVAGE SPEED. BRILLIANTLY SHIMMERING, THIS IS INDEED THE TRUE DUAN TECHNIQUE.
CLOUD MOVES CALMLY AND WITHOUT HURRY RAISES HIS CAPE. IT IS REPELLING PALM'S FIFTH FORM...
Sun Sheltered By Dark Clouds
CLOUD'S CAPE ENCOMPASSES DUAN-LANG'S SWORD. WITH AN IMPENETRABLE INTERNAL FORCE, IT CONCEALS THE SWORD'S BRILLIANCE, COMPLETELY ROUTING THE SWORD'S RAYS.
DUAN-LANG'S ALLIES MERELY LOOK ON, WAITING FOR SWORD SAINT TO JOIN THE FRAY.
DUAN-LANG, I WANT YOU TO KNOW THAT I'VE ALREADY PROVEN YOUR INFERIORITY ONCE, AND WILL PROVE IT AGAIN TODAY.
THE FORCE OF CLOUD'S PALMS BATTERS DUAN-LANG. HE HAS ALREADY LOST, JUST AS HE DID YEARS EARLIER.

ELDER SIR... WHAT CAN I DO FOR YOU? PLEASE... LOOK AT WHICHEVER ONE YOU WANT!

THESE WOODEN SWORDS ARE ALL EXQUISITE BUT THEY ARE NOT DELICATE.

HOW MUCH DO YOU WANT FOR A SWORD?

THREE COINS.

FOR THREE COINS I CAN KILL A YOUNG LAD; IT'S ACTUALLY TOO CHEAP.

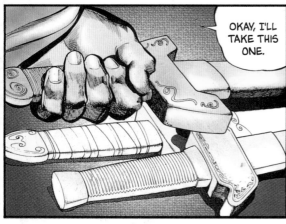

OKAY, I'LL TAKE THIS ONE.

AS HE GRASPS THE SWORD, HIS BODY EMITS A BURST OF LIGHT AND TAKES ON A VENOMOUS APPEARANCE.

SWORD SAINT'S ENERGY IS OVERWHELMING. A HIDDEN FORCE PULLS ALL THE WOODEN SWORDS OUT OF THEIR SCABBARDS IN AN AMAZING DISPLAY OF INTERNAL KUNG FU TECHNIQUE!!

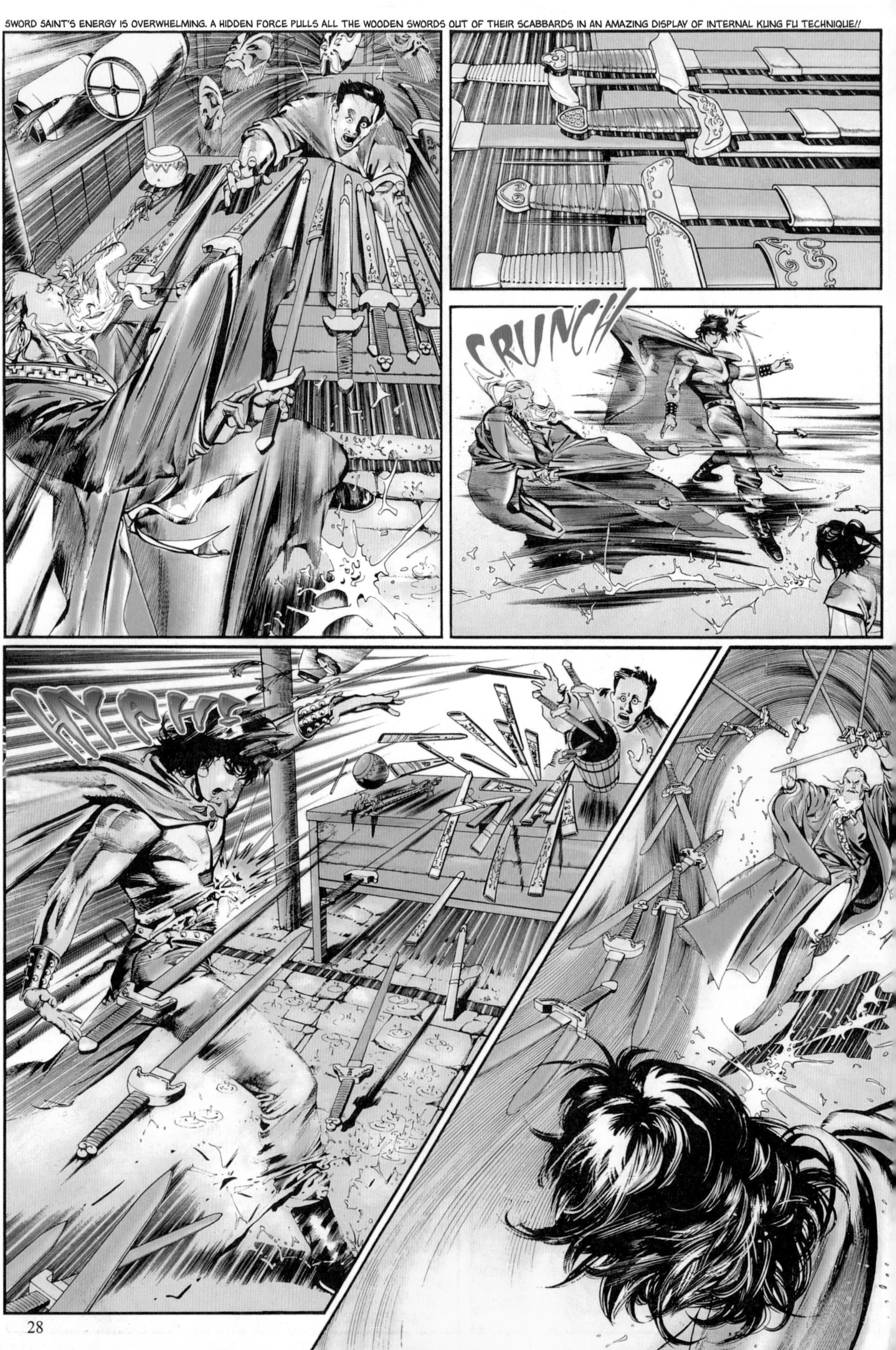

CRUNCH
HYAH!

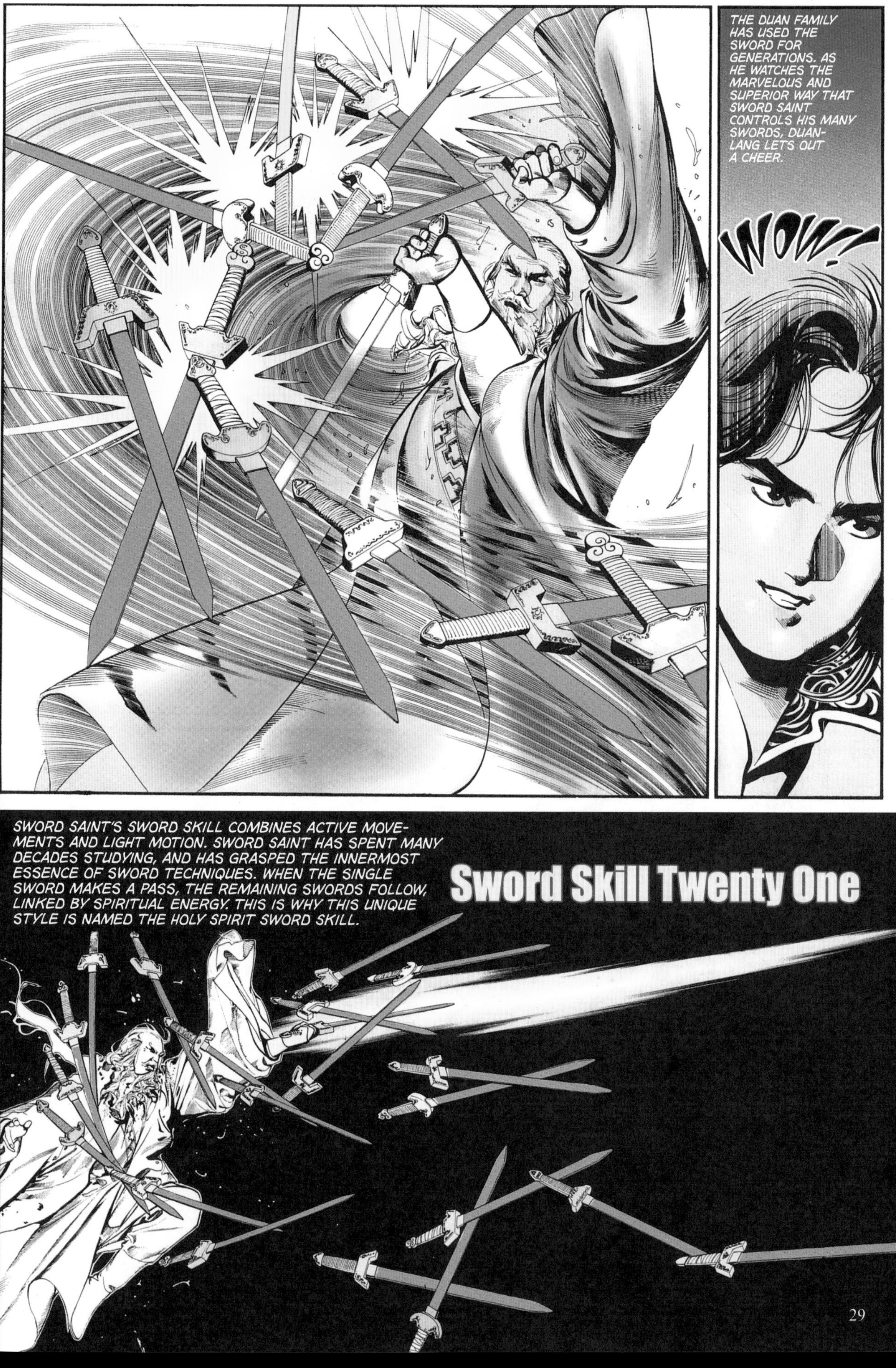
THE DUAN FAMILY HAS USED THE SWORD FOR GENERATIONS. AS HE WATCHES THE MARVELOUS AND SUPERIOR WAY THAT SWORD SAINT CONTROLS HIS MANY SWORDS, DUAN-LANG LETS OUT A CHEER.
WOW!
SWORD SAINT'S SWORD SKILL COMBINES ACTIVE MOVEMENTS AND LIGHT MOTION. SWORD SAINT HAS SPENT MANY DECADES STUDYING, AND HAS GRASPED THE INNERMOST ESSENCE OF SWORD TECHNIQUES. WHEN THE SINGLE SWORD MAKES A PASS, THE REMAINING SWORDS FOLLOW, LINKED BY SPIRITUAL ENERGY. THIS IS WHY THIS UNIQUE STYLE IS NAMED THE HOLY SPIRIT SWORD SKILL.
Sword Skill Twenty One

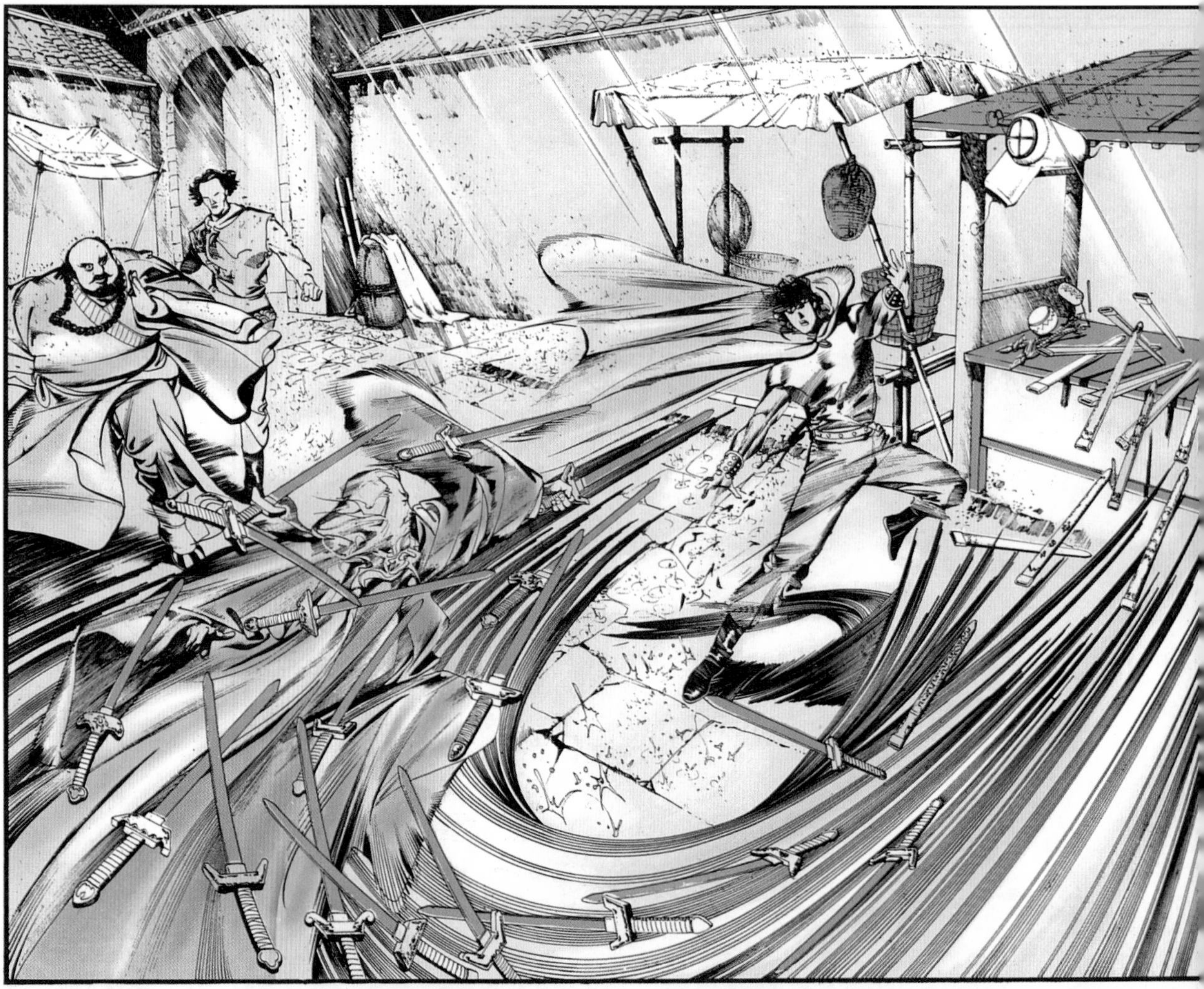

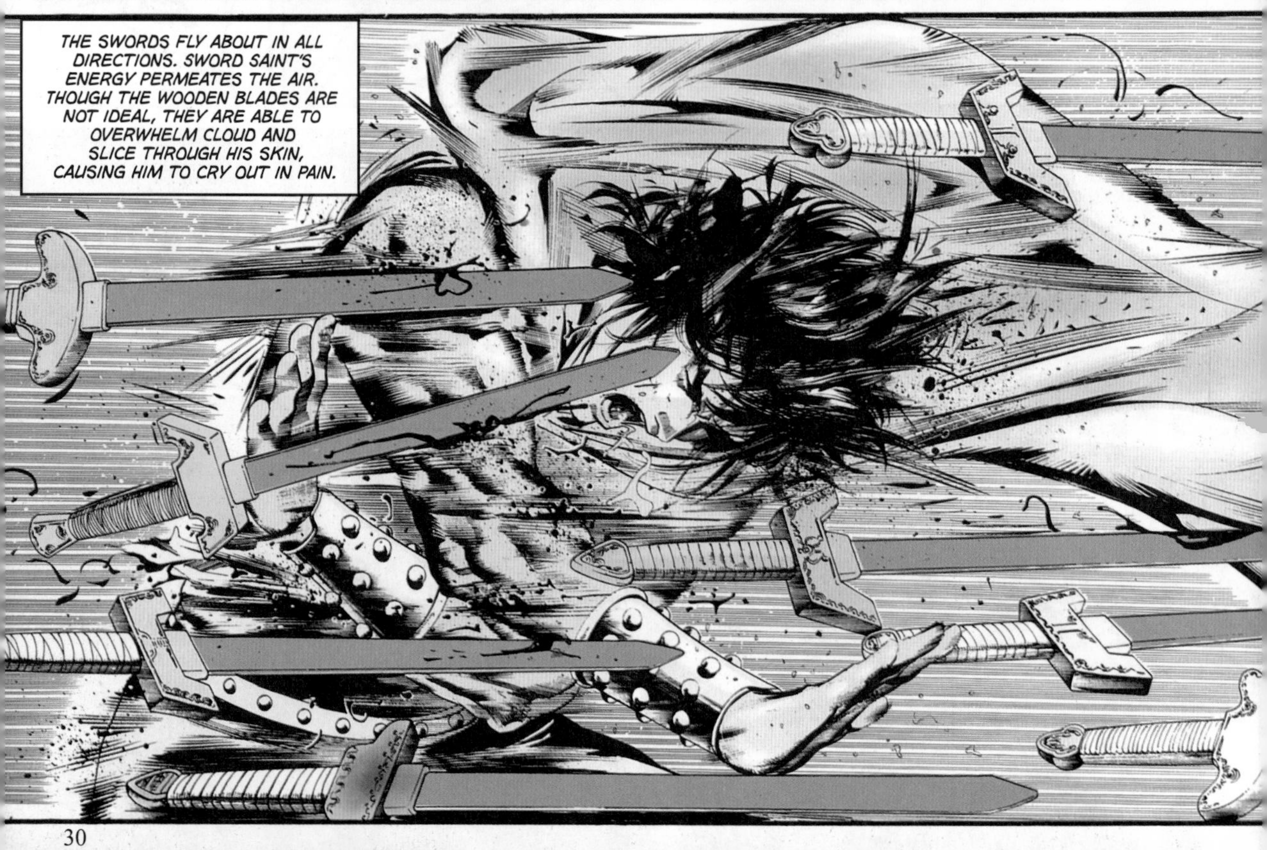
THE SWORDS FLY ABOUT IN ALL DIRECTIONS. SWORD SAINT'S ENERGY PERMEATES THE AIR. THOUGH THE WOODEN BLADES ARE NOT IDEAL, THEY ARE ABLE TO OVERWHELM CLOUD AND SLICE THROUGH HIS SKIN, CAUSING HIM TO CRY OUT IN PAIN.

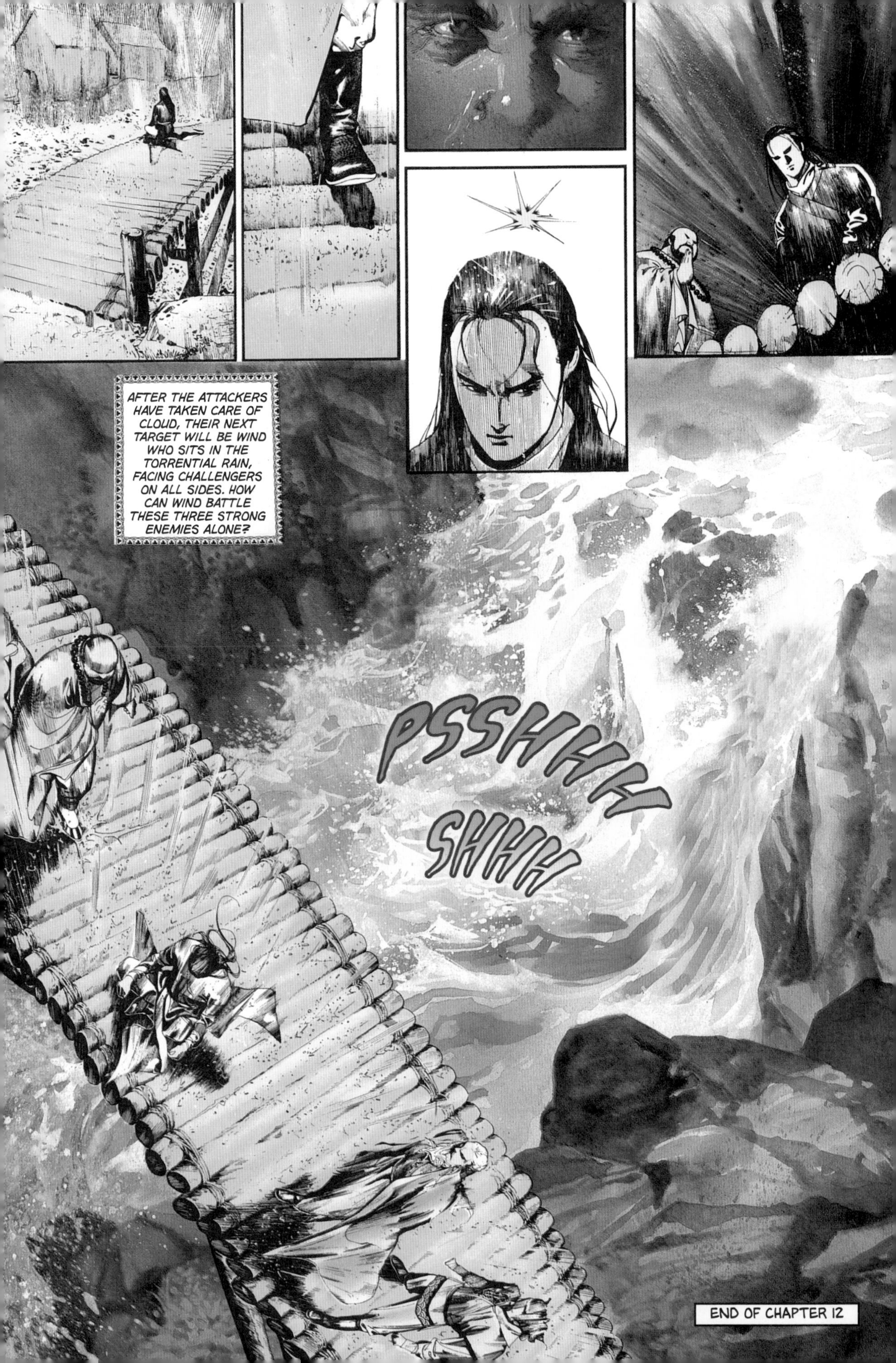
AFTER THE ATTACKERS HAVE TAKEN CARE OF CLOUD, THEIR NEXT TARGET WILL BE WIND WHO SITS IN THE TORRENTIAL RAIN, FACING CHALLENGERS ON ALL SIDES. HOW CAN WIND BATTLE THESE THREE STRONG ENEMIES ALONE?
PSSHHH
SHHH
END OF CHAPTER 12

Chapter 13: Violent Storm

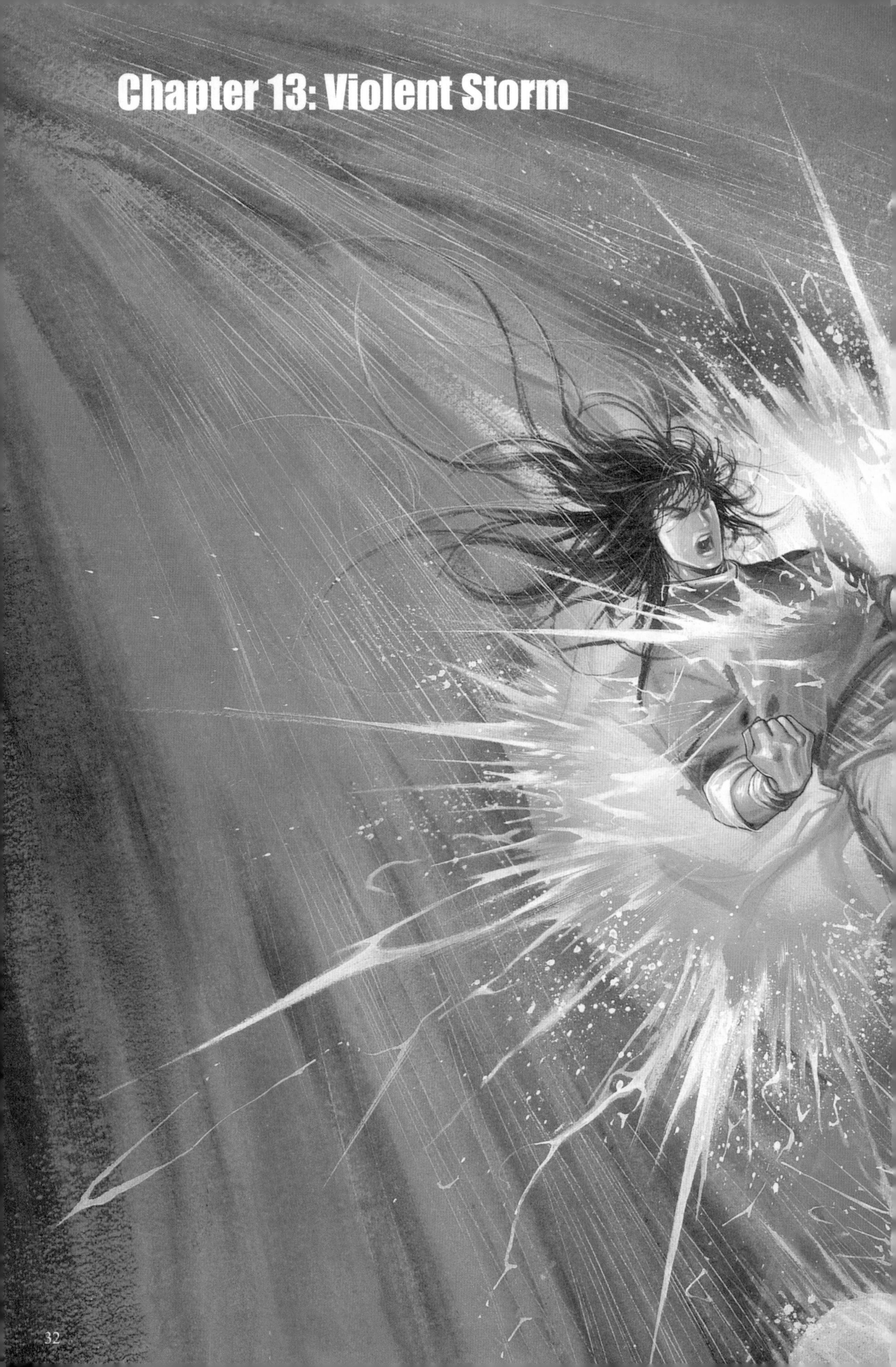

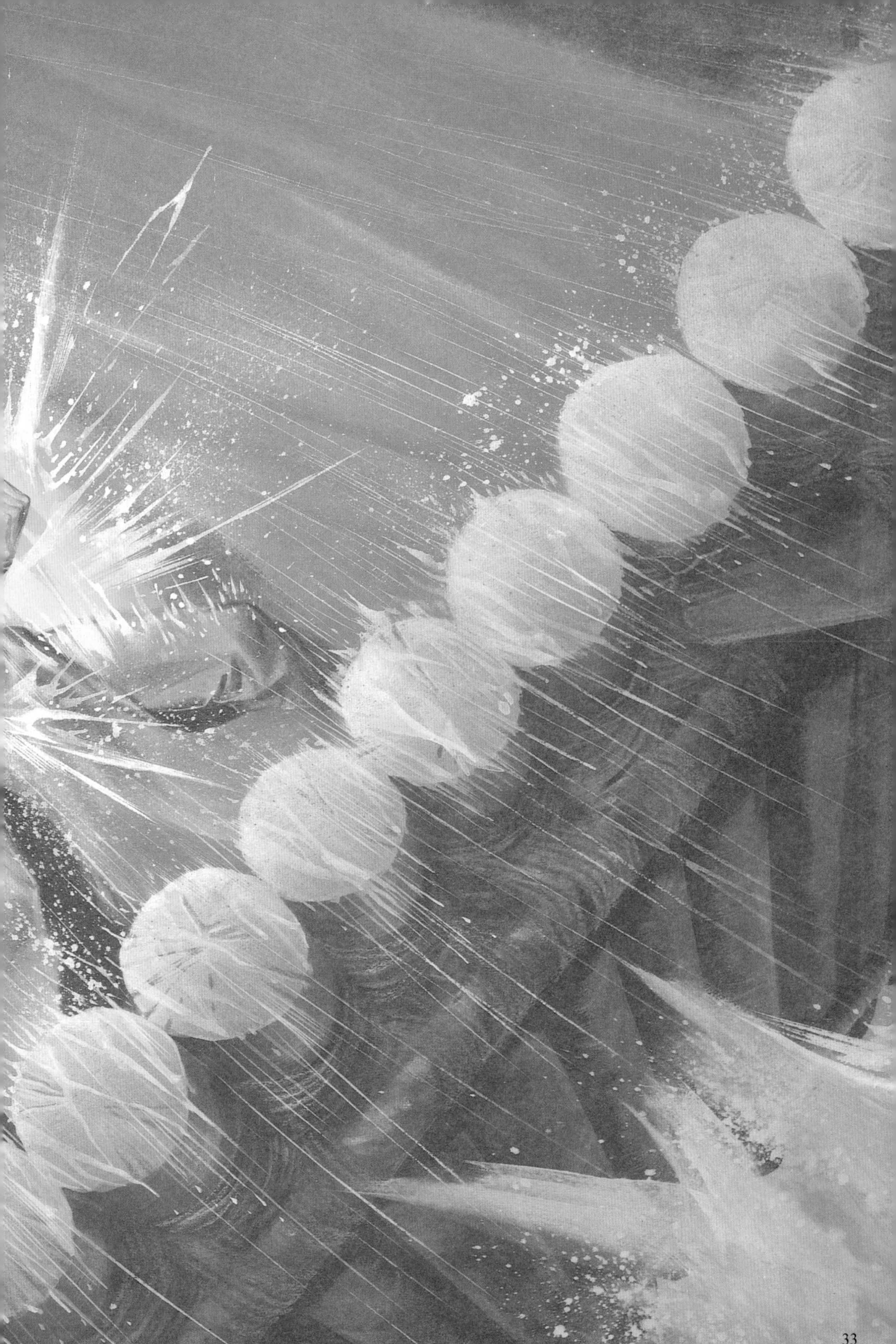

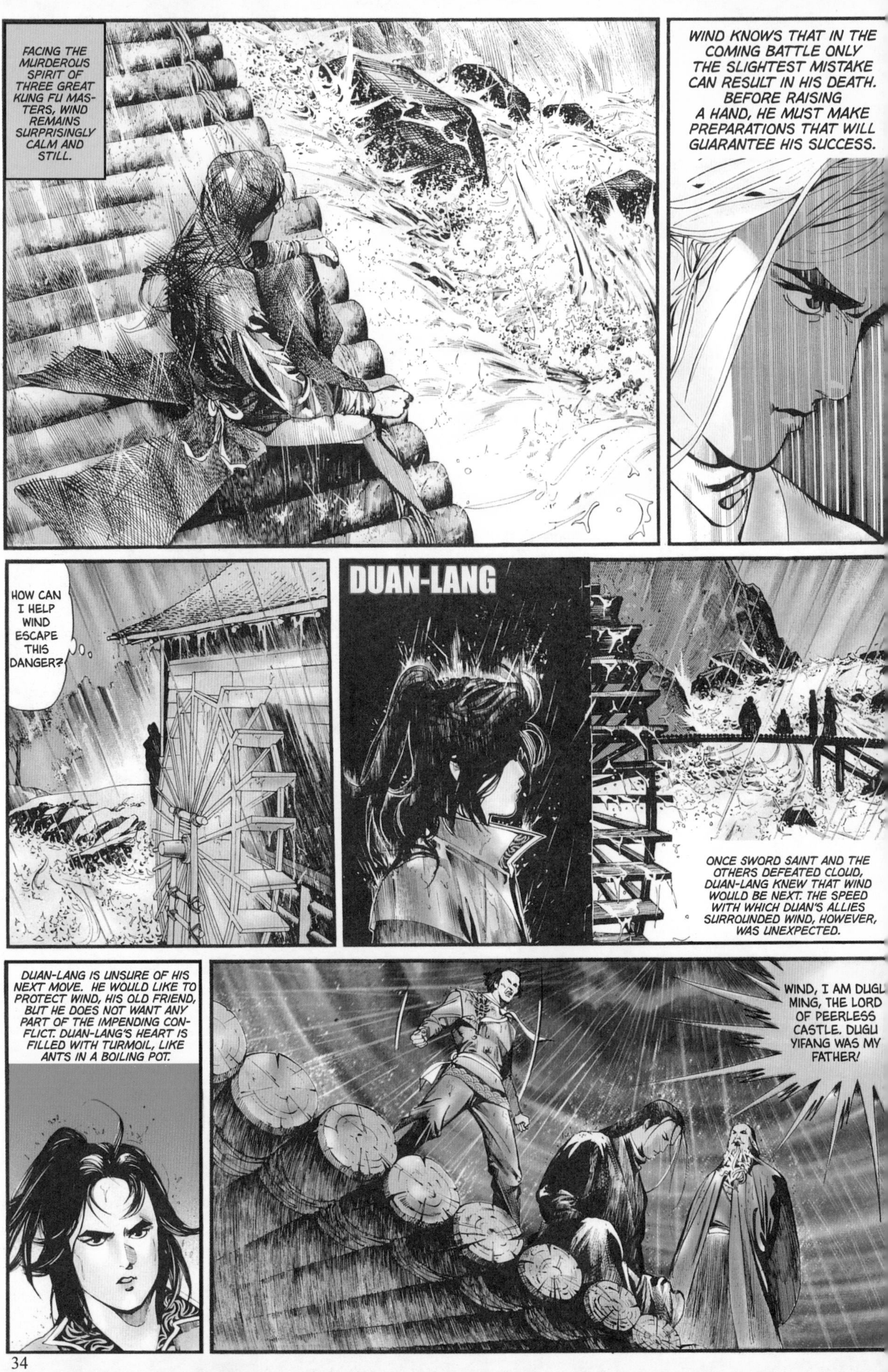
FACING THE MURDEROUS SPIRIT OF THREE GREAT KUNG FU MASTERS, WIND REMAINS SURPRISINGLY CALM AND STILL.
WIND KNOWS THAT IN THE COMING BATTLE ONLY THE SLIGHTEST MISTAKE CAN RESULT IN HIS DEATH. BEFORE RAISING A HAND, HE MUST MAKE PREPARATIONS THAT WILL GUARANTEE HIS SUCCESS.
HOW CAN I HELP WIND ESCAPE THIS DANGER?
DUAN-LANG
ONCE SWORD SAINT AND THE OTHERS DEFEATED CLOUD, DUAN-LANG KNEW THAT WIND WOULD BE NEXT. THE SPEED WITH WHICH DUAN'S ALLIES SURROUNDED WIND, HOWEVER, WAS UNEXPECTED.
DUAN-LANG IS UNSURE OF HIS NEXT MOVE. HE WOULD LIKE TO PROTECT WIND, HIS OLD FRIEND, BUT HE DOES NOT WANT ANY PART OF THE IMPENDING CONFLICT. DUAN-LANG'S HEART IS FILLED WITH TURMOIL, LIKE ANTS IN A BOILING POT.
WIND, I AM DUGU MING, THE LORD OF PEERLESS CASTLE. DUGU YIFANG WAS MY FATHER!

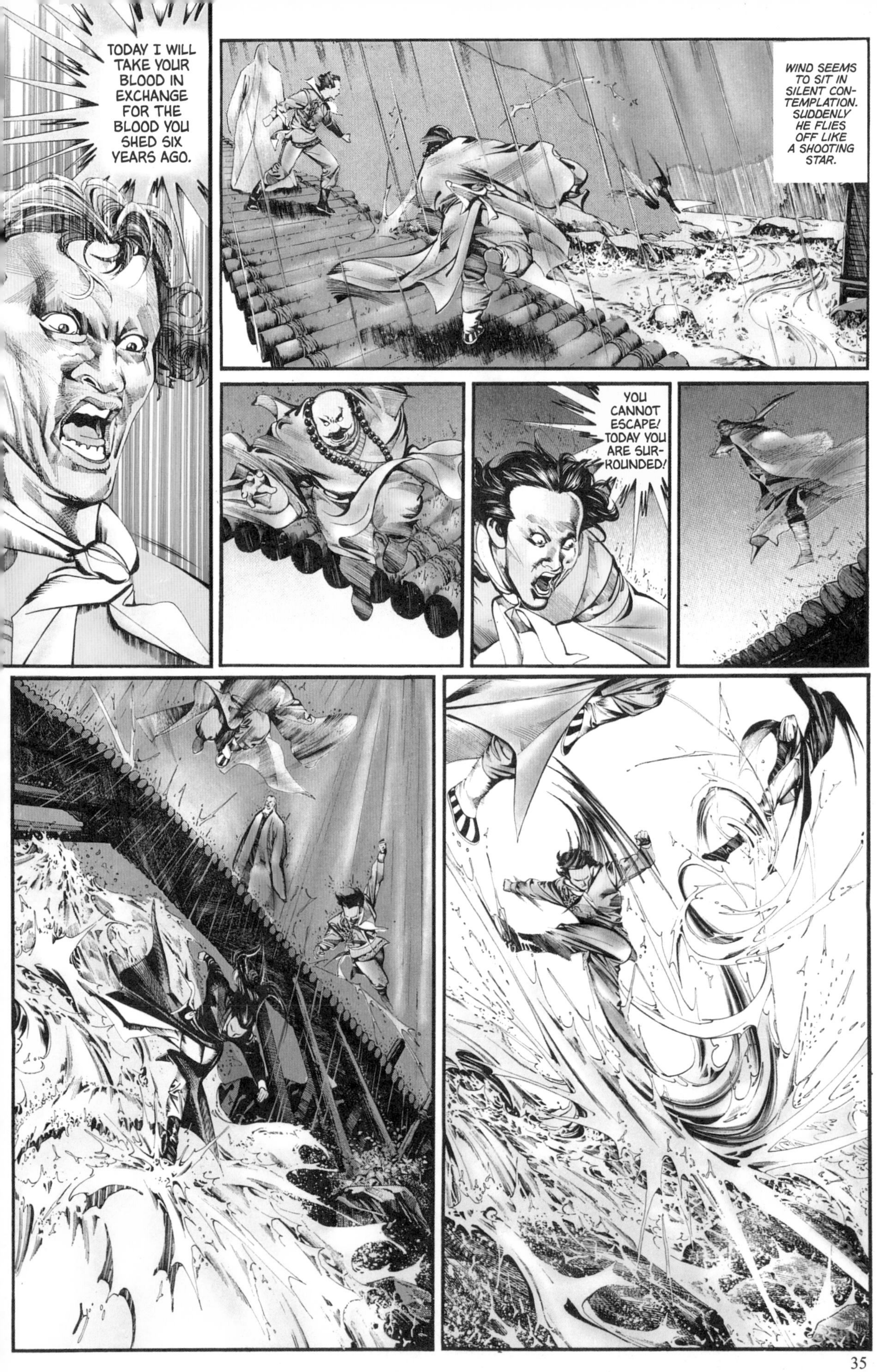
TODAY I WILL TAKE YOUR BLOOD IN EXCHANGE FOR THE BLOOD YOU SHED SIX YEARS AGO.
WIND SEEMS TO SIT IN SILENT CONTEMPLATION. SUDDENLY HE FLIES OFF LIKE A SHOOTING STAR.
YOU CANNOT ESCAPE! TODAY YOU ARE SURROUNDED!

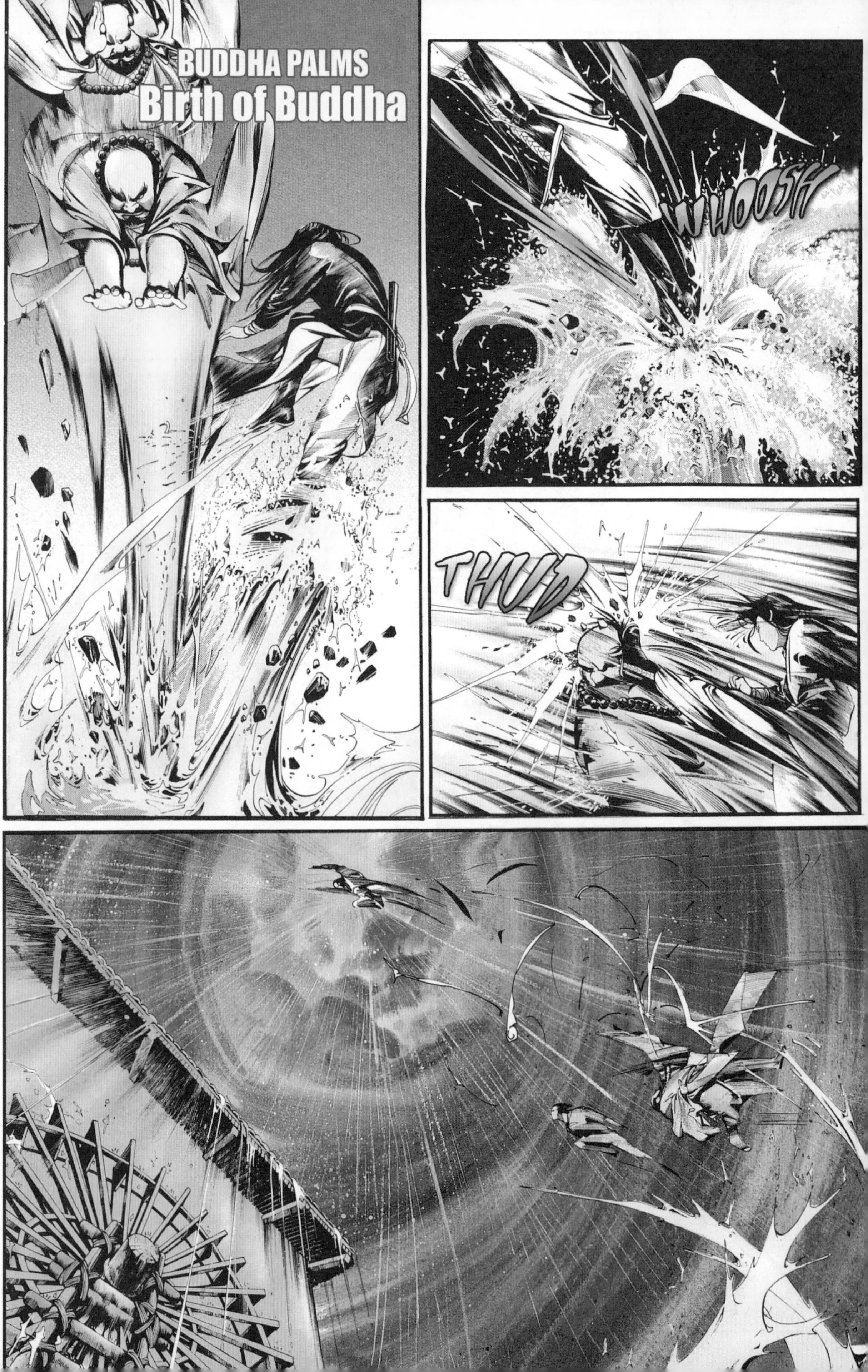
BUDDHA PALMS
Birth of Buddha
WHOOSH
THUD

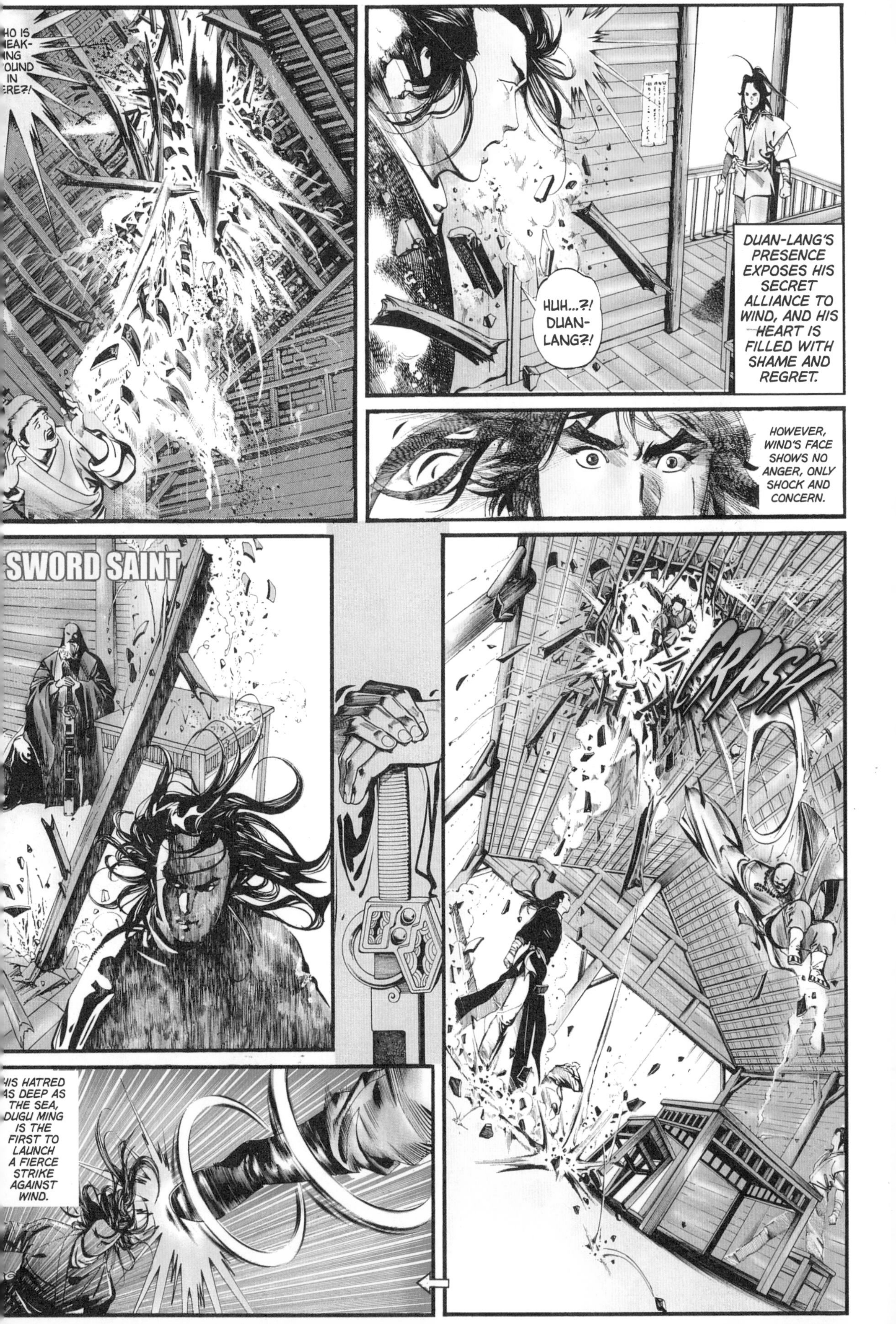
HO IS
EAK-
ING
OUND
IN
ERE?!
HUH...?! DUAN-LANG?!
DUAN-LANG'S PRESENCE EXPOSES HIS SECRET ALLIANCE TO WIND, AND HIS HEART IS FILLED WITH SHAME AND REGRET.
HOWEVER, WIND'S FACE SHOWS NO ANGER, ONLY SHOCK AND CONCERN.
SWORD SAINT
HIS HATRED
AS DEEP AS
THE SEA,
DUGU MING
IS THE
FIRST TO
LAUNCH
A FIERCE
STRIKE
AGAINST
WIND.
CRASH

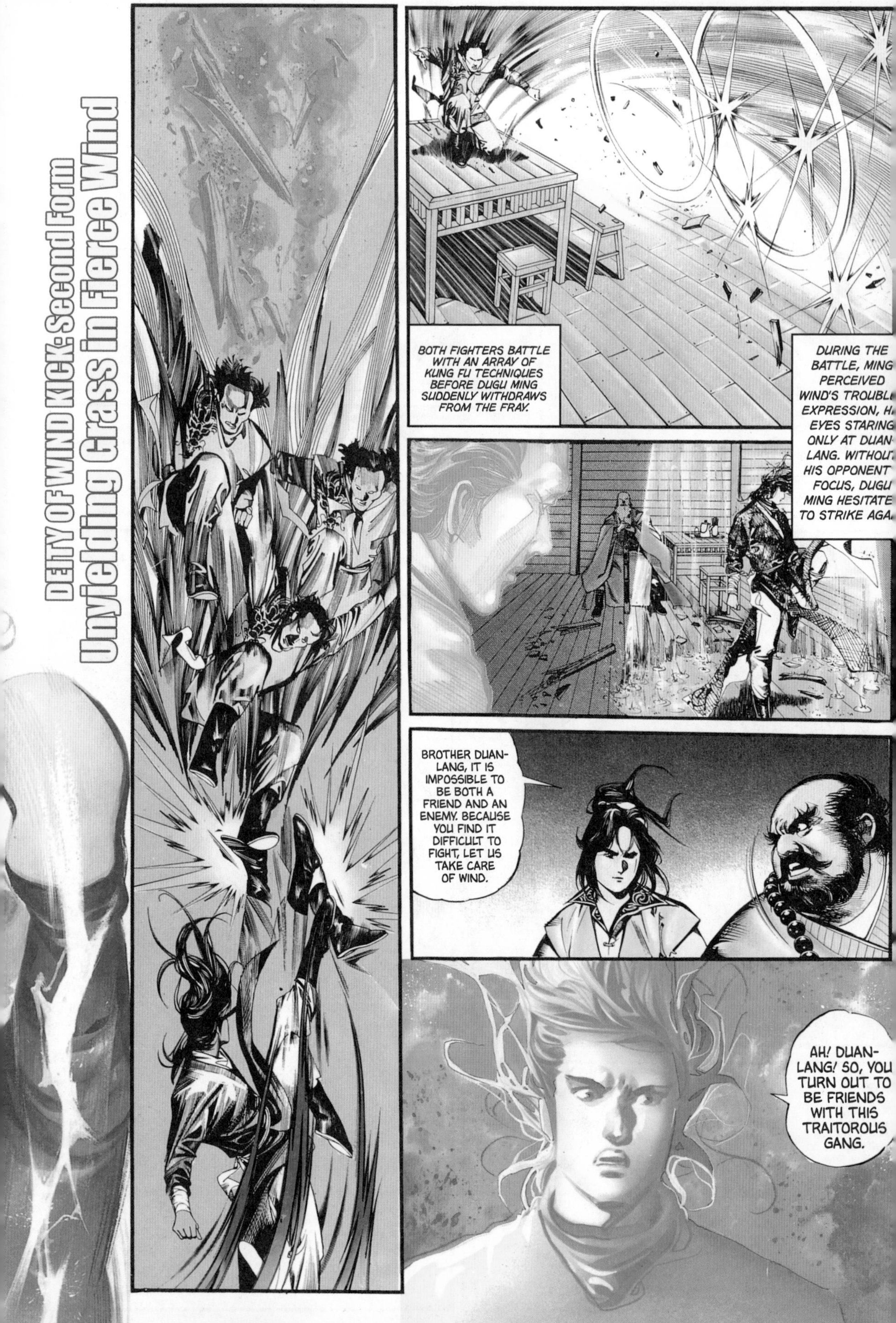
DEITY OF WIND KICK: Second Form
Unyielding Grass in Fierce Wind
BOTH FIGHTERS BATTLE WITH AN ARRAY OF KUNG FU TECHNIQUES BEFORE DUGU MING SUDDENLY WITHDRAWS FROM THE FRAY.
DURING THE BATTLE, MING PERCEIVED WIND'S TROUBL EXPRESSION, H EYES STARING ONLY AT DUAN-LANG. WITHOUT HIS OPPONENT FOCUS, DUGU MING HESITATE TO STRIKE AGA
BROTHER DUAN-LANG, IT IS IMPOSSIBLE TO BE BOTH A FRIEND AND AN ENEMY. BECAUSE YOU FIND IT DIFFICULT TO FIGHT, LET US TAKE CARE OF WIND.
AH! DUAN-LANG! SO, YOU TURN OUT TO BE FRIENDS WITH THIS TRAITOROUS GANG.

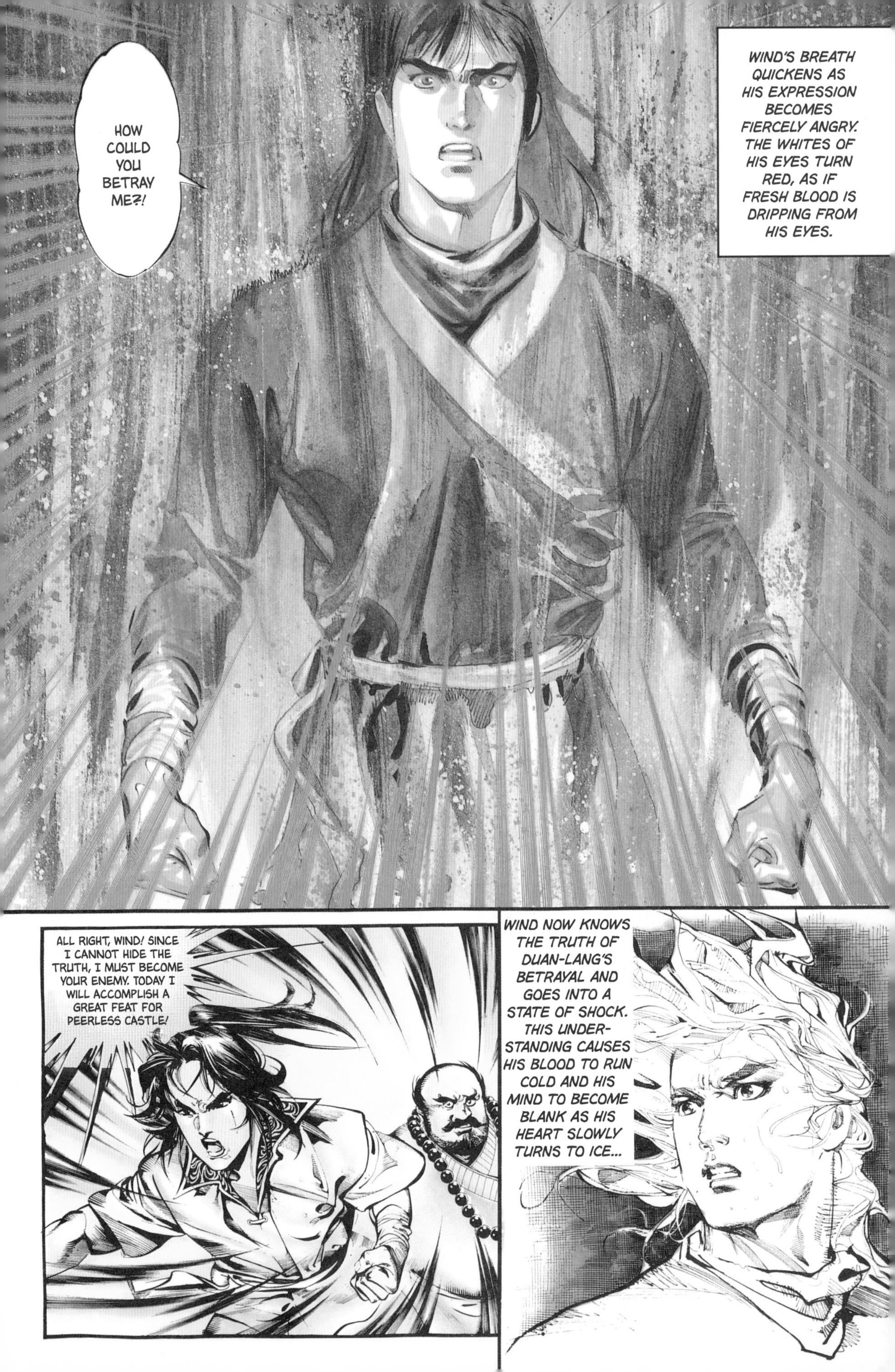
HOW COULD YOU BETRAY ME?!
WIND'S BREATH QUICKENS AS HIS EXPRESSION BECOMES FIERCELY ANGRY. THE WHITES OF HIS EYES TURN RED, AS IF FRESH BLOOD IS DRIPPING FROM HIS EYES.
ALL RIGHT, WIND! SINCE I CANNOT HIDE THE TRUTH, I MUST BECOME YOUR ENEMY. TODAY I WILL ACCOMPLISH A GREAT FEAT FOR PEERLESS CASTLE!
WIND NOW KNOWS THE TRUTH OF DUAN-LANG'S BETRAYAL AND GOES INTO A STATE OF SHOCK. THIS UNDER-STANDING CAUSES HIS BLOOD TO RUN COLD AND HIS MIND TO BECOME BLANK AS HIS HEART SLOWLY TURNS TO ICE...

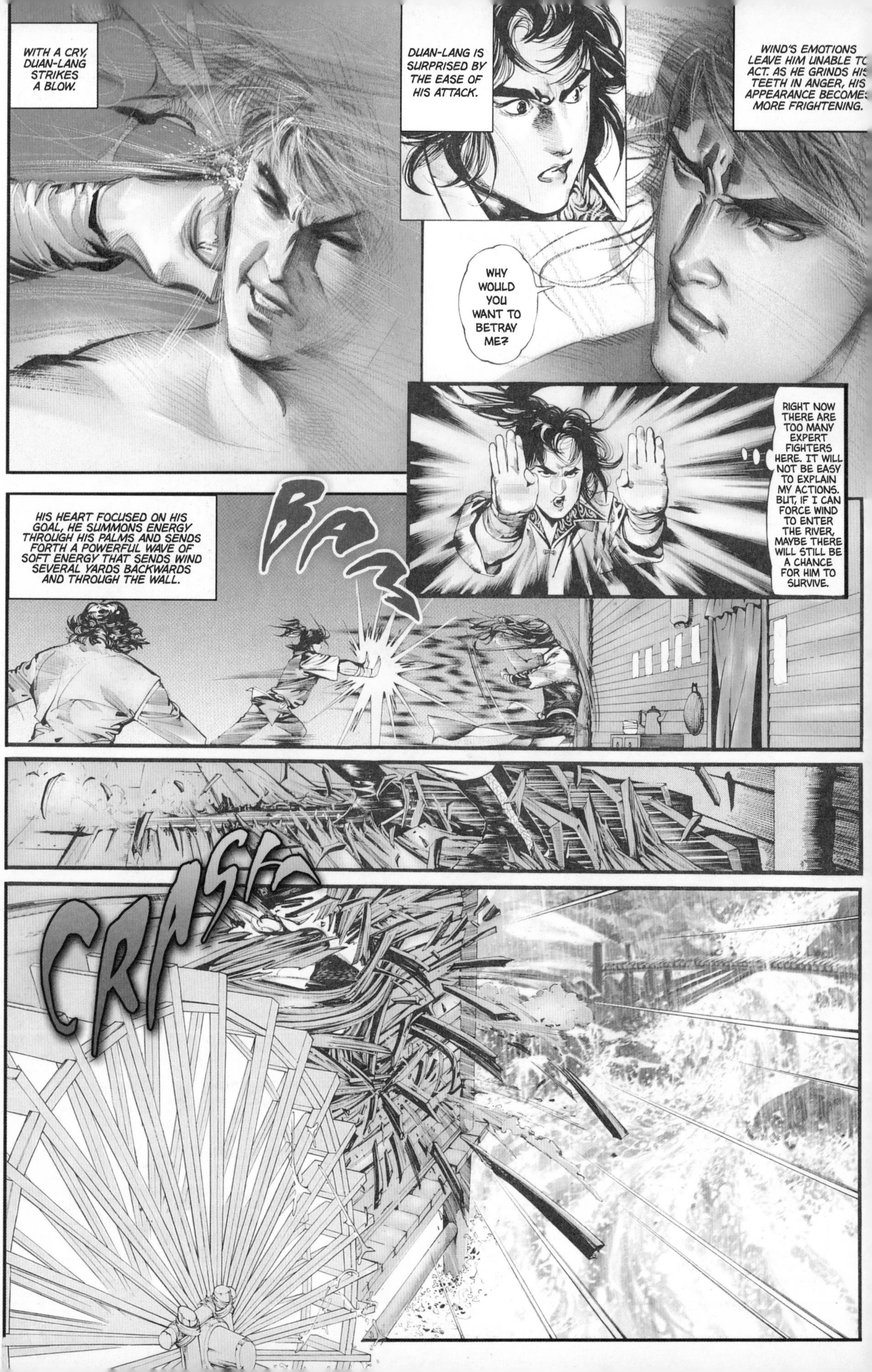
WITH A CRY, DUAN-LANG STRIKES A BLOW.
DUAN-LANG IS SURPRISED BY THE EASE OF HIS ATTACK.
WIND'S EMOTIONS LEAVE HIM UNABLE TO ACT. AS HE GRINDS HIS TEETH IN ANGER, HIS APPEARANCE BECOMES MORE FRIGHTENING.
WHY WOULD YOU WANT TO BETRAY ME?
...
RIGHT NOW THERE ARE TOO MANY EXPERT FIGHTERS HERE. IT WILL NOT BE EASY TO EXPLAIN MY ACTIONS. BUT, IF I CAN FORCE WIND TO ENTER THE RIVER, MAYBE THERE WILL STILL BE A CHANCE FOR HIM TO SURVIVE.
HIS HEART FOCUSED ON HIS GOAL, HE SUMMONS ENERGY THROUGH HIS PALMS AND SENDS FORTH A POWERFUL WAVE OF SOFT ENERGY THAT SENDS WIND SEVERAL YARDS BACKWARDS AND THROUGH THE WALL.
BAM
CRASH

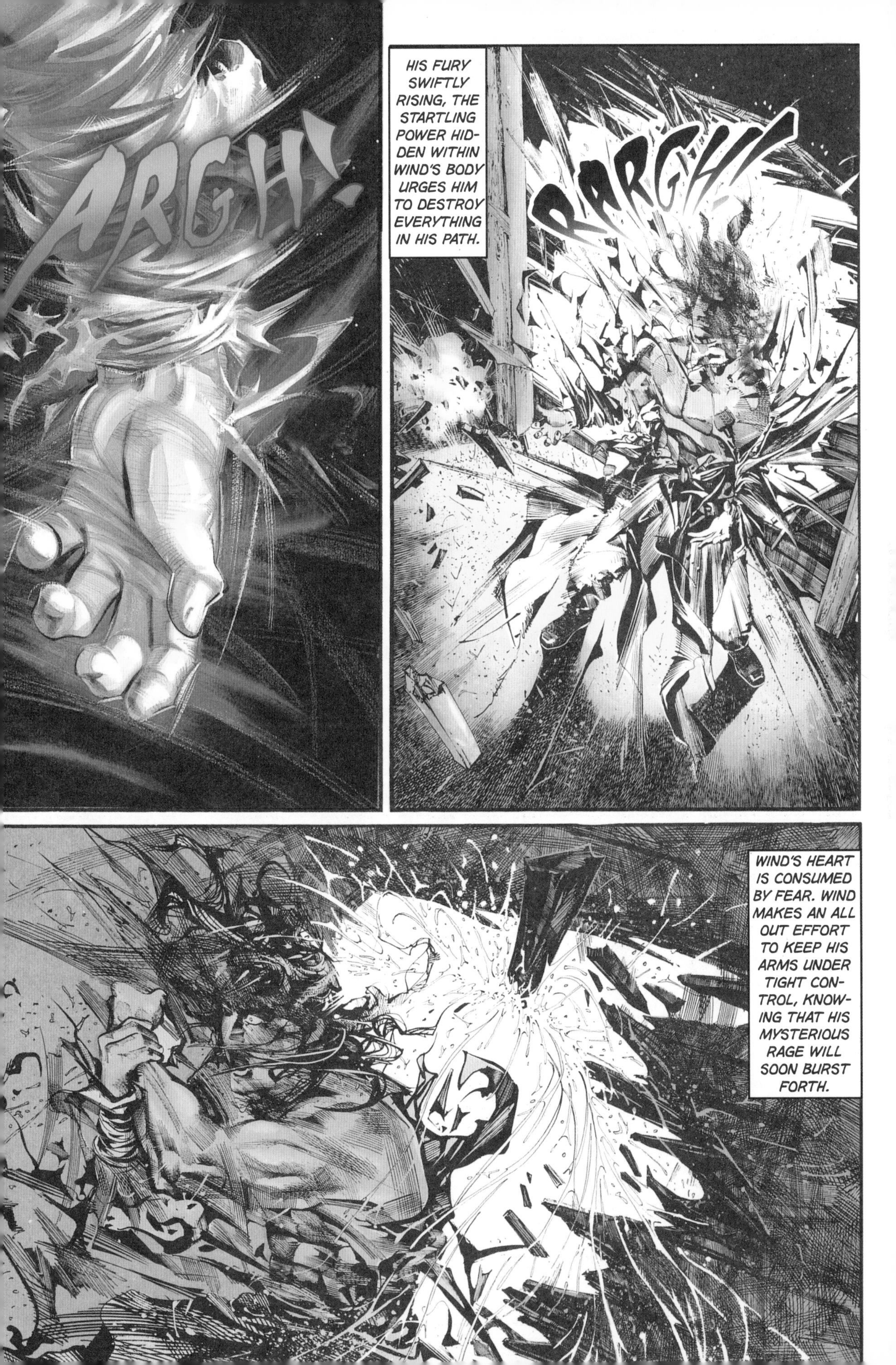
ARGH!
HIS FURY SWIFTLY RISING, THE STARTLING POWER HIDDEN WITHIN WIND'S BODY URGES HIM TO DESTROY EVERYTHING IN HIS PATH.
RARGH!!
WIND'S HEART IS CONSUMED BY FEAR. WIND MAKES AN ALL OUT EFFORT TO KEEP HIS ARMS UNDER TIGHT CONTROL, KNOWING THAT HIS MYSTERIOUS RAGE WILL SOON BURST FORTH.

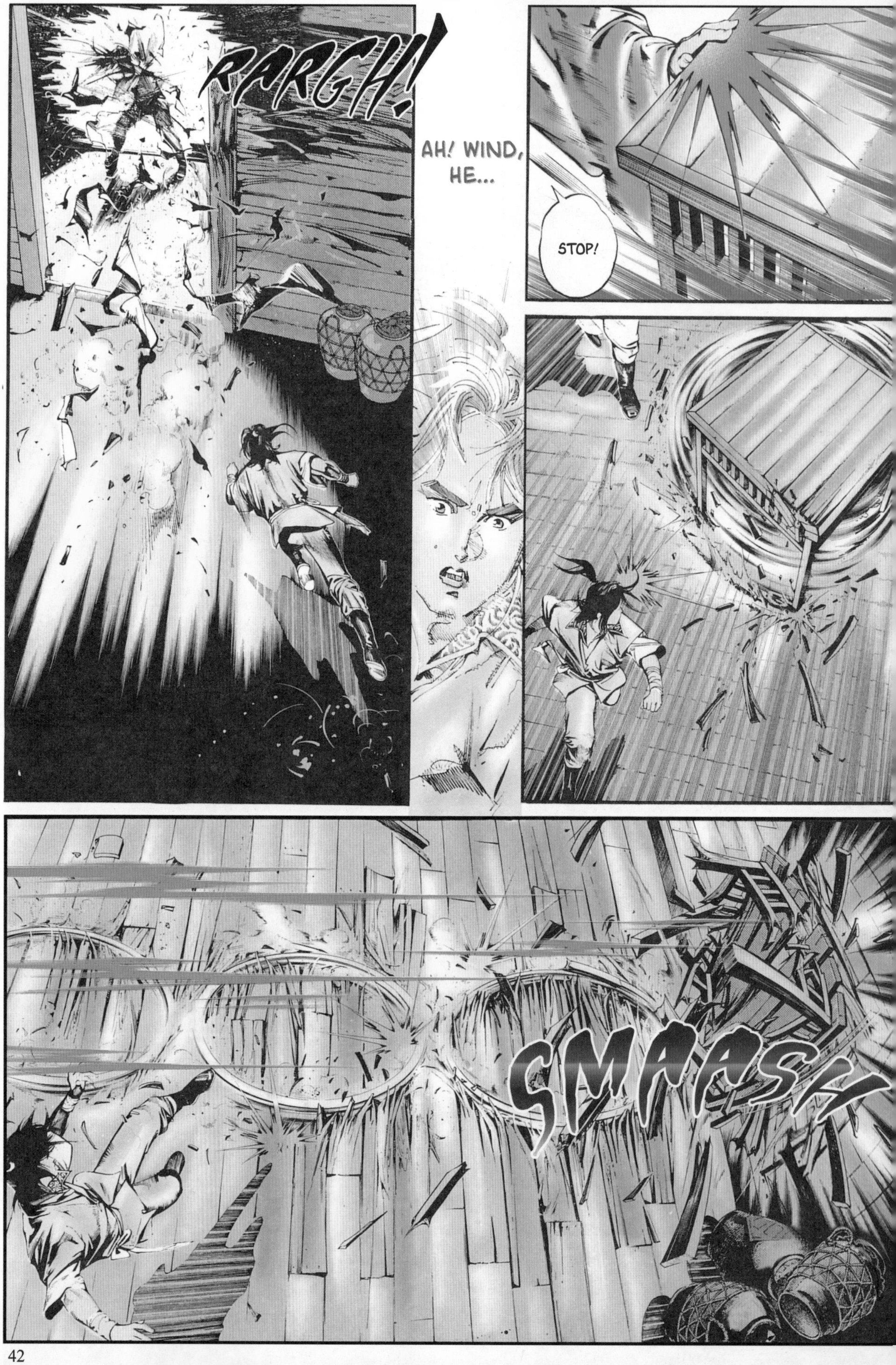
RARGH!
AH! WIND, HE...
STOP!
SMAASH

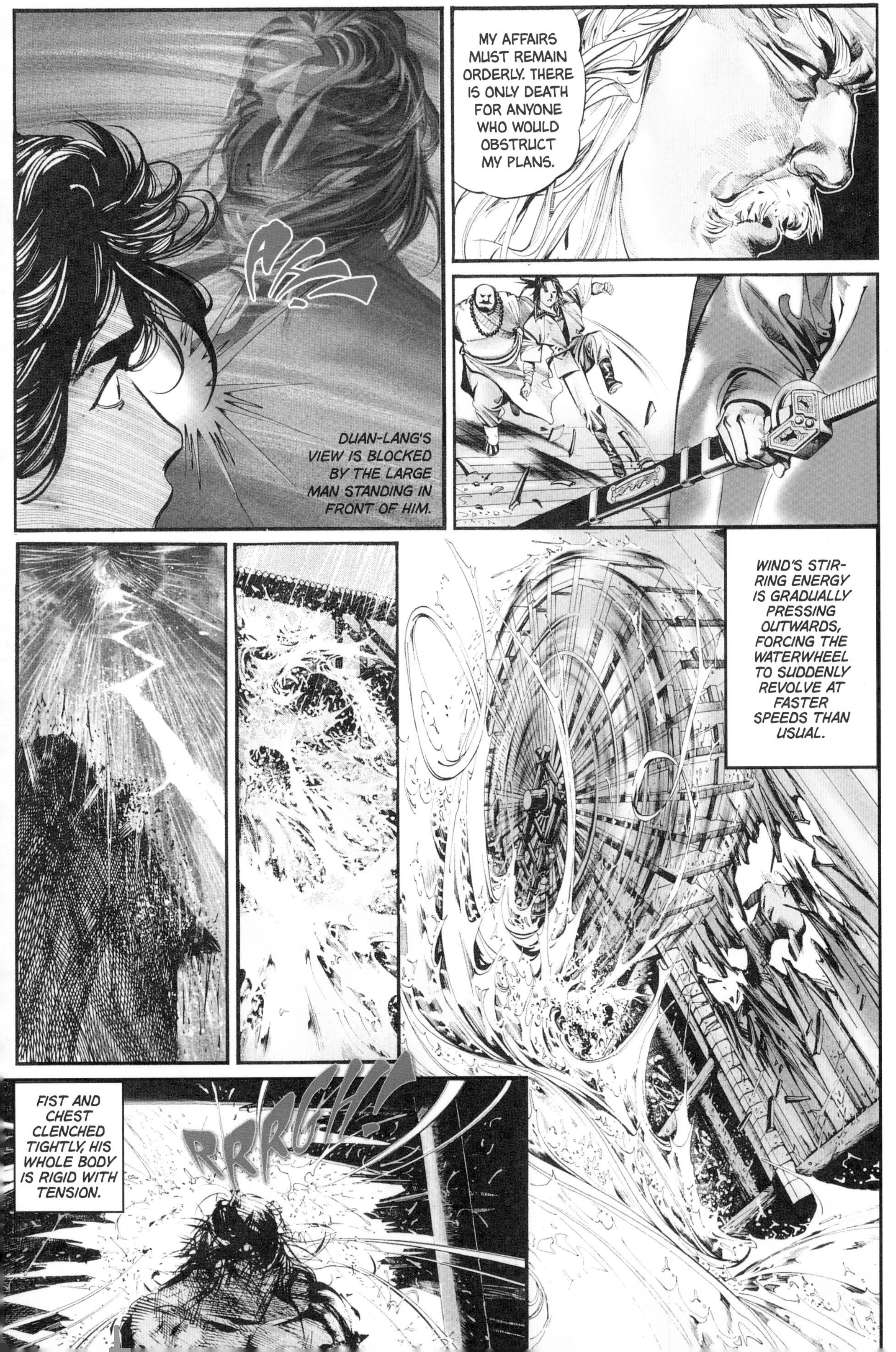
AKK!
DUAN-LANG'S VIEW IS BLOCKED BY THE LARGE MAN STANDING IN FRONT OF HIM.
MY AFFAIRS MUST REMAIN ORDERLY. THERE IS ONLY DEATH FOR ANYONE WHO WOULD OBSTRUCT MY PLANS.
WIND'S STIR-RING ENERGY IS GRADUALLY PRESSING OUTWARDS, FORCING THE WATERWHEEL TO SUDDENLY REVOLVE AT FASTER SPEEDS THAN USUAL.
FIST AND CHEST CLENCHED TIGHTLY, HIS WHOLE BODY IS RIGID WITH TENSION.
RRRGH!!

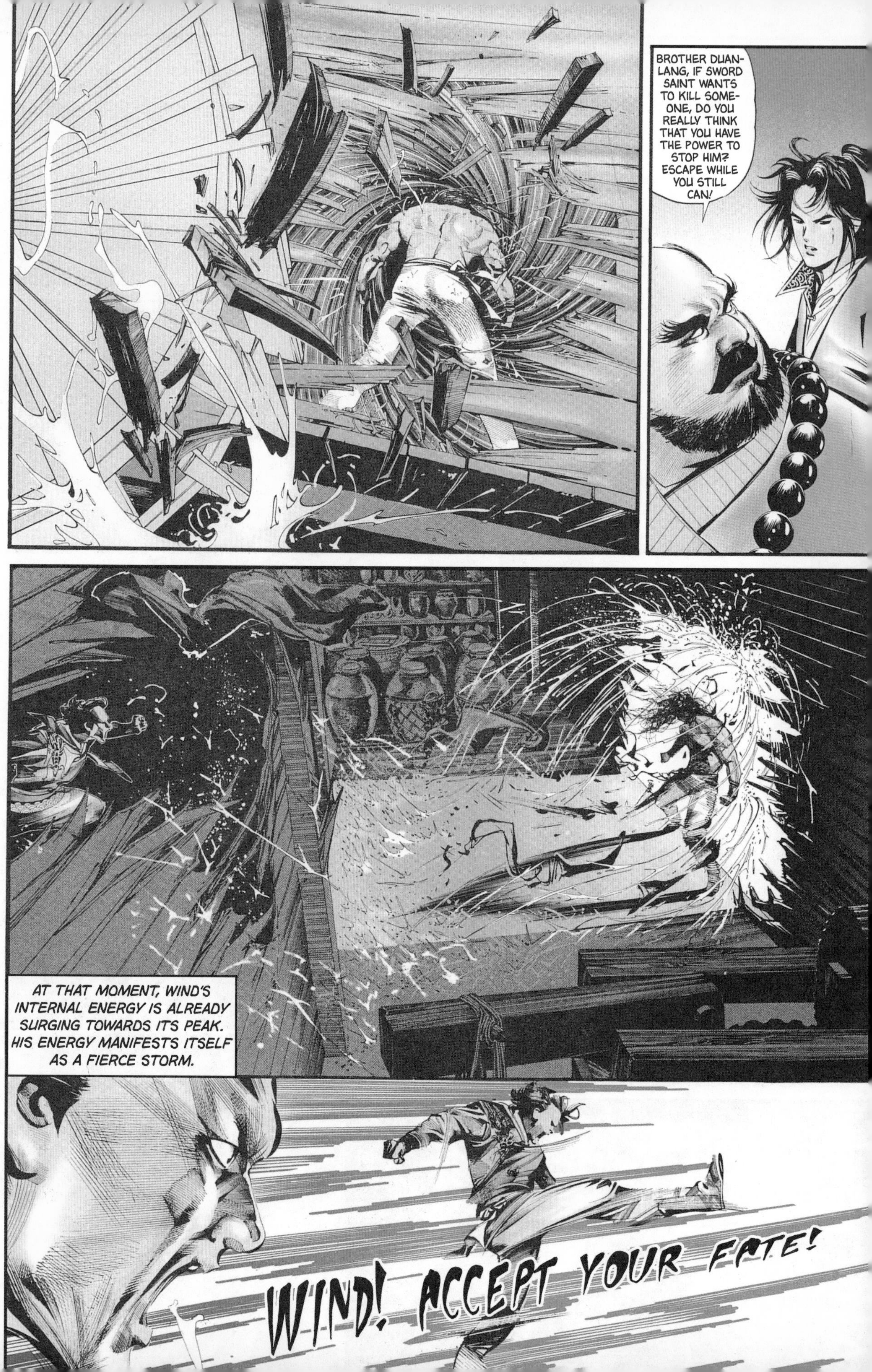
BROTHER DUANLANG, IF SWORD SAINT WANTS TO KILL SOMEONE, DO YOU REALLY THINK THAT YOU HAVE THE POWER TO STOP HIM? ESCAPE WHILE YOU STILL CAN!
AT THAT MOMENT, WIND'S INTERNAL ENERGY IS ALREADY SURGING TOWARDS ITS PEAK. HIS ENERGY MANIFESTS ITSELF AS A FIERCE STORM.
WIND! ACCEPT YOUR FATE!

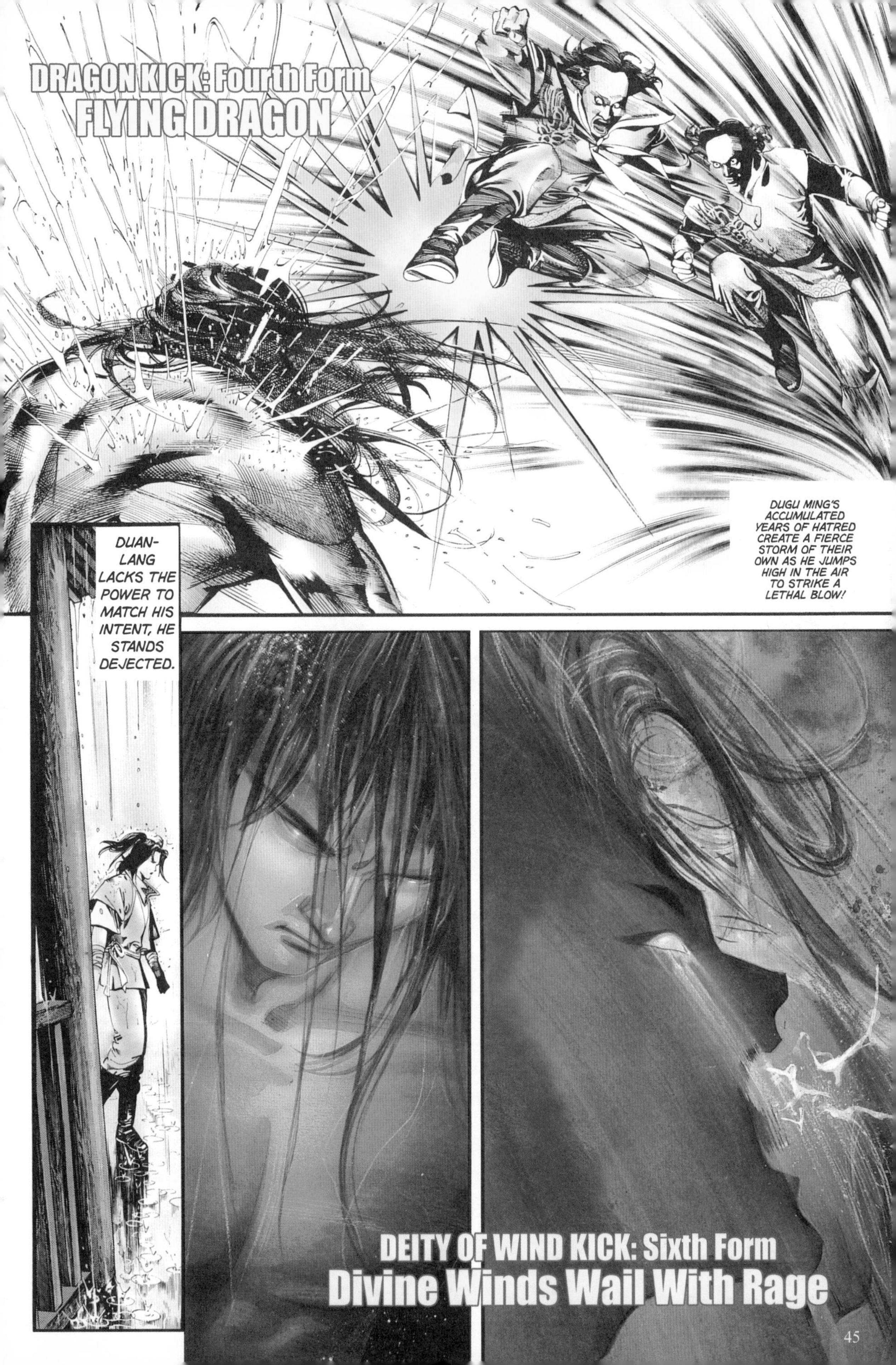
DRAGON KICK: Fourth Form
FLYING DRAGON
DUGU MING'S ACCUMULATED YEARS OF HATRED CREATE A FIERCE STORM OF THEIR OWN AS HE JUMPS HIGH IN THE AIR TO STRIKE A LETHAL BLOW!
DUAN-LANG LACKS THE POWER TO MATCH HIS INTENT, HE STANDS DEJECTED.
DEITY OF WIND KICK: Sixth Form
Divine Winds Wail With Rage

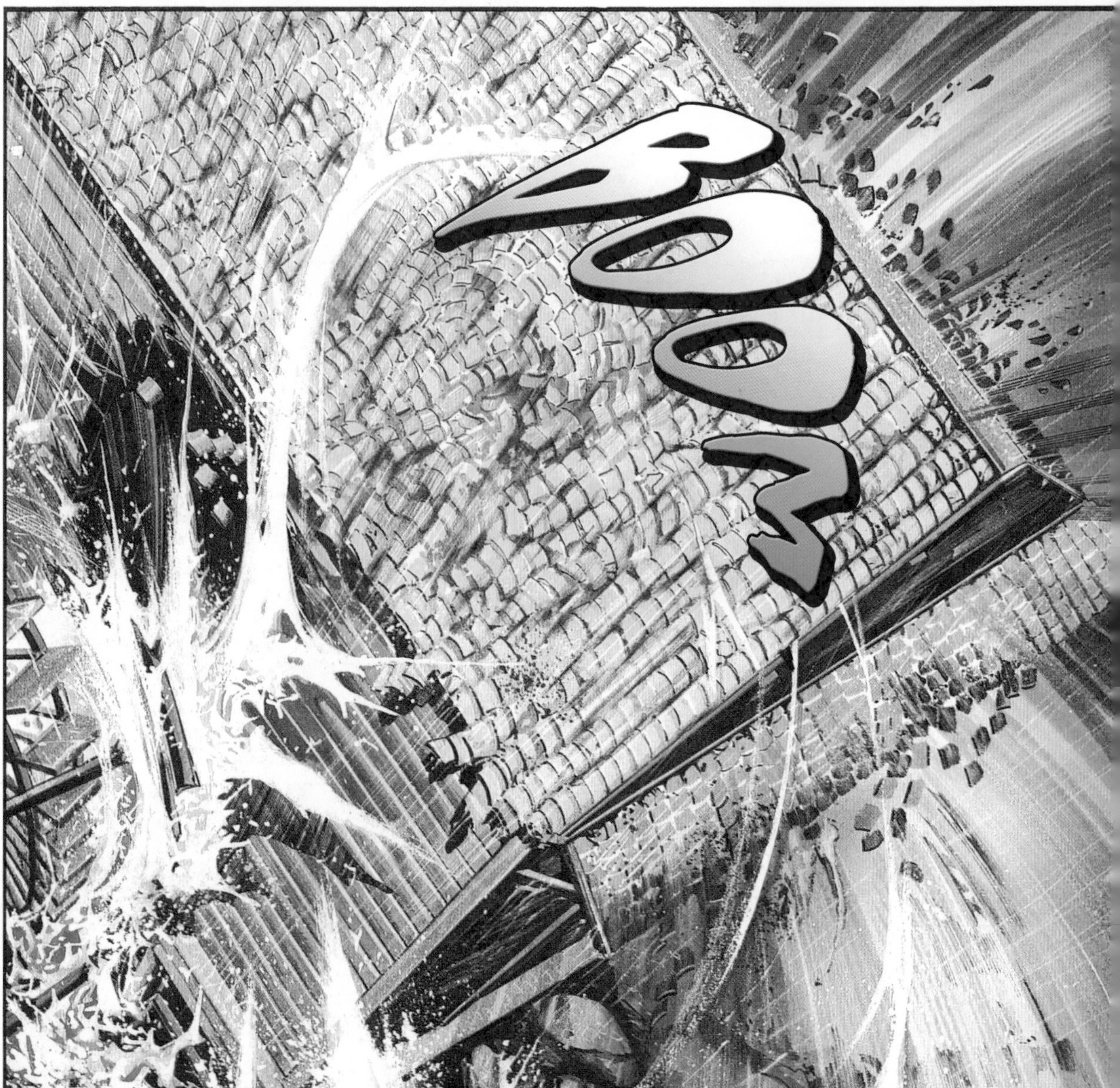
BOOM
WIND'S EARTH-SHAKING ROAR CAUSES THE WATERWHEEL TO INSTANTLY BREAK FREE.

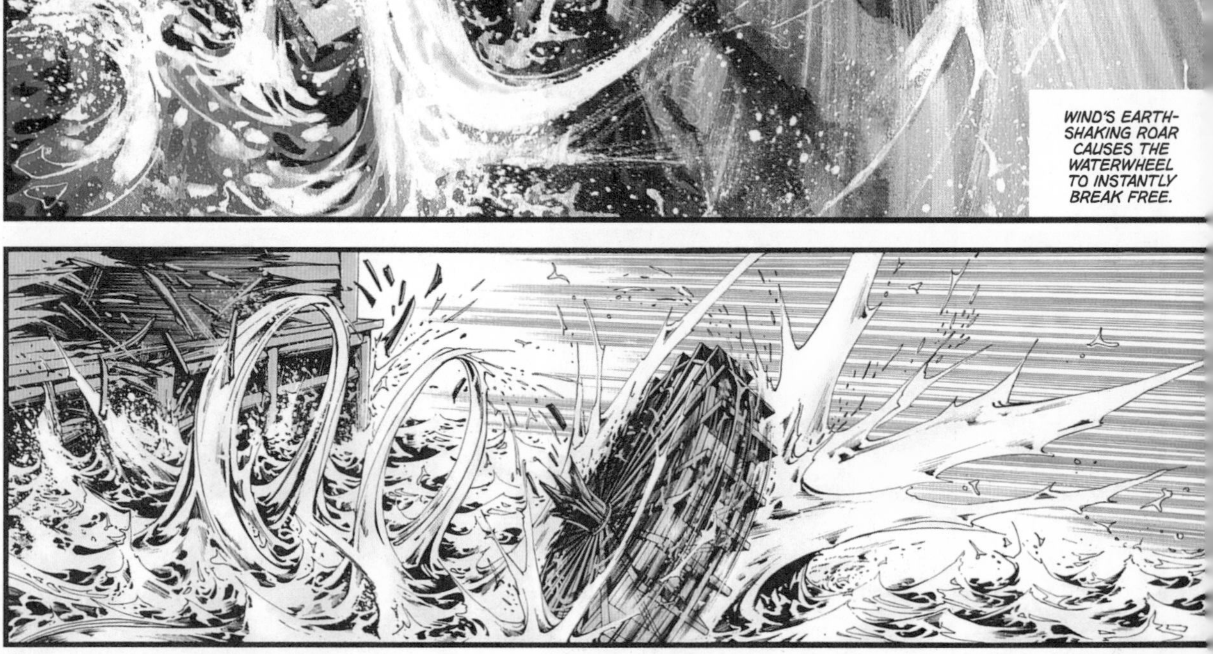

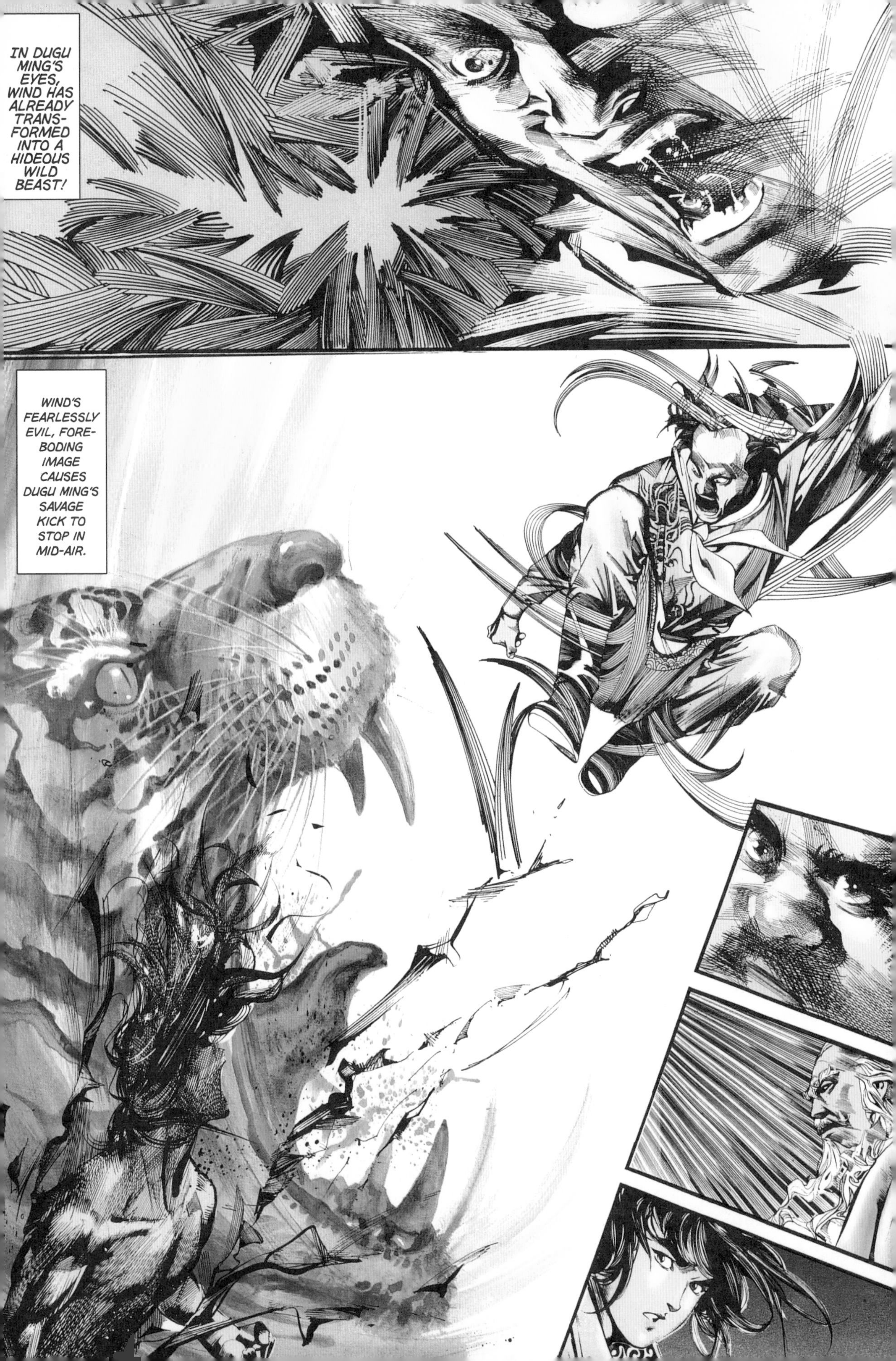
IN DUGU MING'S EYES, WIND HAS ALREADY TRANSFORMED INTO A HIDEOUS WILD BEAST!
WIND'S FEARLESSLY EVIL, FOREBODING IMAGE CAUSES DUGU MING'S SAVAGE KICK TO STOP IN MID-AIR.

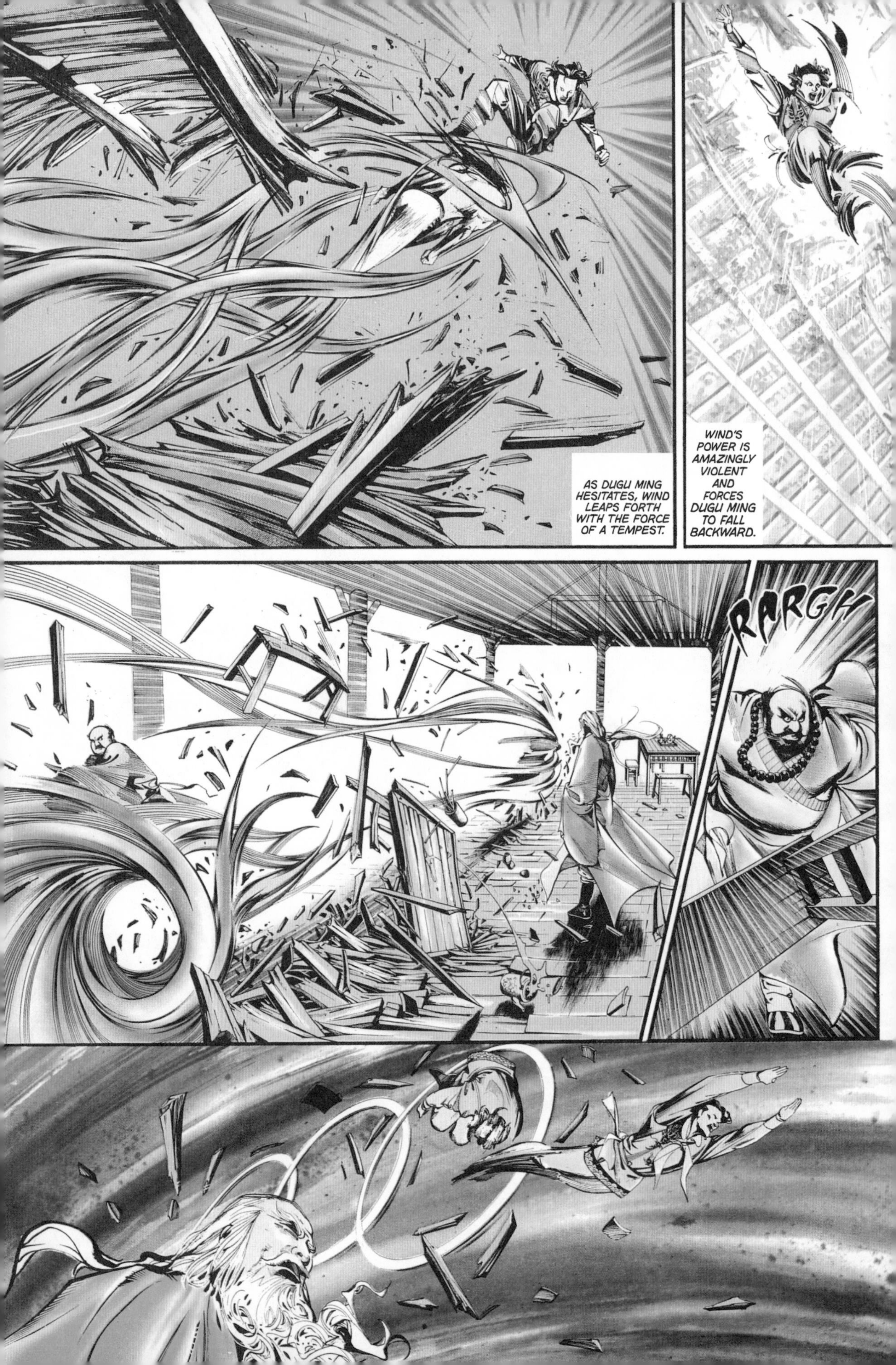
AS DUGU MING HESITATES, WIND LEAPS FORTH WITH THE FORCE OF A TEMPEST.
WIND'S POWER IS AMAZINGLY VIOLENT AND FORCES DUGU MING TO FALL BACKWARD.
RARGH

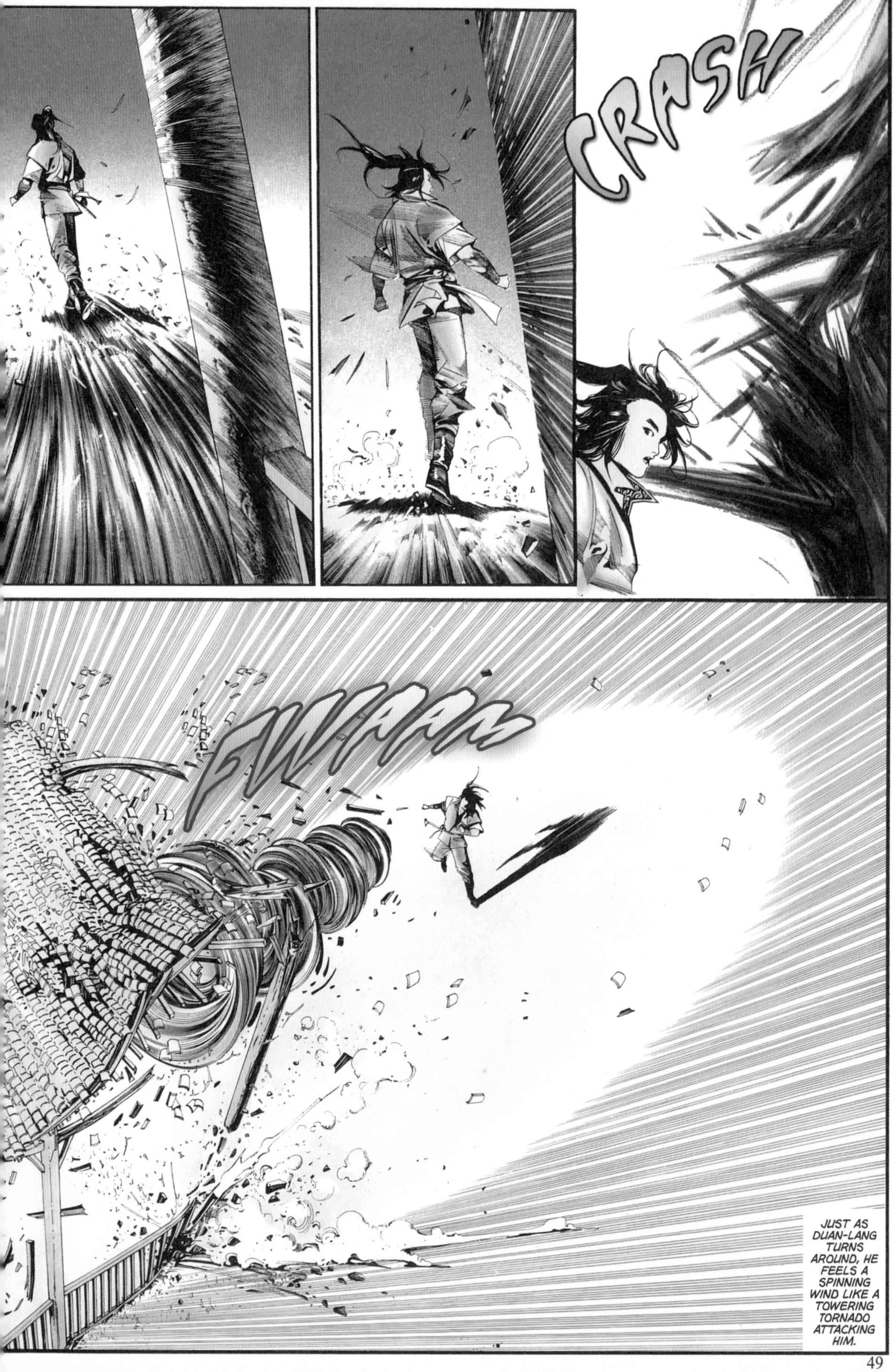
CRASH
FWAAM
JUST AS DUAN-LANG TURNS AROUND, HE FEELS A SPINNING WIND LIKE A TOWERING TORNADO ATTACKING HIM.

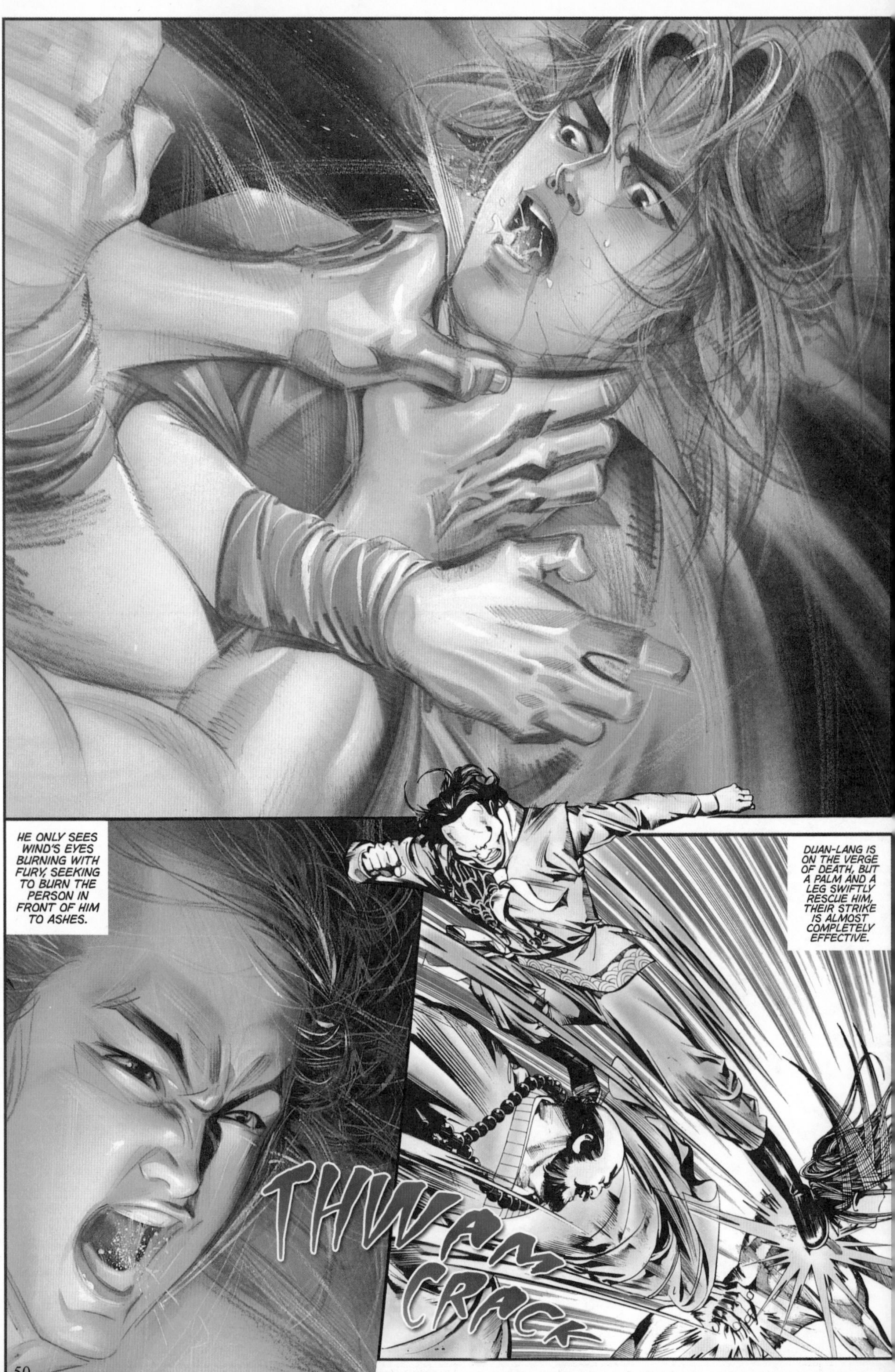
HE ONLY SEES WIND'S EYES BURNING WITH FURY, SEEKING TO BURN THE PERSON IN FRONT OF HIM TO ASHES.
DUAN-LANG IS ON THE VERGE OF DEATH, BUT A PALM AND A LEG SWIFTLY RESCUE HIM, THEIR STRIKE IS ALMOST COMPLETELY EFFECTIVE.
THWAM
CRACK

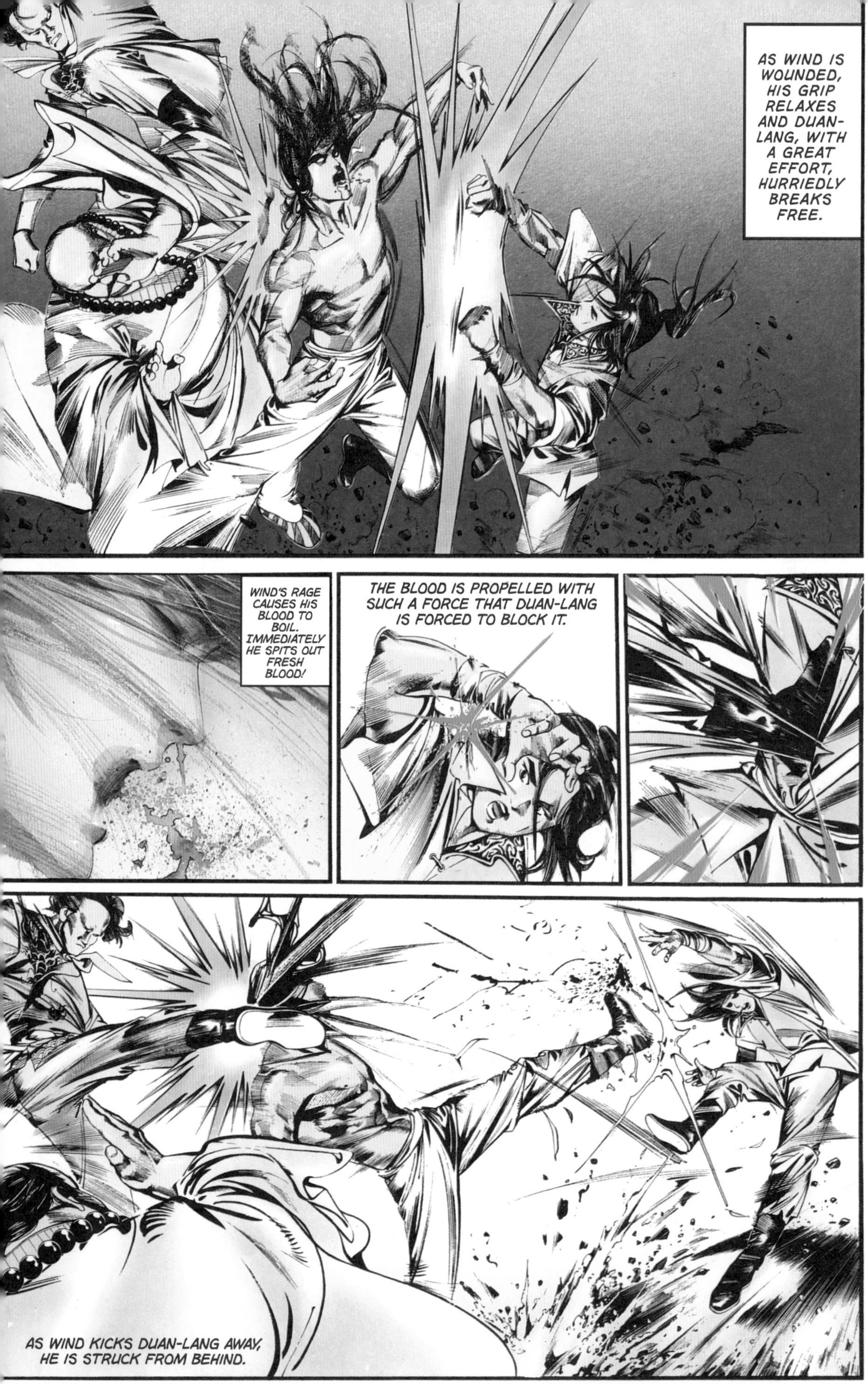
AS WIND IS WOUNDED, HIS GRIP RELAXES AND DUAN-LANG, WITH A GREAT EFFORT, HURRIEDLY BREAKS FREE.
WIND'S RAGE CAUSES HIS BLOOD TO BOIL. IMMEDIATELY HE SPITS OUT FRESH BLOOD!
THE BLOOD IS PROPELLED WITH SUCH A FORCE THAT DUAN-LANG IS FORCED TO BLOCK IT.
AS WIND KICKS DUAN-LANG AWAY, HE IS STRUCK FROM BEHIND.

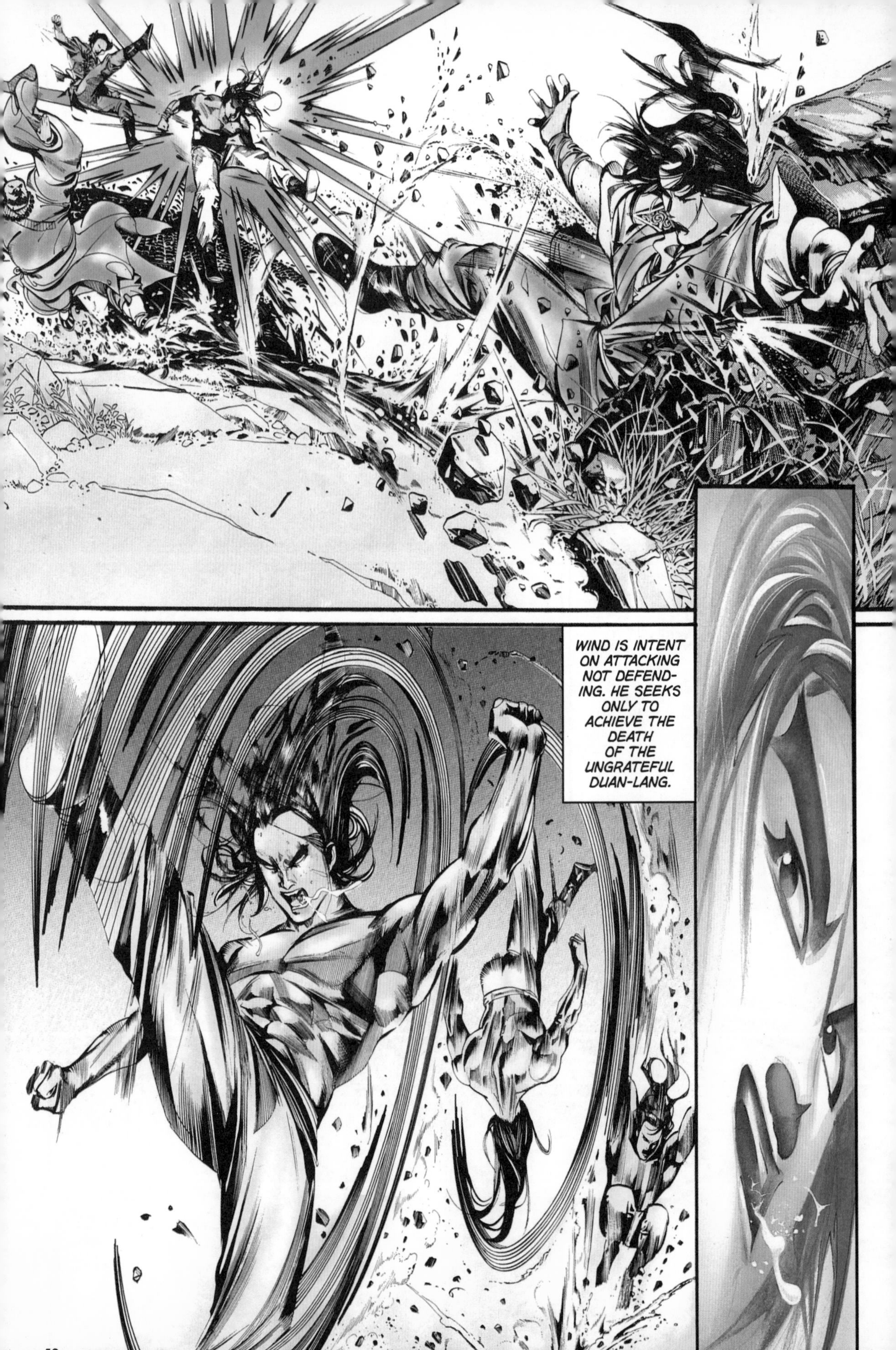
WIND IS INTENT ON ATTACKING NOT DEFENDING. HE SEEKS ONLY TO ACHIEVE THE DEATH OF THE UNGRATEFUL DUAN-LANG.

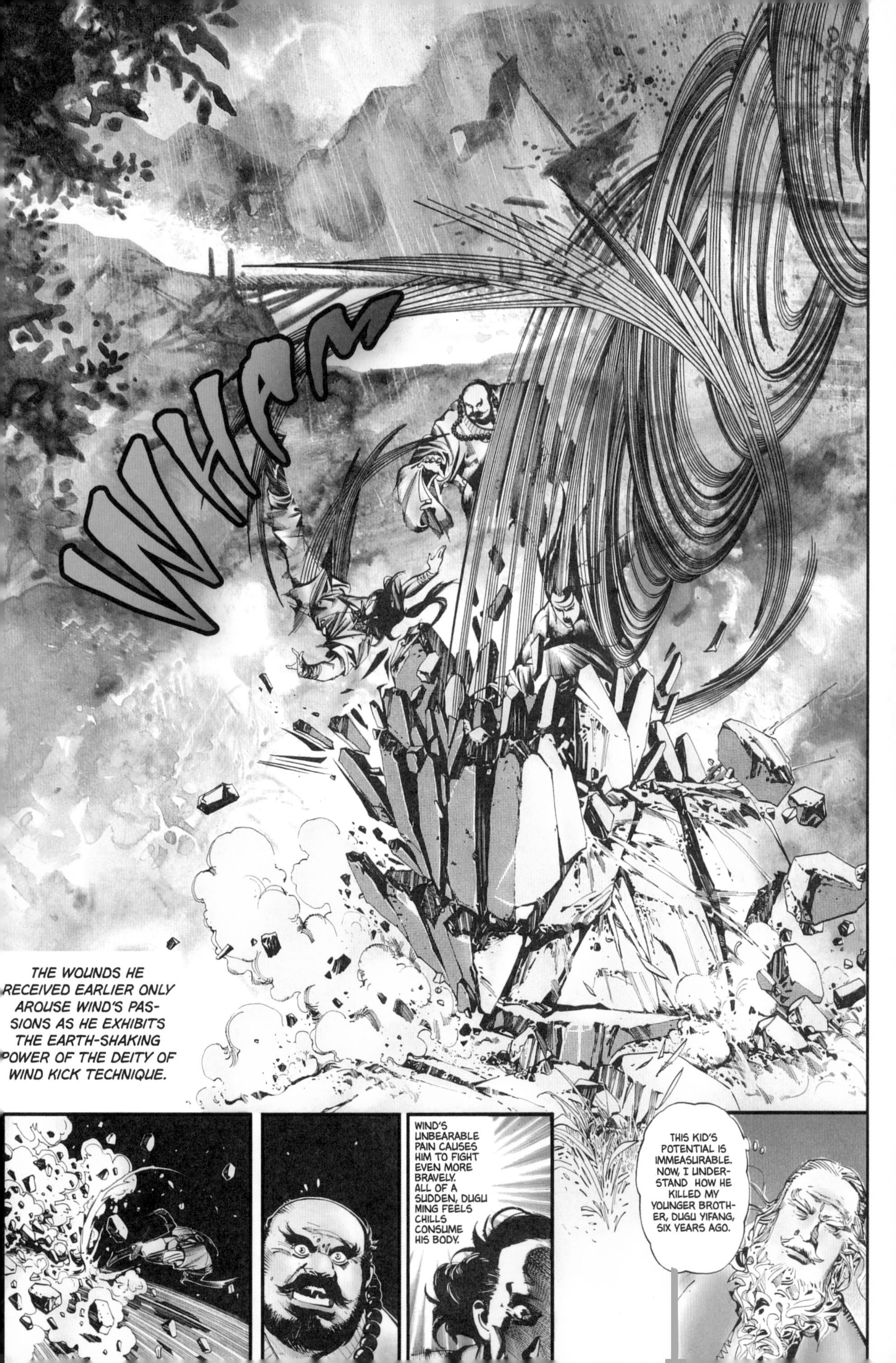
WHAM
THE WOUNDS HE RECEIVED EARLIER ONLY AROUSE WIND'S PASSIONS AS HE EXHIBITS THE EARTH-SHAKING POWER OF THE DEITY OF WIND KICK TECHNIQUE.
WIND'S UNBEARABLE PAIN CAUSES HIM TO FIGHT EVEN MORE BRAVELY. ALL OF A SUDDEN, DUGU MING FEELS CHILLS CONSUME HIS BODY.
THIS KID'S POTENTIAL IS IMMEASURABLE. NOW, I UNDERSTAND HOW HE KILLED MY YOUNGER BROTHER, DUGU YIFANG, SIX YEARS AGO.

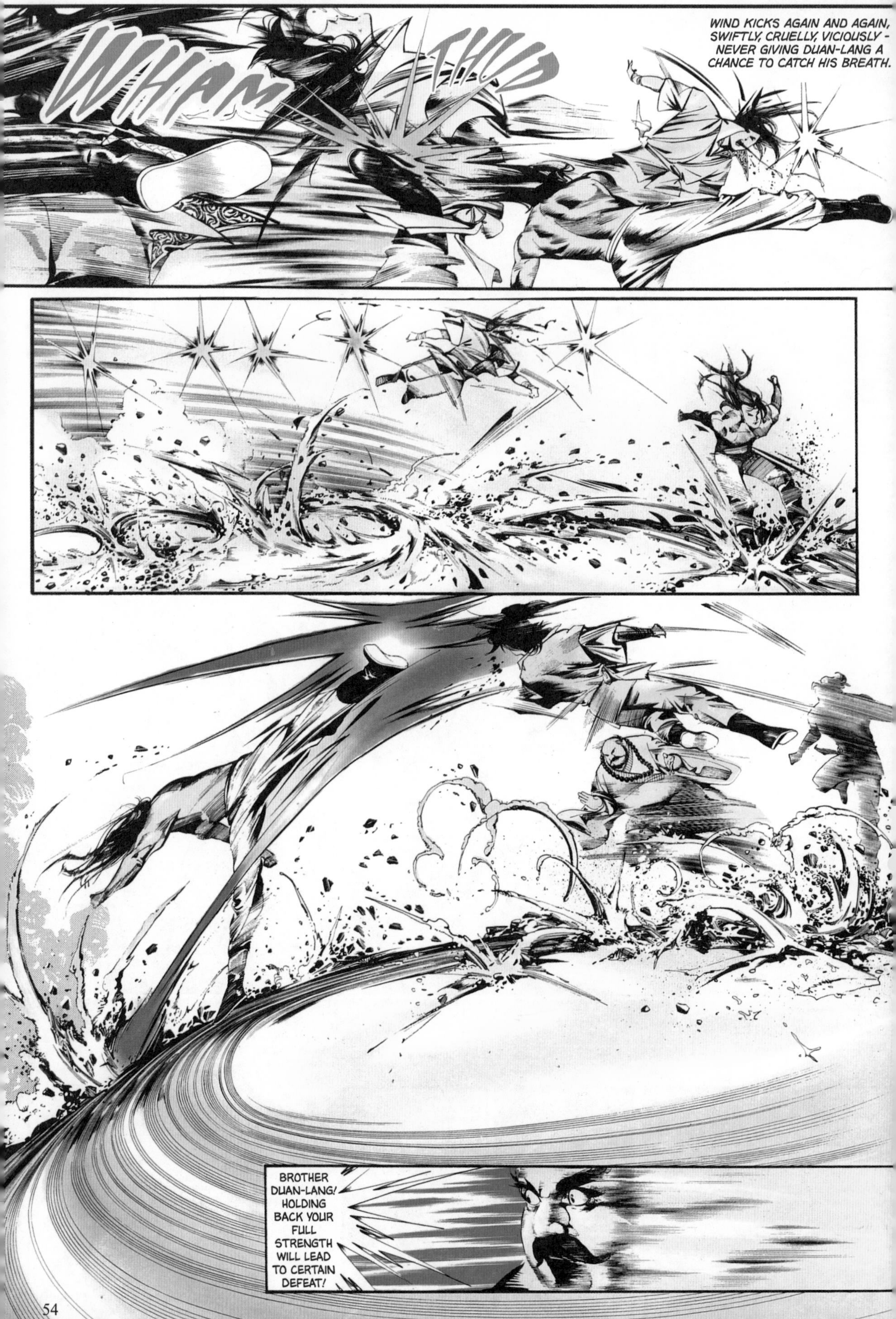
WHAM
THUD
WIND KICKS AGAIN AND AGAIN, SWIFTLY, CRUELLY, VICIOUSLY - NEVER GIVING DUAN-LANG A CHANCE TO CATCH HIS BREATH.
BROTHER DUAN-LANG! HOLDING BACK YOUR FULL STRENGTH WILL LEAD TO CERTAIN DEFEAT!

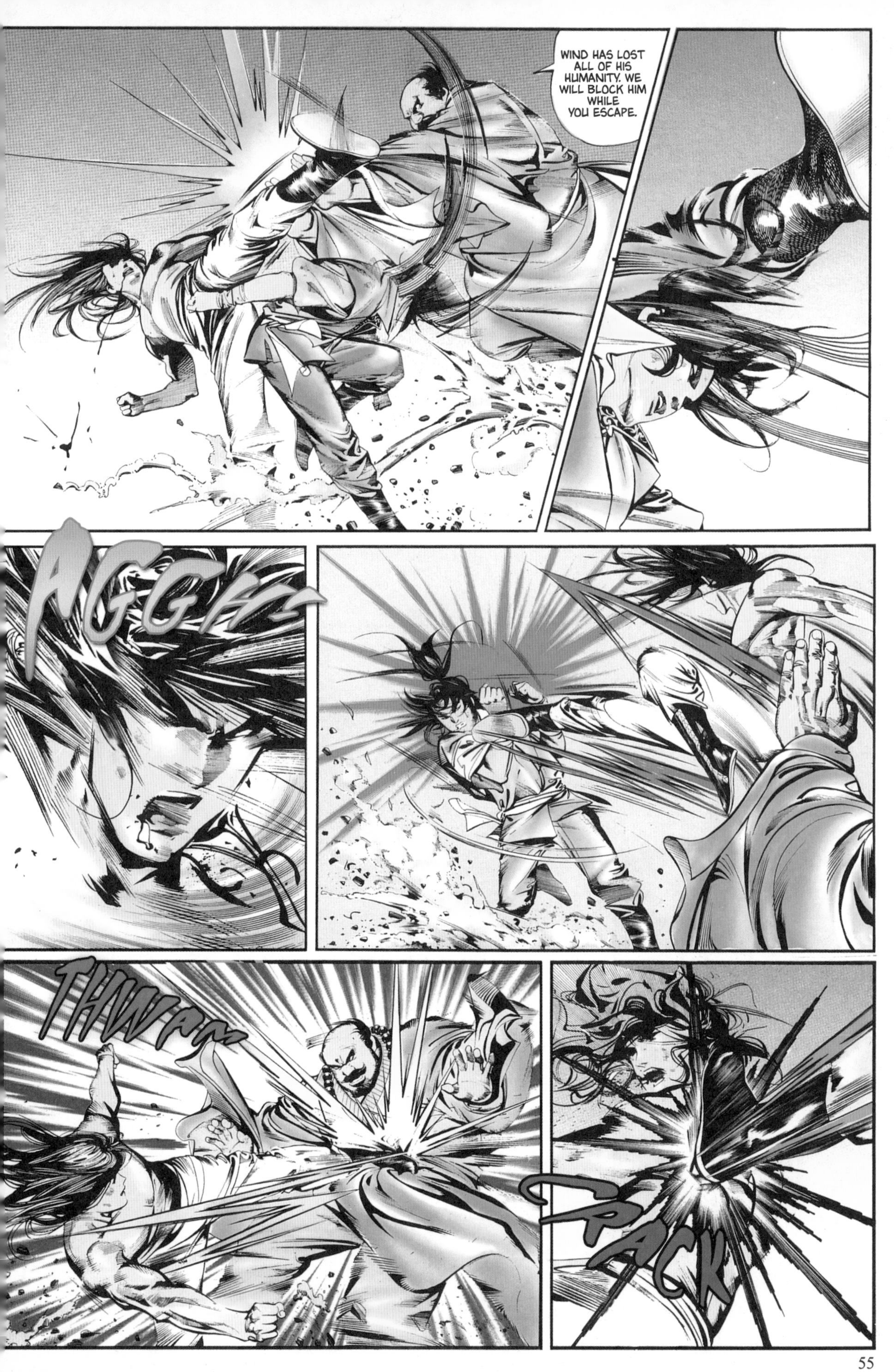
WIND HAS LOST ALL OF HIS HUMANITY. WE WILL BLOCK HIM WHILE YOU ESCAPE.
AGGH
THWAM
CRACK

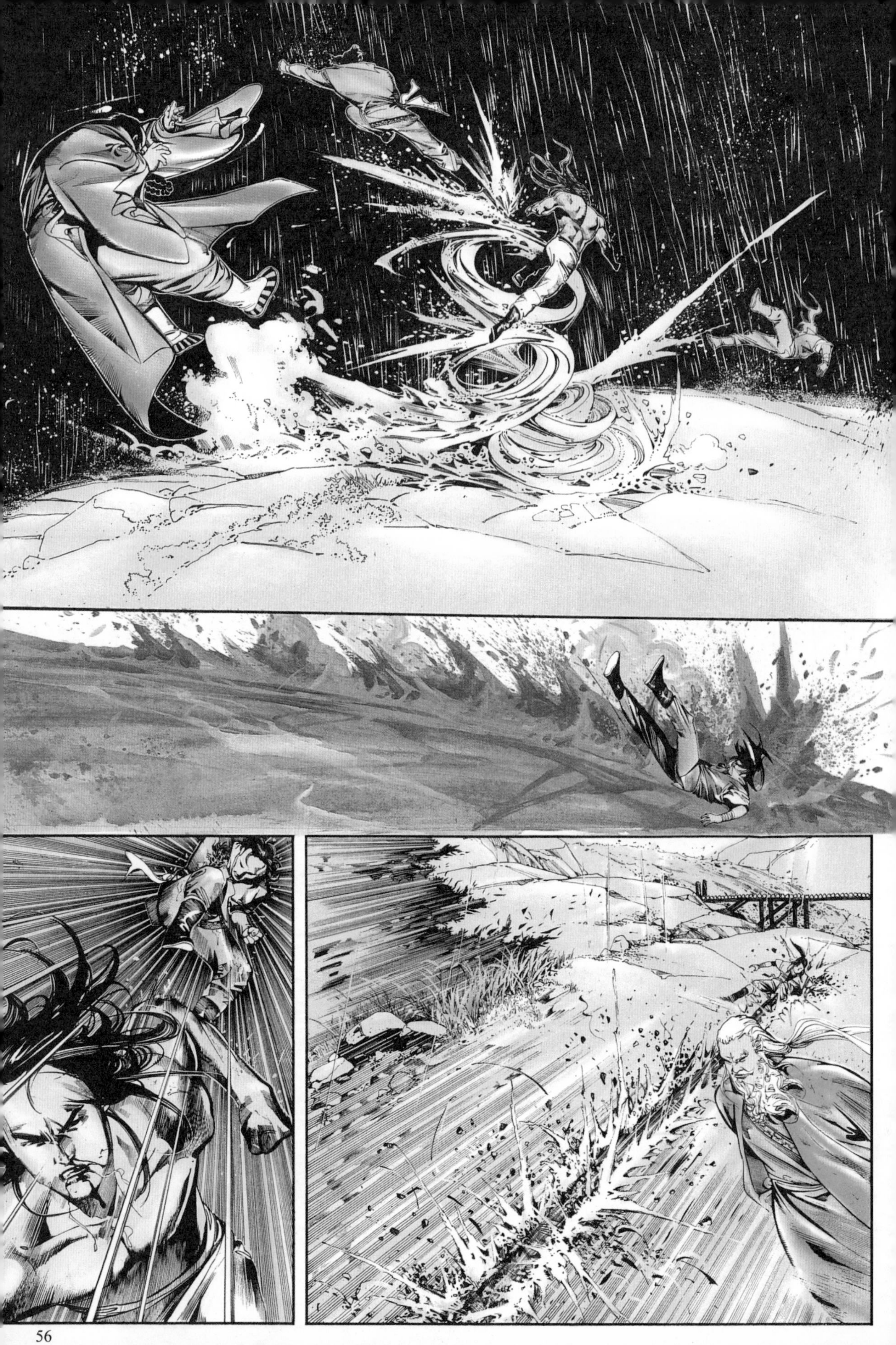

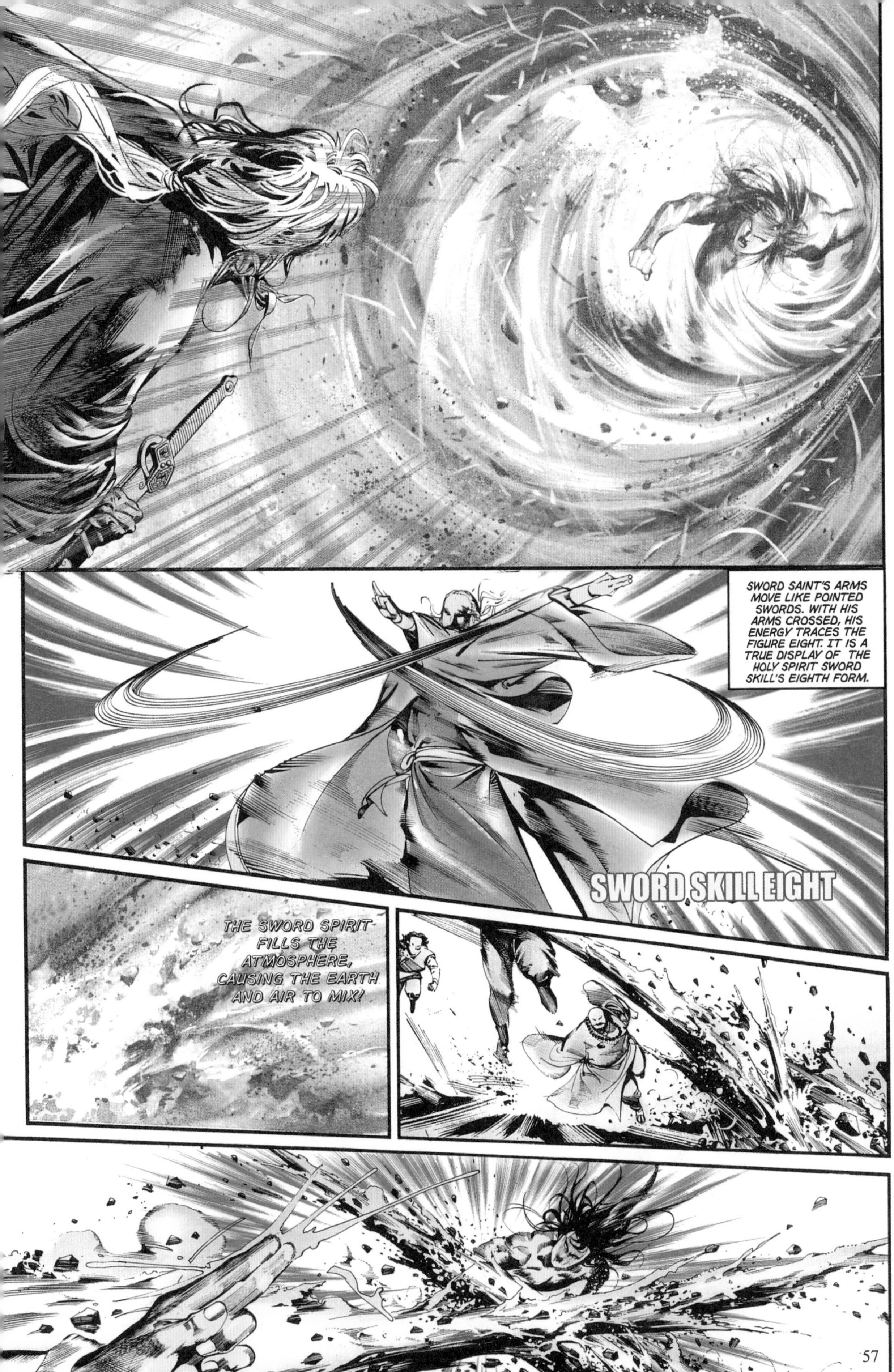
SWORD SAINT'S ARMS MOVE LIKE POINTED SWORDS. WITH HIS ARMS CROSSED, HIS ENERGY TRACES THE FIGURE EIGHT. IT IS A TRUE DISPLAY OF THE HOLY SPIRIT SWORD SKILL'S EIGHTH FORM.
SWORD SKILL EIGHT
THE SWORD SPIRIT FILLS THE ATMOSPHERE, CAUSING THE EARTH AND AIR TO MIX!

WIND'S MURDEROUS RAGE HAS ALREADY REACHED ITS BOILING POINT! NO MATTER WHO STANDS IN FRONT OF HIM, HE THINKS ONLY OF ATTACKING!

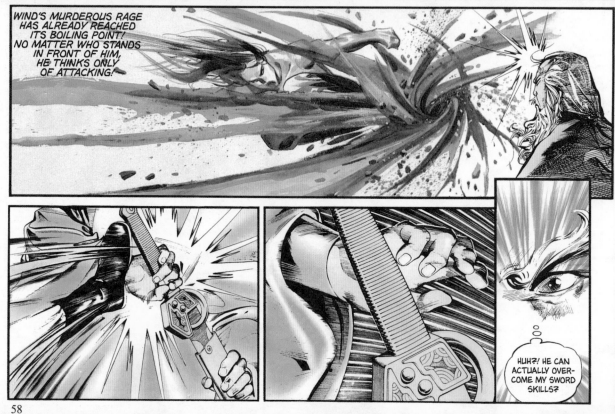

HUH?! HE CAN ACTUALLY OVER-COME MY SWORD SKILLS?

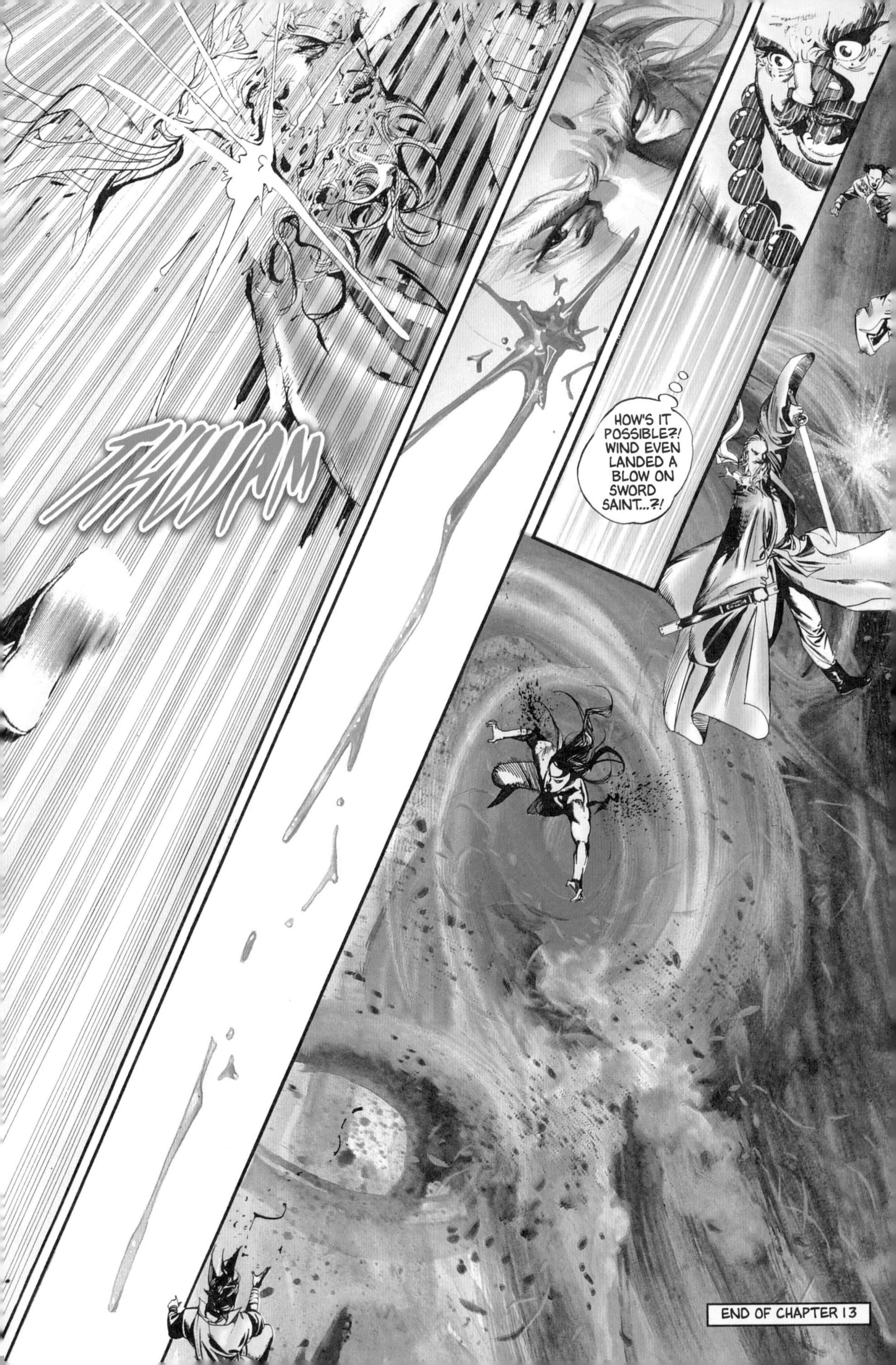
THMAM
HOW'S IT POSSIBLE?! WIND EVEN LANDED A BLOW ON SWORD SAINT...?!
END OF CHAPTER 13

Chapter 14: Blood of Insanity

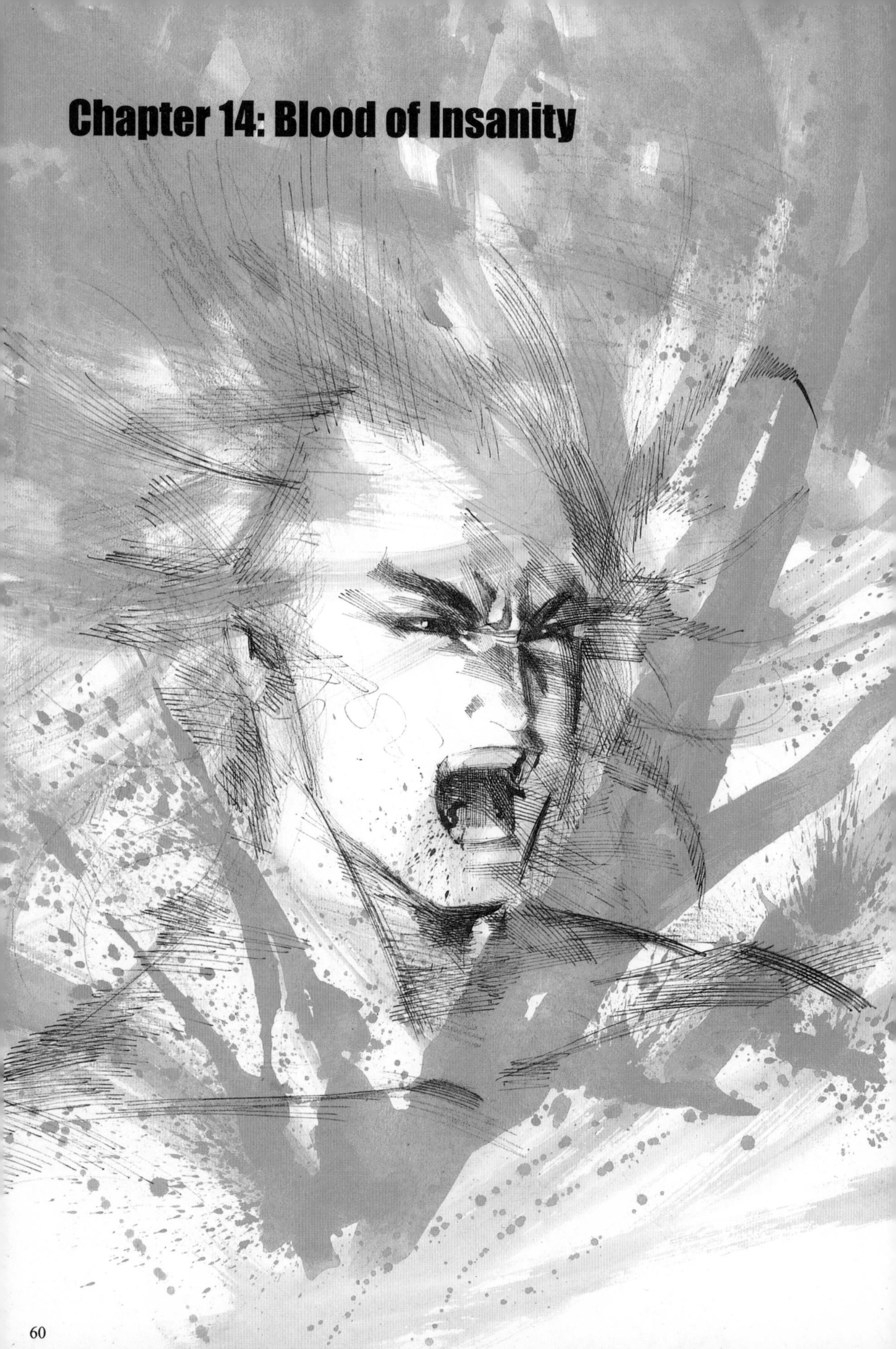

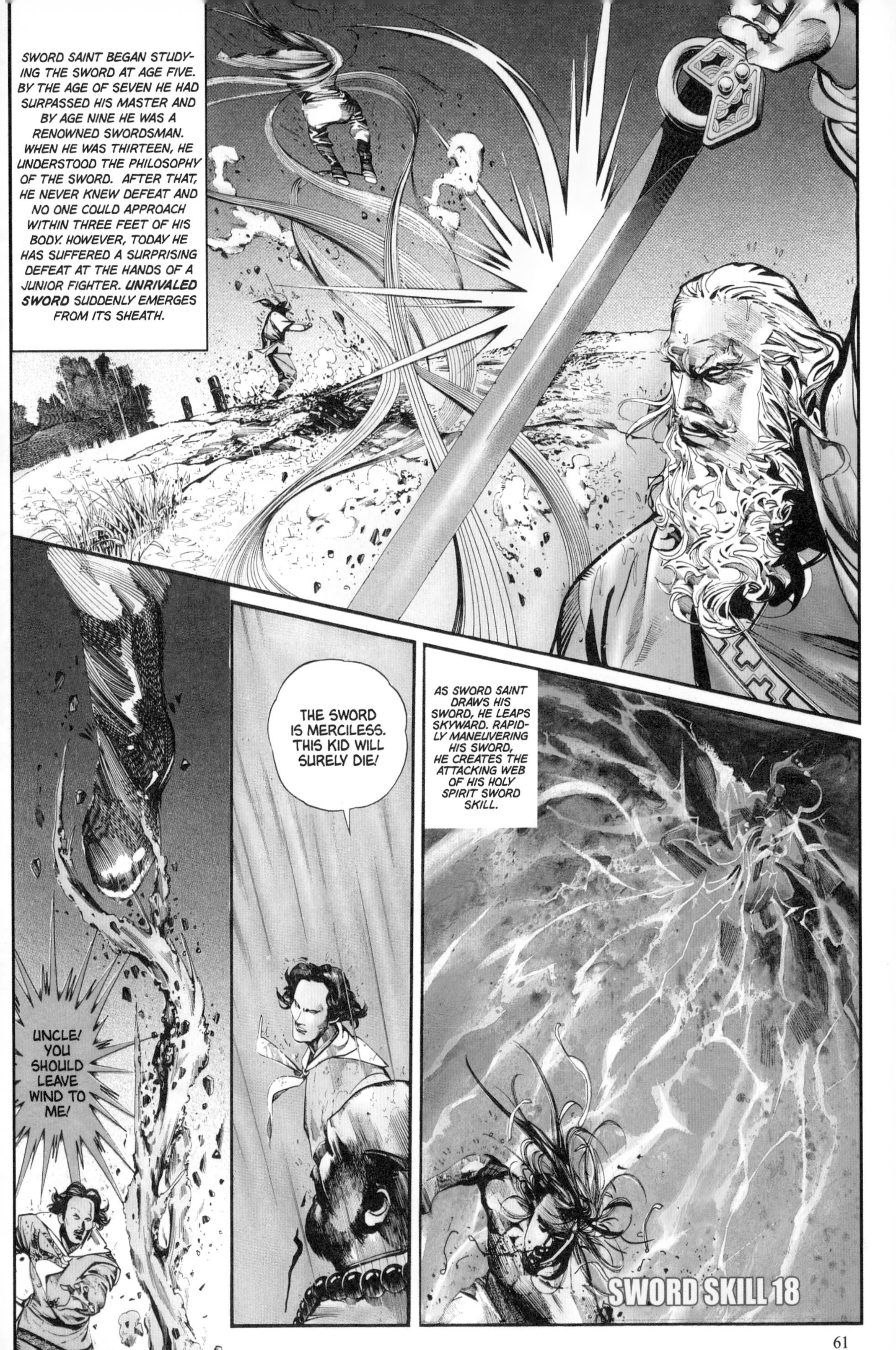

SWORD SAINT BEGAN STUDYING THE SWORD AT AGE FIVE. BY THE AGE OF SEVEN HE HAD SURPASSED HIS MASTER AND BY AGE NINE HE WAS A RENOWNED SWORDSMAN. WHEN HE WAS THIRTEEN, HE UNDERSTOOD THE PHILOSOPHY OF THE SWORD. AFTER THAT, HE NEVER KNEW DEFEAT AND NO ONE COULD APPROACH WITHIN THREE FEET OF HIS BODY. HOWEVER, TODAY HE HAS SUFFERED A SURPRISING DEFEAT AT THE HANDS OF A JUNIOR FIGHTER. **UNRIVALED SWORD** SUDDENLY EMERGES FROM ITS SHEATH.
UNCLE! YOU SHOULD LEAVE WIND TO ME!
THE SWORD IS MERCILESS. THIS KID WILL SURELY DIE!
AS SWORD SAINT DRAWS HIS SWORD, HE LEAPS SKYWARD. RAPIDLY MANEUVERING HIS SWORD, HE CREATES THE ATTACKING WEB OF HIS HOLY SPIRIT SWORD SKILL.
SWORD SKILL 18

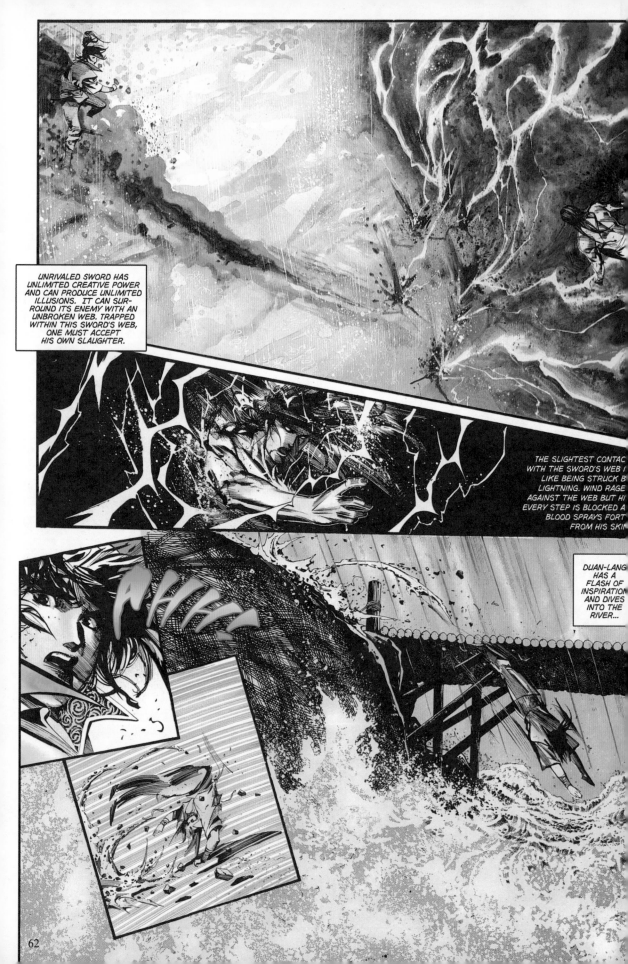

UNRIVALED SWORD HAS UNLIMITED CREATIVE POWER AND CAN PRODUCE UNLIMITED ILLUSIONS. IT CAN SURROUND ITS ENEMY WITH AN UNBROKEN WEB. TRAPPED WITHIN THIS SWORD'S WEB, ONE MUST ACCEPT HIS OWN SLAUGHTER.

THE SLIGHTEST CONTAC WITH THE SWORD'S WEB I LIKE BEING STRUCK B LIGHTNING. WIND RAGE AGAINST THE WEB BUT HI EVERY STEP IS BLOCKED A BLOOD SPRAYS FORT FROM HIS SKI

DUAN-LANG HAS A FLASH OF INSPIRATION AND DIVES INTO THE RIVER...

AHHH

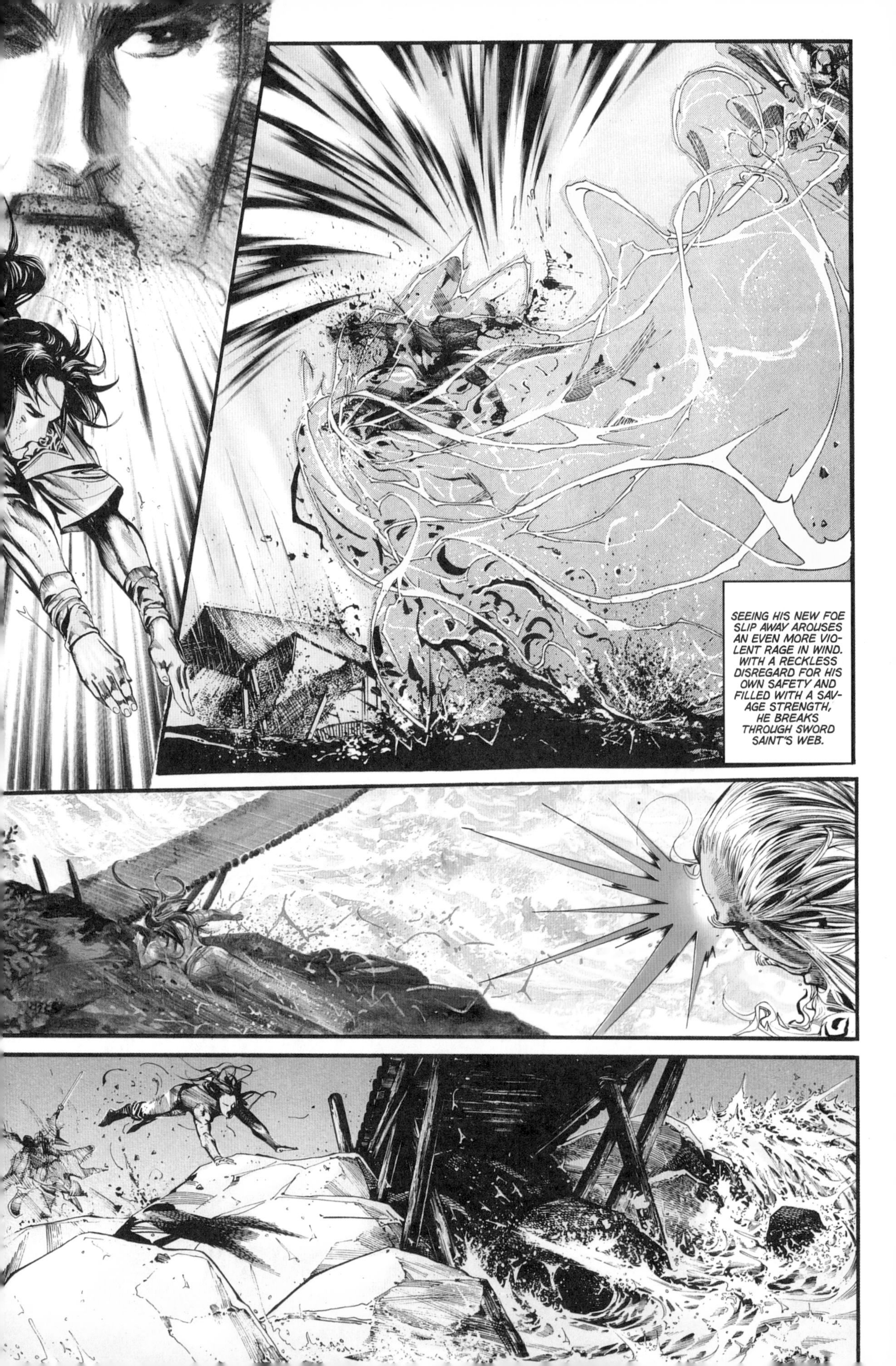
SEEING HIS NEW FOE SLIP AWAY AROUSES AN EVEN MORE VIOLENT RAGE IN WIND. WITH A RECKLESS DISREGARD FOR HIS OWN SAFETY AND FILLED WITH A SAVAGE STRENGTH, HE BREAKS THROUGH SWORD SAINT'S WEB.

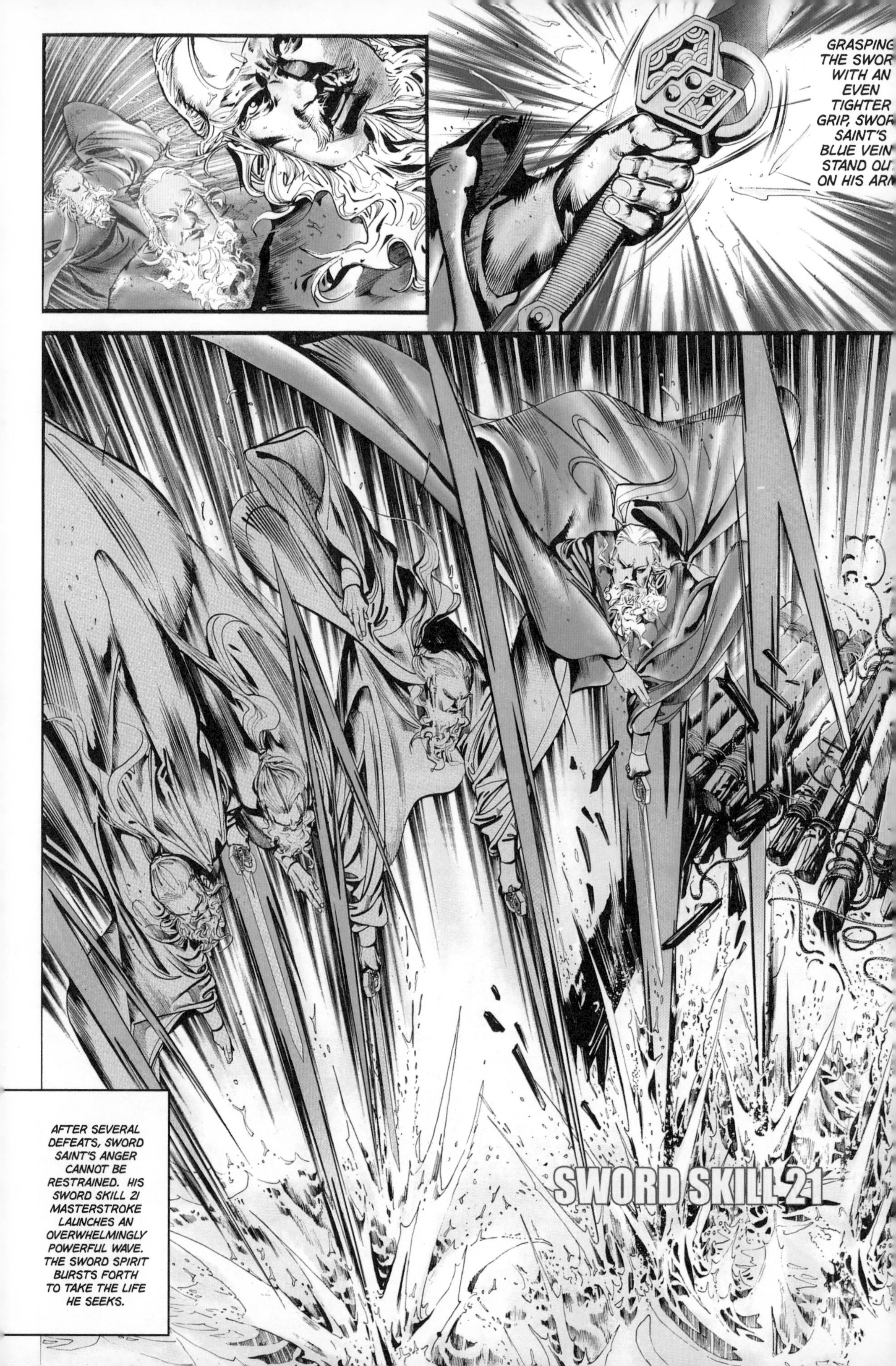
GRASPING THE SWOR WITH AN EVEN TIGHTER GRIP, SWOR SAINT'S BLUE VEIN STAND OU ON HIS ARM
AFTER SEVERAL DEFEATS, SWORD SAINT'S ANGER CANNOT BE RESTRAINED. HIS SWORD SKILL 21 MASTERSTROKE LAUNCHES AN OVERWHELMINGLY POWERFUL WAVE. THE SWORD SPIRIT BURSTS FORTH TO TAKE THE LIFE HE SEEKS.
SWORD SKILL 21

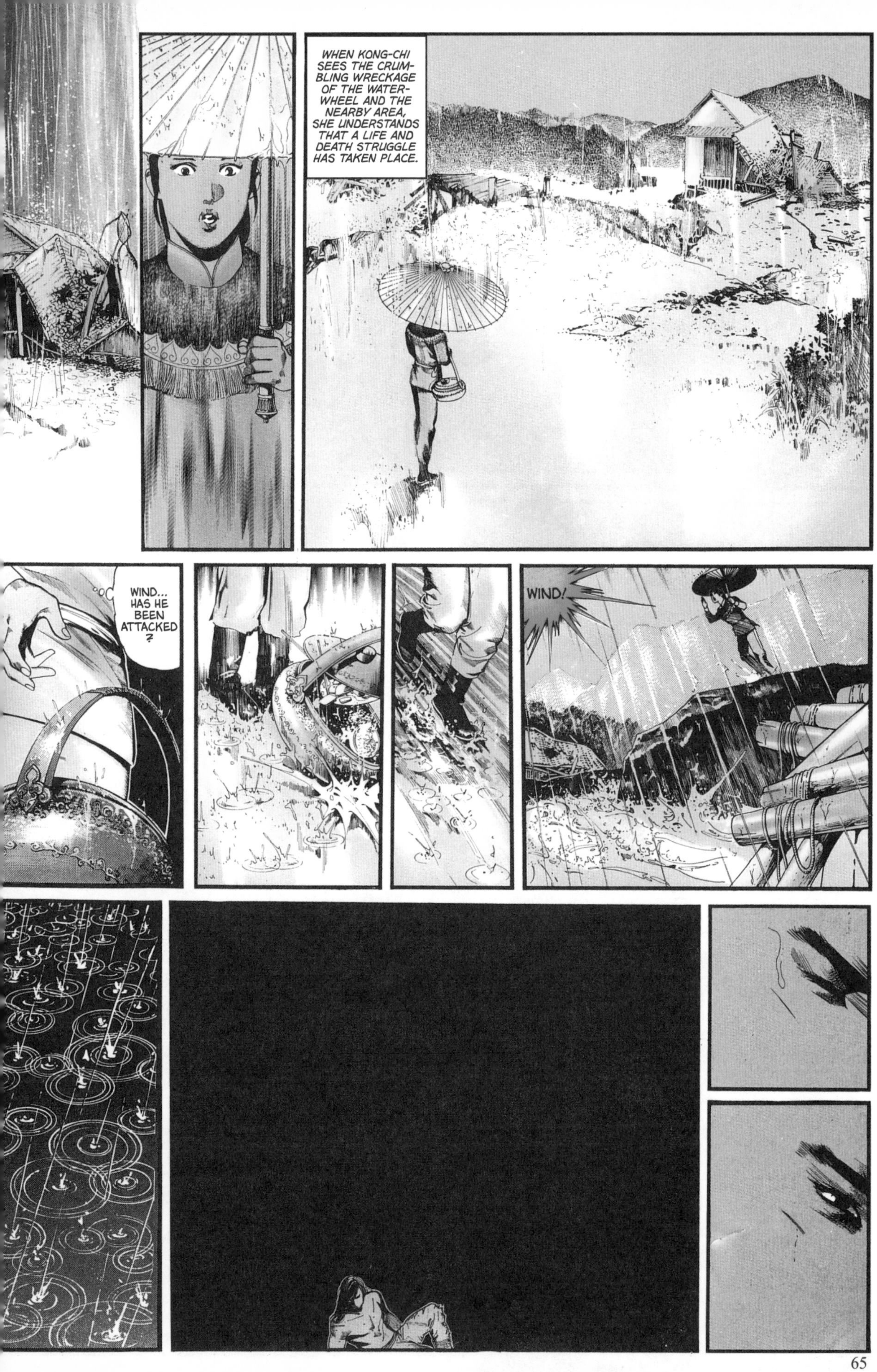
WHEN KONG-CHI SEES THE CRUMBLING WRECKAGE OF THE WATER-WHEEL AND THE NEARBY AREA, SHE UNDERSTANDS THAT A LIFE AND DEATH STRUGGLE HAS TAKEN PLACE.
WIND... HAS HE BEEN ATTACKED?
WIND!

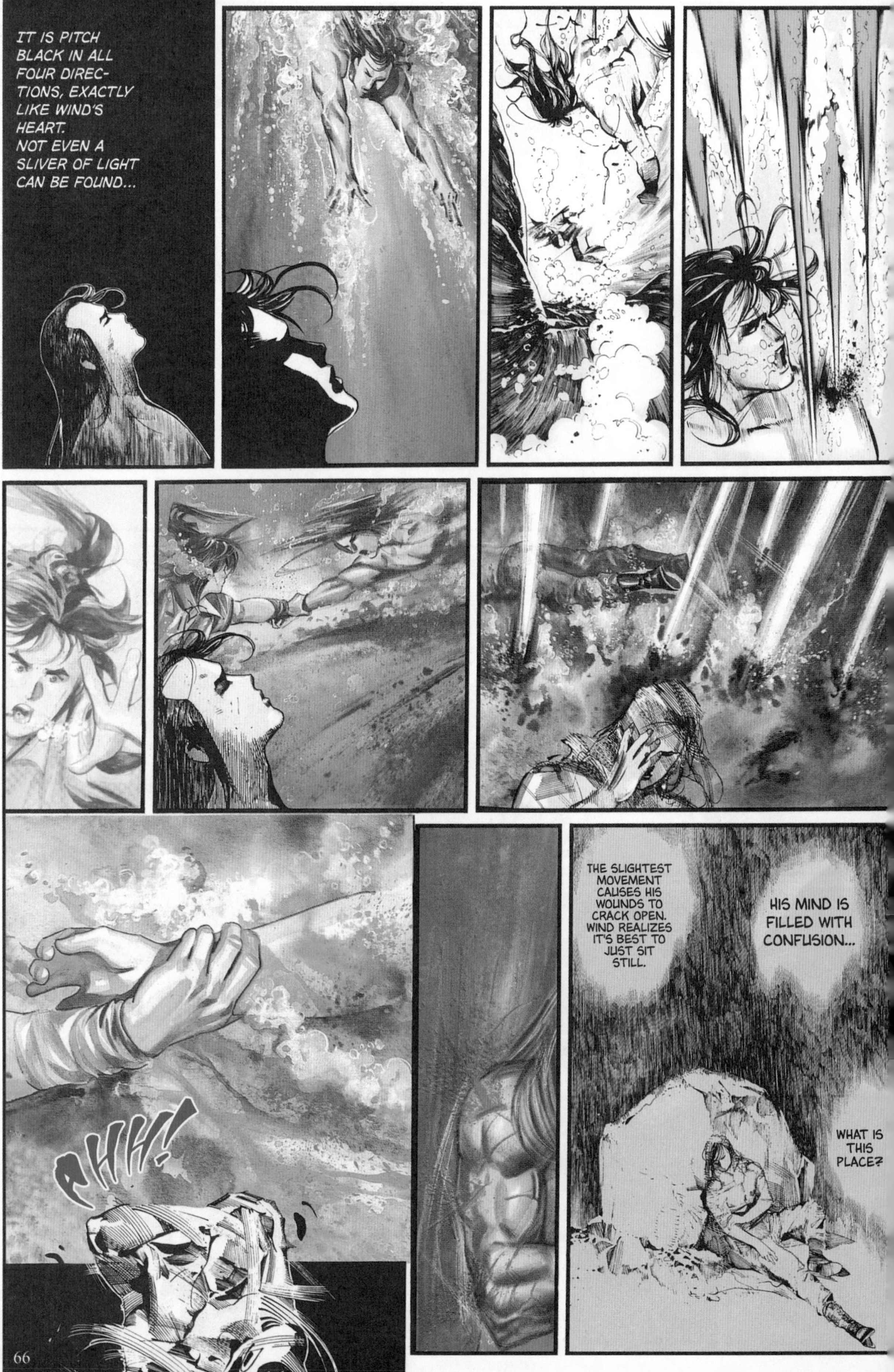
IT IS PITCH BLACK IN ALL FOUR DIRECTIONS, EXACTLY LIKE WIND'S HEART.
NOT EVEN A SLIVER OF LIGHT CAN BE FOUND...
AHH!
THE SLIGHTEST MOVEMENT CAUSES HIS WOUNDS TO CRACK OPEN. WIND REALIZES IT'S BEST TO JUST SIT STILL.
HIS MIND IS FILLED WITH CONFUSION...
WHAT IS THIS PLACE?

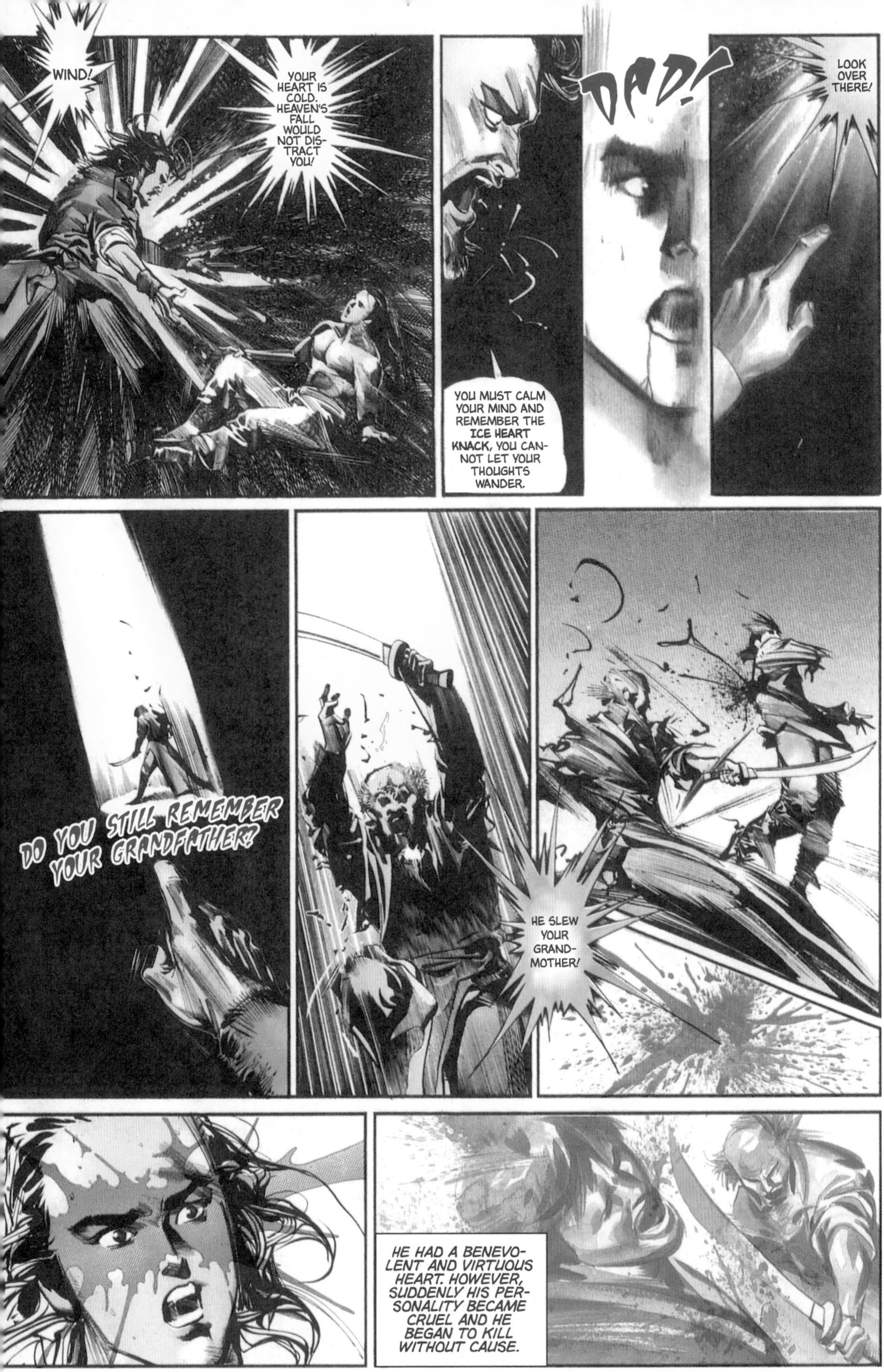
WIND!
YOUR HEART IS COLD. HEAVEN'S FALL WOULD NOT DISTRACT YOU!
YOU MUST CALM YOUR MIND AND REMEMBER THE ICE HEART KNACK, YOU CANNOT LET YOUR THOUGHTS WANDER.
DAD!
LOOK OVER THERE!
DO YOU STILL REMEMBER YOUR GRANDFATHER?
HE SLEW YOUR GRAND-MOTHER!
HE HAD A BENEVOLENT AND VIRTUOUS HEART. HOWEVER, SUDDENLY HIS PERSONALITY BECAME CRUEL AND HE BEGAN TO KILL WITHOUT CAUSE.

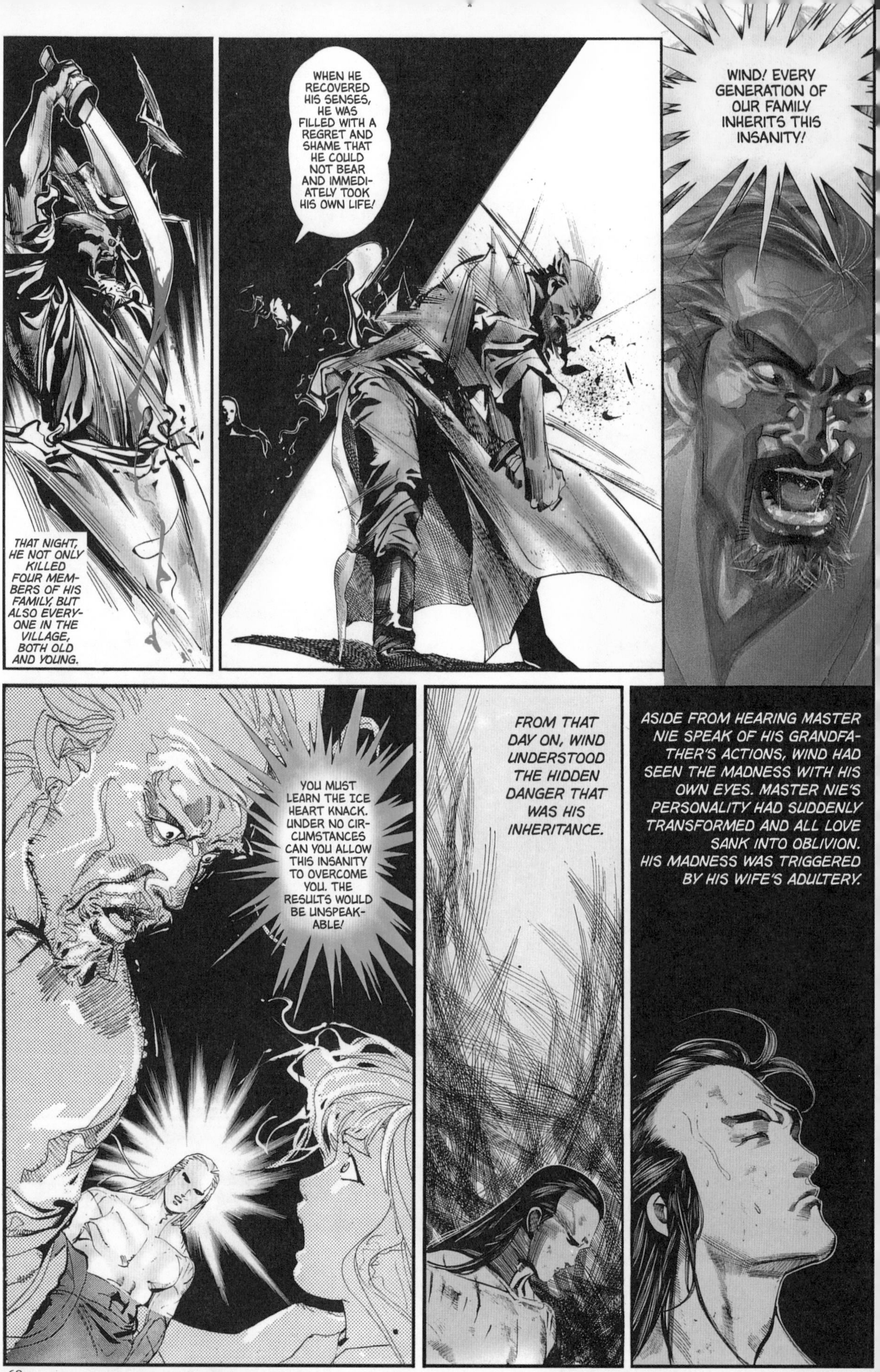
THAT NIGHT, HE NOT ONLY KILLED FOUR MEMBERS OF HIS FAMILY, BUT ALSO EVERYONE IN THE VILLAGE, BOTH OLD AND YOUNG.
WHEN HE RECOVERED HIS SENSES, HE WAS FILLED WITH A REGRET AND SHAME THAT HE COULD NOT BEAR AND IMMEDIATELY TOOK HIS OWN LIFE!
WIND! EVERY GENERATION OF OUR FAMILY INHERITS THIS INSANITY!
YOU MUST LEARN THE ICE HEART KNACK. UNDER NO CIRCUMSTANCES CAN YOU ALLOW THIS INSANITY TO OVERCOME YOU. THE RESULTS WOULD BE UNSPEAKABLE!
FROM THAT DAY ON, WIND UNDERSTOOD THE HIDDEN DANGER THAT WAS HIS INHERITANCE.
ASIDE FROM HEARING MASTER NIE SPEAK OF HIS GRANDFATHER'S ACTIONS, WIND HAD SEEN THE MADNESS WITH HIS OWN EYES. MASTER NIE'S PERSONALITY HAD SUDDENLY TRANSFORMED AND ALL LOVE SANK INTO OBLIVION. HIS MADNESS WAS TRIGGERED BY HIS WIFE'S ADULTERY.

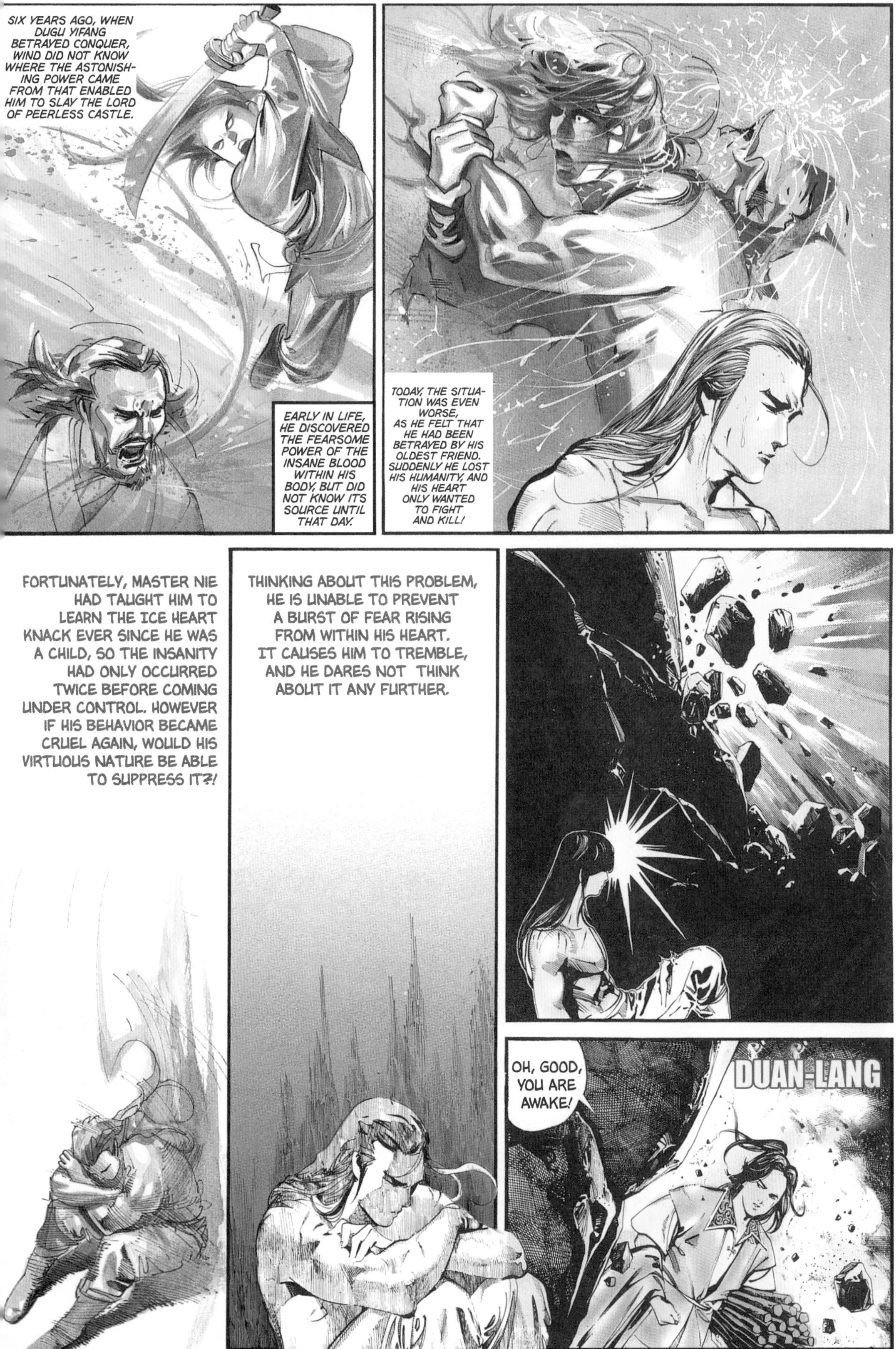
SIX YEARS AGO, WHEN DUGU YIFANG BETRAYED CONQUER, WIND DID NOT KNOW WHERE THE ASTONISHING POWER CAME FROM THAT ENABLED HIM TO SLAY THE LORD OF PEERLESS CASTLE.
EARLY IN LIFE, HE DISCOVERED THE FEARSOME POWER OF THE INSANE BLOOD WITHIN HIS BODY, BUT DID NOT KNOW ITS SOURCE UNTIL THAT DAY.
TODAY, THE SITUATION WAS EVEN WORSE, AS HE FELT THAT HE HAD BEEN BETRAYED BY HIS OLDEST FRIEND. SUDDENLY HE LOST HIS HUMANITY, AND HIS HEART ONLY WANTED TO FIGHT AND KILL!
FORTUNATELY, MASTER NIE HAD TAUGHT HIM TO LEARN THE ICE HEART KNACK EVER SINCE HE WAS A CHILD, SO THE INSANITY HAD ONLY OCCURRED TWICE BEFORE COMING UNDER CONTROL. HOWEVER IF HIS BEHAVIOR BECAME CRUEL AGAIN, WOULD HIS VIRTUOUS NATURE BE ABLE TO SUPPRESS IT?!
THINKING ABOUT THIS PROBLEM, HE IS UNABLE TO PREVENT A BURST OF FEAR RISING FROM WITHIN HIS HEART. IT CAUSES HIM TO TREMBLE, AND HE DARES NOT THINK ABOUT IT ANY FURTHER.
DUAN-LANG
OH, GOOD, YOU ARE AWAKE!

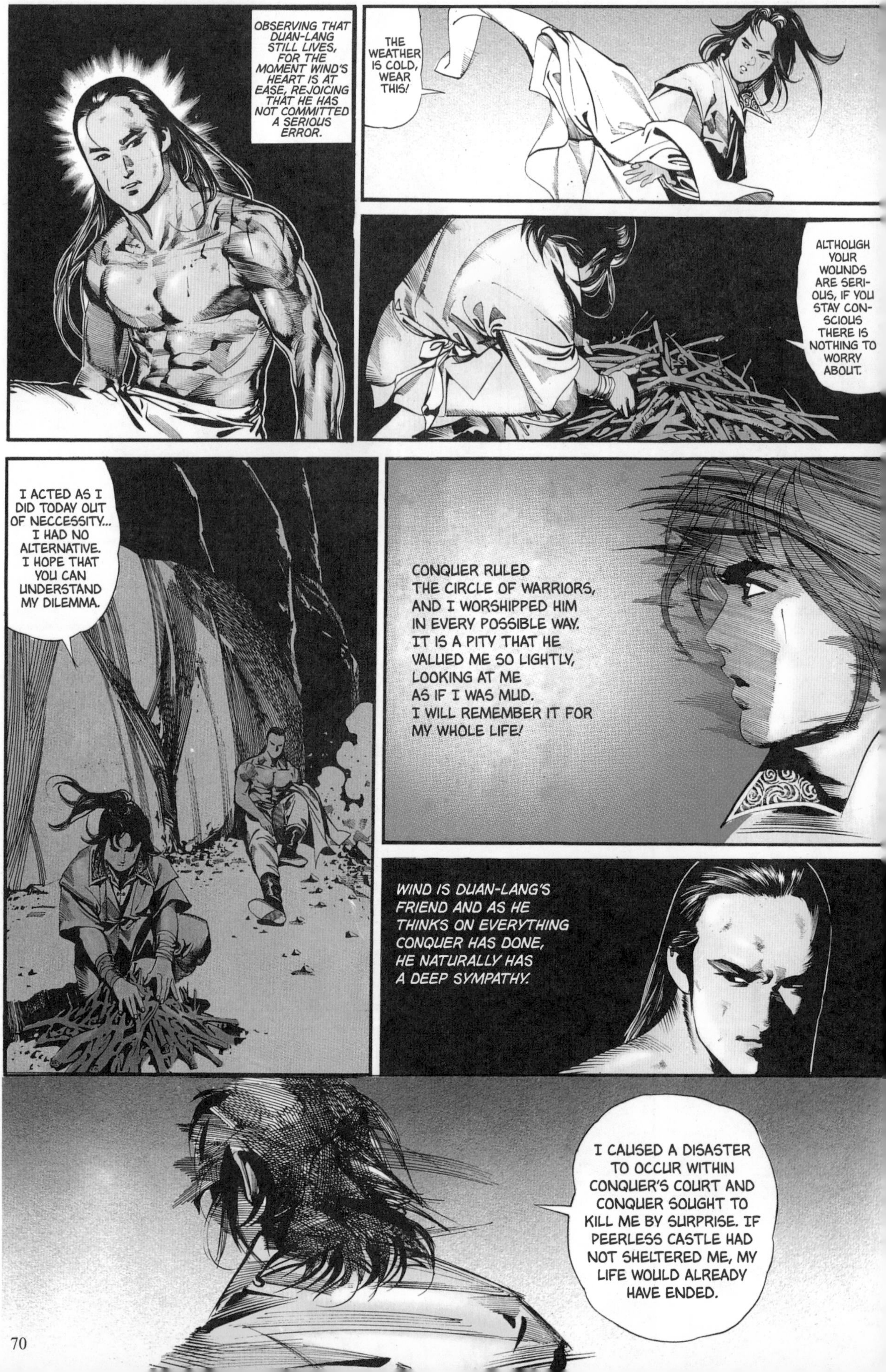
OBSERVING THAT DUAN-LANG STILL LIVES, FOR THE MOMENT WIND'S HEART IS AT EASE, REJOICING THAT HE HAS NOT COMMITTED A SERIOUS ERROR.
THE WEATHER IS COLD, WEAR THIS!
ALTHOUGH YOUR WOUNDS ARE SERIOUS, IF YOU STAY CONSCIOUS THERE IS NOTHING TO WORRY ABOUT.
I ACTED AS I DID TODAY OUT OF NECCESSITY... I HAD NO ALTERNATIVE. I HOPE THAT YOU CAN UNDERSTAND MY DILEMMA.
CONQUER RULED THE CIRCLE OF WARRIORS, AND I WORSHIPPED HIM IN EVERY POSSIBLE WAY. IT IS A PITY THAT HE VALUED ME SO LIGHTLY, LOOKING AT ME AS IF I WAS MUD. I WILL REMEMBER IT FOR MY WHOLE LIFE!
WIND IS DUAN-LANG'S FRIEND AND AS HE THINKS ON EVERYTHING CONQUER HAS DONE, HE NATURALLY HAS A DEEP SYMPATHY.
I CAUSED A DISASTER TO OCCUR WITHIN CONQUER'S COURT AND CONQUER SOUGHT TO KILL ME BY SURPRISE. IF PEERLESS CASTLE HAD NOT SHELTERED ME, MY LIFE WOULD ALREADY HAVE ENDED.

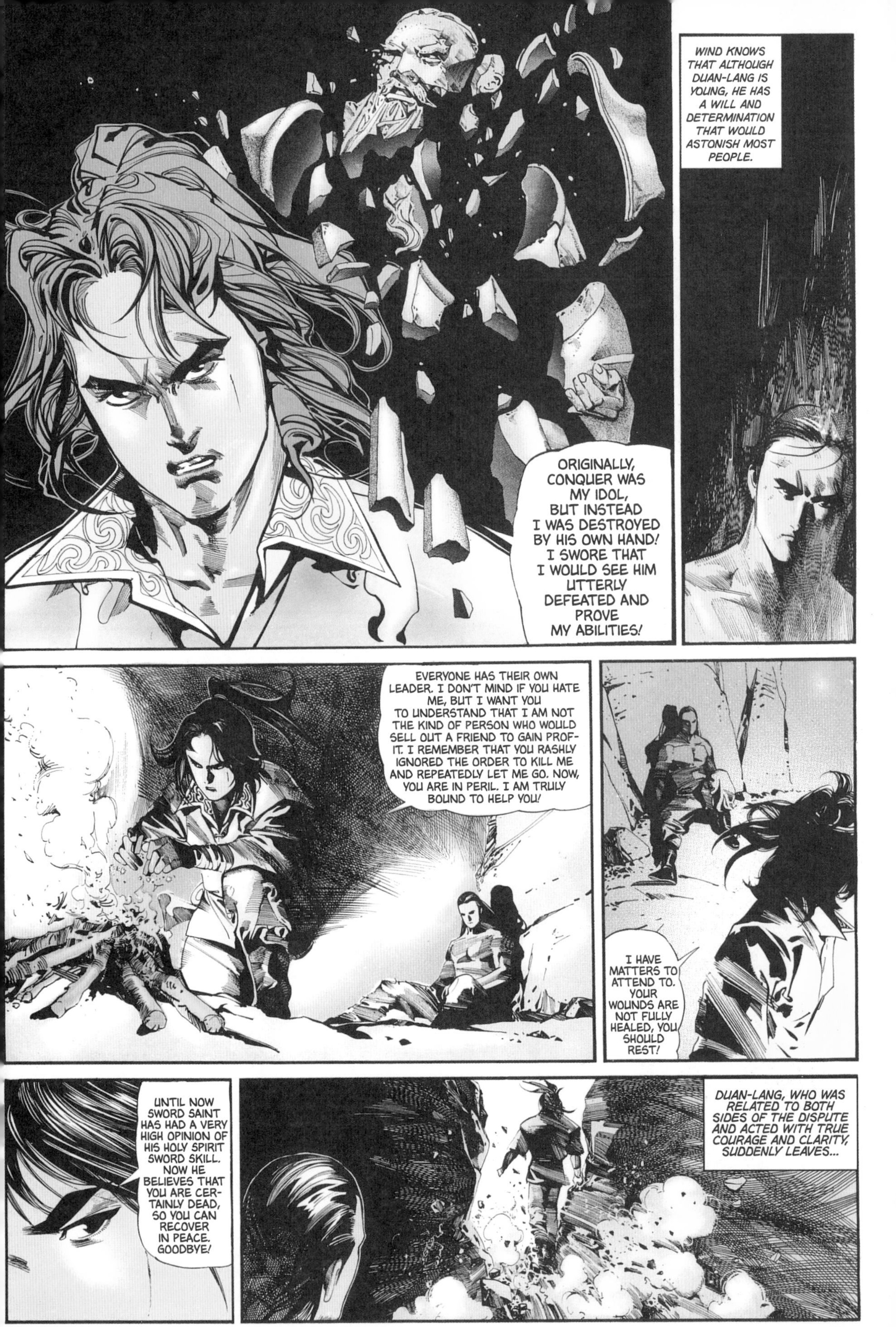
WIND KNOWS THAT ALTHOUGH DUAN-LANG IS YOUNG, HE HAS A WILL AND DETERMINATION THAT WOULD ASTONISH MOST PEOPLE.
ORIGINALLY, CONQUER WAS MY IDOL, BUT INSTEAD I WAS DESTROYED BY HIS OWN HAND! I SWORE THAT I WOULD SEE HIM UTTERLY DEFEATED AND PROVE MY ABILITIES!
EVERYONE HAS THEIR OWN LEADER. I DON'T MIND IF YOU HATE ME, BUT I WANT YOU TO UNDERSTAND THAT I AM NOT THE KIND OF PERSON WHO WOULD SELL OUT A FRIEND TO GAIN PROFIT. I REMEMBER THAT YOU RASHLY IGNORED THE ORDER TO KILL ME AND REPEATEDLY LET ME GO. NOW, YOU ARE IN PERIL. I AM TRULY BOUND TO HELP YOU!
I HAVE MATTERS TO ATTEND TO. YOUR WOUNDS ARE NOT FULLY HEALED, YOU SHOULD REST!
UNTIL NOW SWORD SAINT HAS HAD A VERY HIGH OPINION OF HIS HOLY SPIRIT SWORD SKILL. NOW HE BELIEVES THAT YOU ARE CERTAINLY DEAD, SO YOU CAN RECOVER IN PEACE. GOODBYE!
DUAN-LANG, WHO WAS RELATED TO BOTH SIDES OF THE DISPUTE AND ACTED WITH TRUE COURAGE AND CLARITY, SUDDENLY LEAVES...

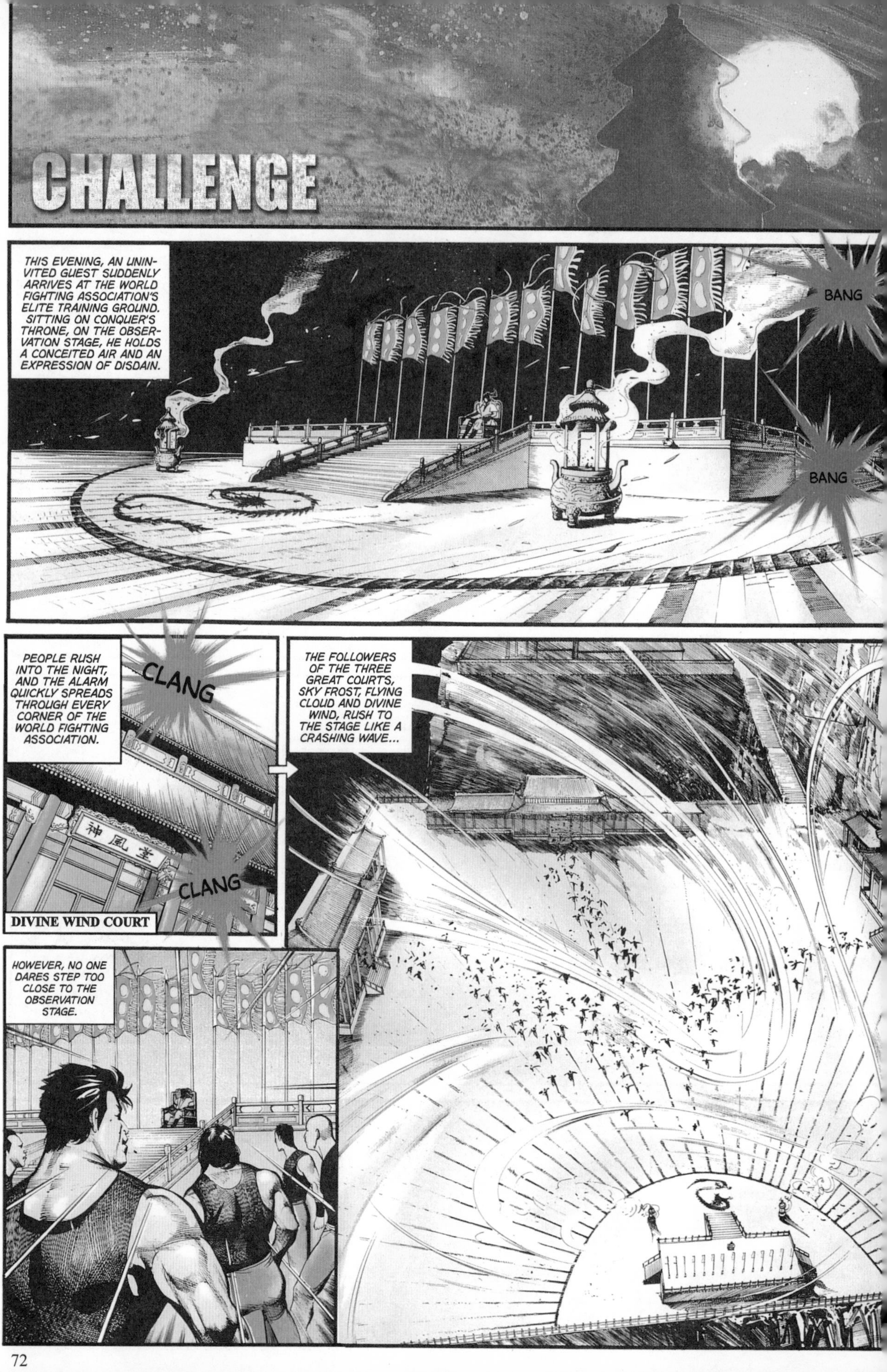
CHALLENGE
THIS EVENING, AN UNINVITED GUEST SUDDENLY ARRIVES AT THE WORLD FIGHTING ASSOCIATION'S ELITE TRAINING GROUND. SITTING ON CONQUER'S THRONE, ON THE OBSERVATION STAGE, HE HOLDS A CONCEITED AIR AND AN EXPRESSION OF DISDAIN.
BANG
BANG
PEOPLE RUSH INTO THE NIGHT, AND THE ALARM QUICKLY SPREADS THROUGH EVERY CORNER OF THE WORLD FIGHTING ASSOCIATION.
CLANG
神風堂
CLANG
DIVINE WIND COURT
THE FOLLOWERS OF THE THREE GREAT COURTS, SKY FROST, FLYING CLOUD AND DIVINE WIND, RUSH TO THE STAGE LIKE A CRASHING WAVE...
HOWEVER, NO ONE DARES STEP TOO CLOSE TO THE OBSERVATION STAGE.

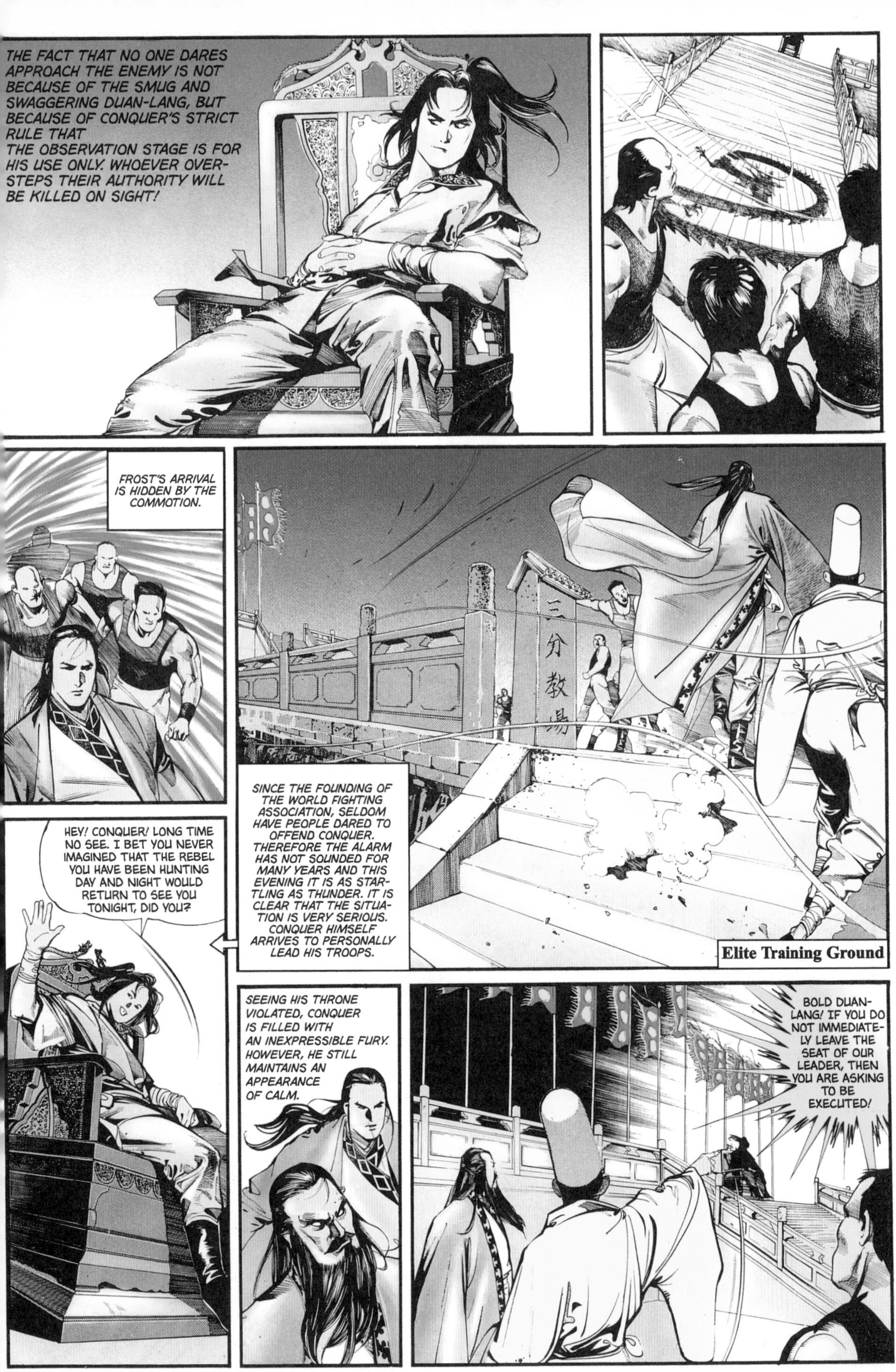
THE FACT THAT NO ONE DARES APPROACH THE ENEMY IS NOT BECAUSE OF THE SMUG AND SWAGGERING DUAN-LANG, BUT BECAUSE OF CONQUER'S STRICT RULE THAT
THE OBSERVATION STAGE IS FOR HIS USE ONLY. WHOEVER OVER-STEPS THEIR AUTHORITY WILL BE KILLED ON SIGHT!
FROST'S ARRIVAL IS HIDDEN BY THE COMMOTION.
三分教場
SINCE THE FOUNDING OF THE WORLD FIGHTING ASSOCIATION, SELDOM HAVE PEOPLE DARED TO OFFEND CONQUER. THEREFORE THE ALARM HAS NOT SOUNDED FOR MANY YEARS AND THIS EVENING IT IS AS STAR-TLING AS THUNDER. IT IS CLEAR THAT THE SITUA-TION IS VERY SERIOUS. CONQUER HIMSELF ARRIVES TO PERSONALLY LEAD HIS TROOPS.
Elite Training Ground
HEY! CONQUER! LONG TIME NO SEE. I BET YOU NEVER IMAGINED THAT THE REBEL YOU HAVE BEEN HUNTING DAY AND NIGHT WOULD RETURN TO SEE YOU TONIGHT, DID YOU?
SEEING HIS THRONE VIOLATED, CONQUER IS FILLED WITH AN INEXPRESSIBLE FURY. HOWEVER, HE STILL MAINTAINS AN APPEARANCE OF CALM.
BOLD DUAN-LANG! IF YOU DO NOT IMMEDIATE-LY LEAVE THE SEAT OF OUR LEADER, THEN YOU ARE ASKING TO BE EXECUTED!

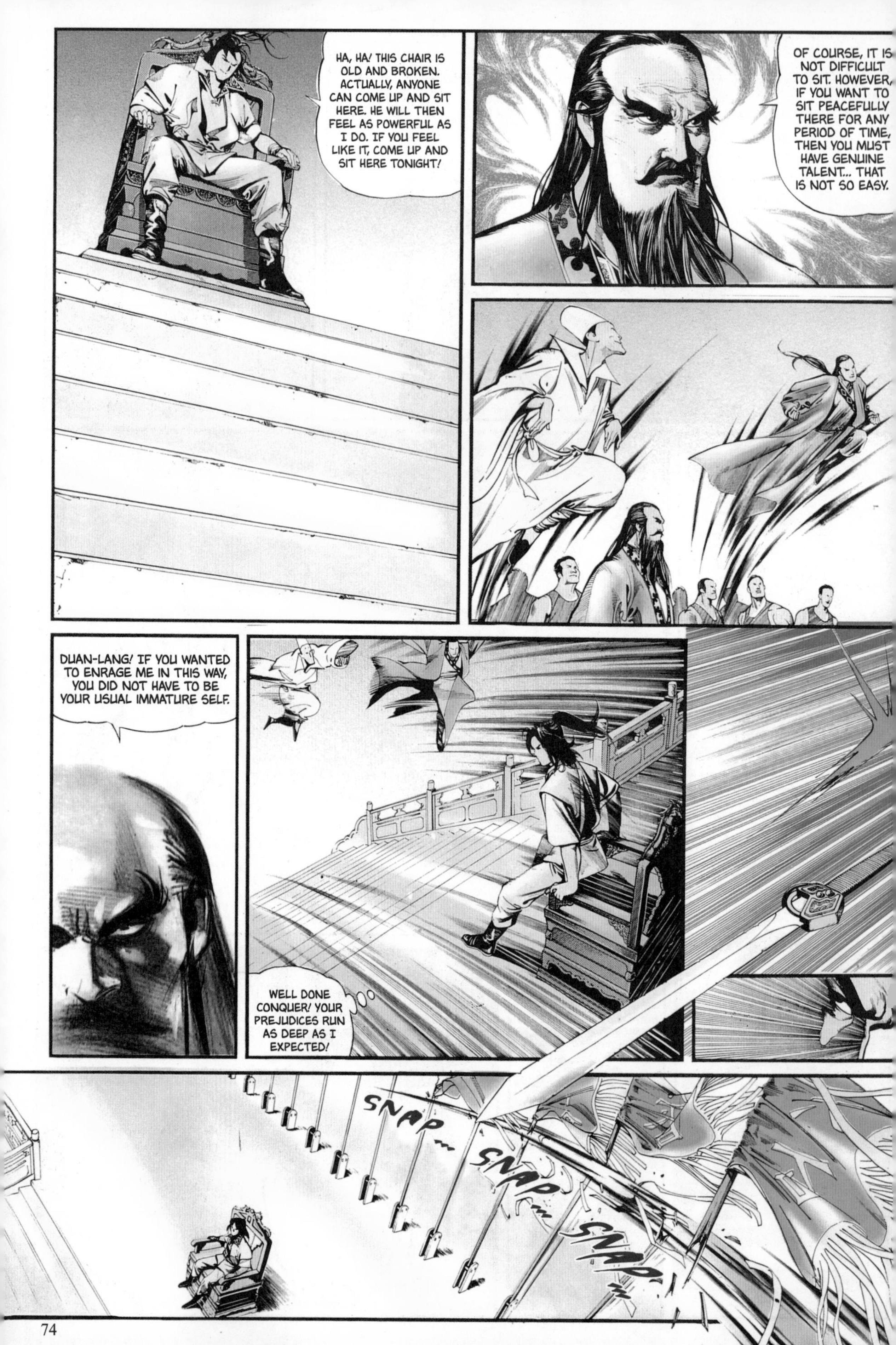
HA, HA! THIS CHAIR IS OLD AND BROKEN. ACTUALLY, ANYONE CAN COME UP AND SIT HERE. HE WILL THEN FEEL AS POWERFUL AS I DO. IF YOU FEEL LIKE IT, COME UP AND SIT HERE TONIGHT!
OF COURSE, IT IS NOT DIFFICULT TO SIT. HOWEVER, IF YOU WANT TO SIT PEACEFULLY THERE FOR ANY PERIOD OF TIME, THEN YOU MUST HAVE GENUINE TALENT... THAT IS NOT SO EASY.
DUAN-LANG! IF YOU WANTED TO ENRAGE ME IN THIS WAY, YOU DID NOT HAVE TO BE YOUR USUAL IMMATURE SELF.
WELL DONE CONQUER! YOUR PREJUDICES RUN AS DEEP AS I EXPECTED!
SNAP...
SNAP...
SNAP...

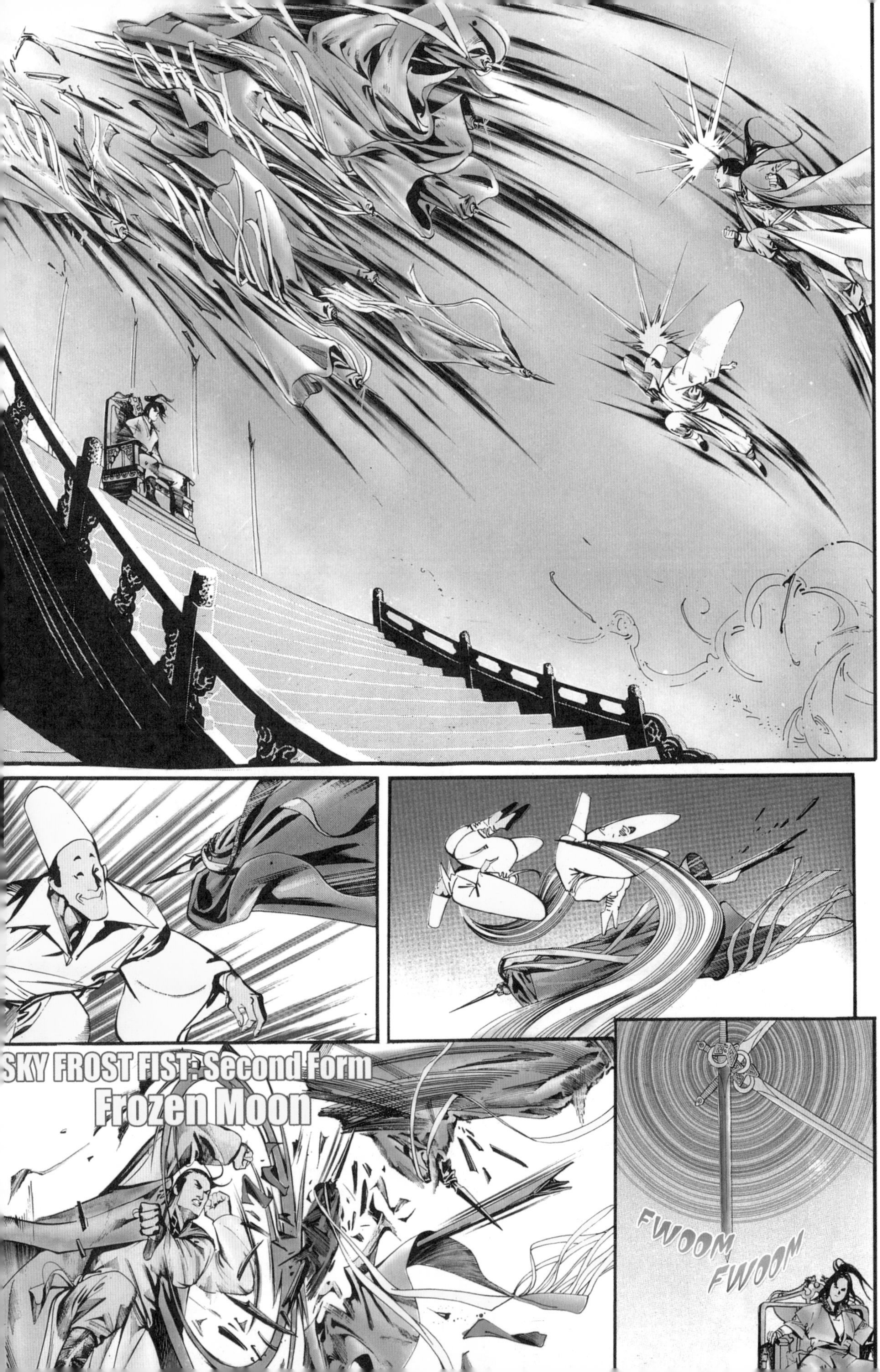

SKY FROST FIST: Second Form
Frozen Moon
FWOOM
FWOOM

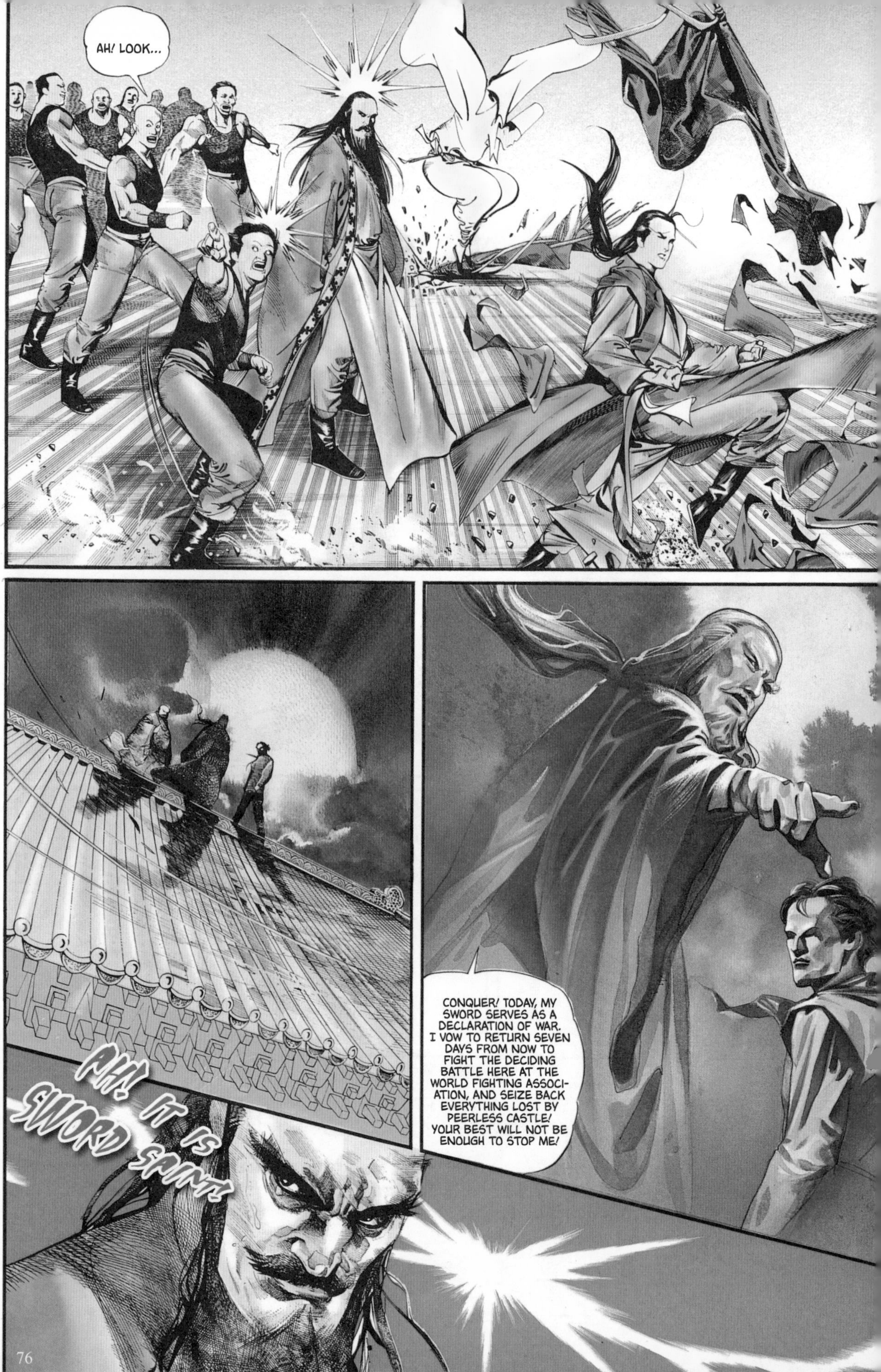

AH! LOOK...
CONQUER! TODAY, MY SWORD SERVES AS A DECLARATION OF WAR. I VOW TO RETURN SEVEN DAYS FROM NOW TO FIGHT THE DECIDING BATTLE HERE AT THE WORLD FIGHTING ASSOCIATION, AND SEIZE BACK EVERYTHING LOST BY PEERLESS CASTLE! YOUR BEST WILL NOT BE ENOUGH TO STOP ME!
AH! IT IS SWORD SPIRIT!

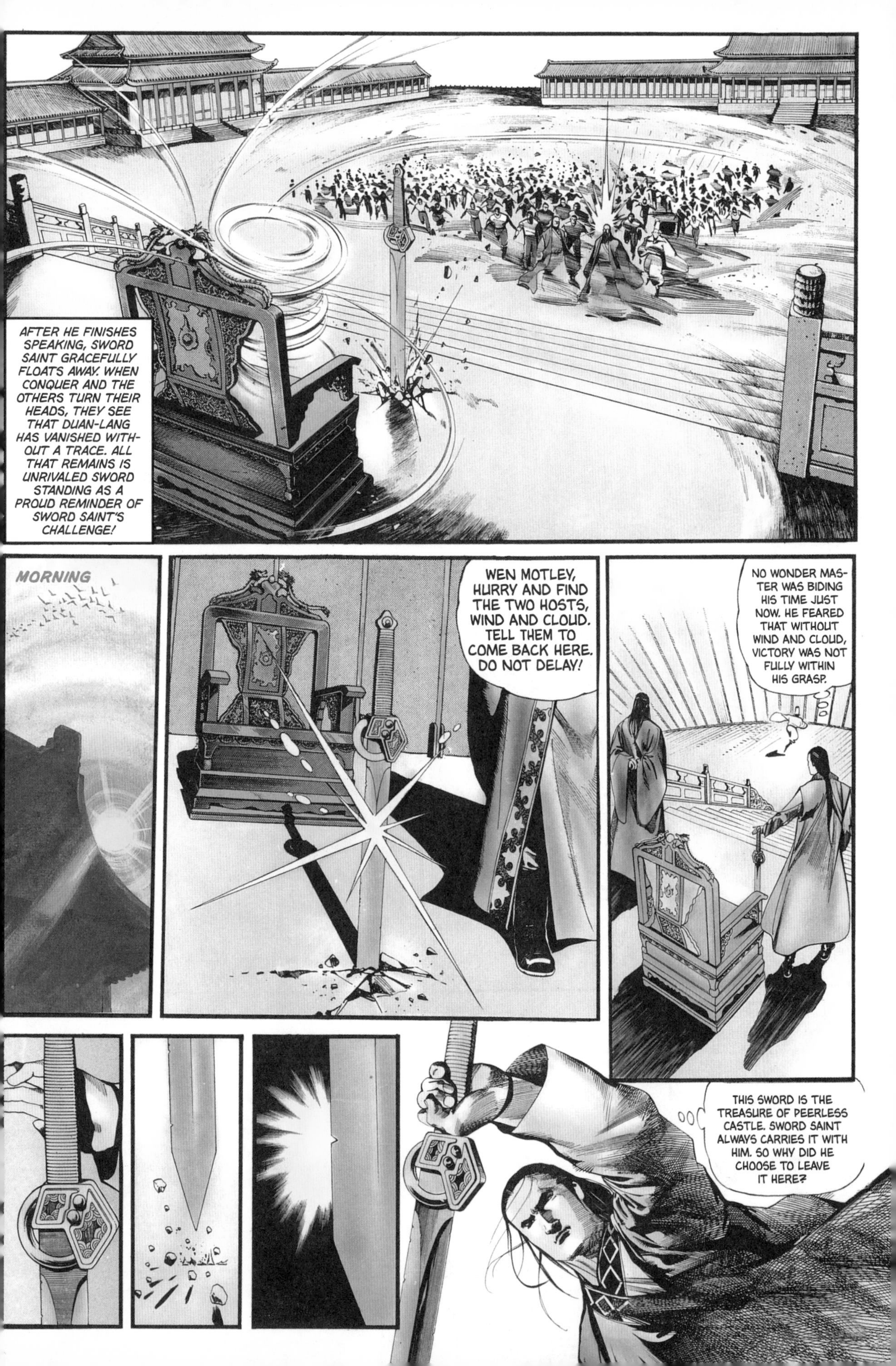

AFTER HE FINISHES SPEAKING, SWORD SAINT GRACEFULLY FLOATS AWAY. WHEN CONQUER AND THE OTHERS TURN THEIR HEADS, THEY SEE THAT DUAN-LANG HAS VANISHED WITHOUT A TRACE. ALL THAT REMAINS IS UNRIVALED SWORD STANDING AS A PROUD REMINDER OF SWORD SAINT'S CHALLENGE!
MORNING
WEN MOTLEY, HURRY AND FIND THE TWO HOSTS, WIND AND CLOUD. TELL THEM TO COME BACK HERE. DO NOT DELAY!
NO WONDER MASTER WAS BIDING HIS TIME JUST NOW. HE FEARED THAT WITHOUT WIND AND CLOUD, VICTORY WAS NOT FULLY WITHIN HIS GRASP.
THIS SWORD IS THE TREASURE OF PEERLESS CASTLE. SWORD SAINT ALWAYS CARRIES IT WITH HIM. SO WHY DID HE CHOOSE TO LEAVE IT HERE?

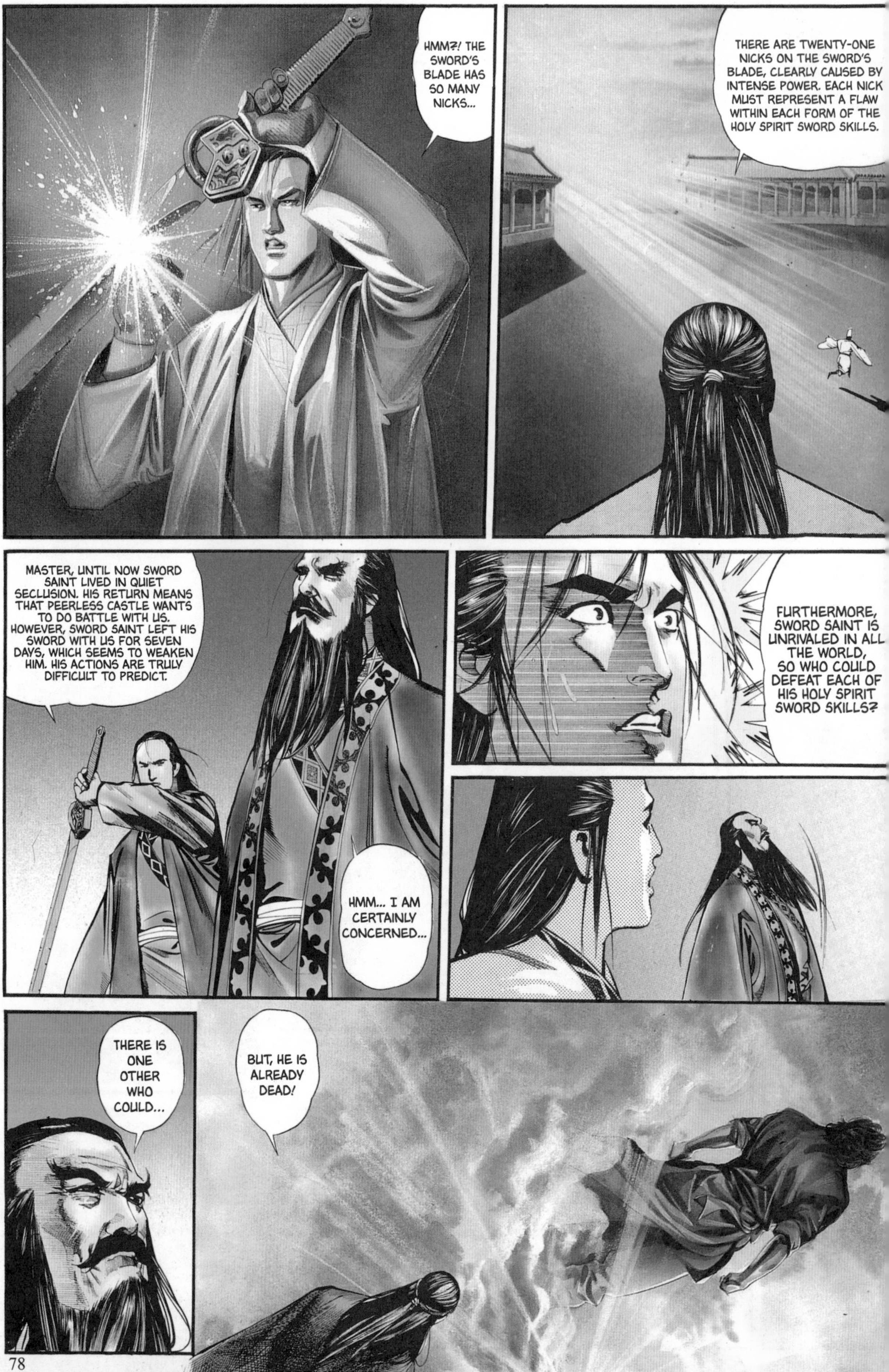
HMM?! THE SWORD'S BLADE HAS SO MANY NICKS...
THERE ARE TWENTY-ONE NICKS ON THE SWORD'S BLADE, CLEARLY CAUSED BY INTENSE POWER. EACH NICK MUST REPRESENT A FLAW WITHIN EACH FORM OF THE HOLY SPIRIT SWORD SKILLS.
MASTER, UNTIL NOW SWORD SAINT LIVED IN QUIET SECLUSION. HIS RETURN MEANS THAT PEERLESS CASTLE WANTS TO DO BATTLE WITH US. HOWEVER, SWORD SAINT LEFT HIS SWORD WITH US FOR SEVEN DAYS, WHICH SEEMS TO WEAKEN HIM. HIS ACTIONS ARE TRULY DIFFICULT TO PREDICT.
HMM... I AM CERTAINLY CONCERNED...
FURTHERMORE, SWORD SAINT IS UNRIVALED IN ALL THE WORLD, SO WHO COULD DEFEAT EACH OF HIS HOLY SPIRIT SWORD SKILLS?
THERE IS ONE OTHER WHO COULD...
BUT, HE IS ALREADY DEAD!

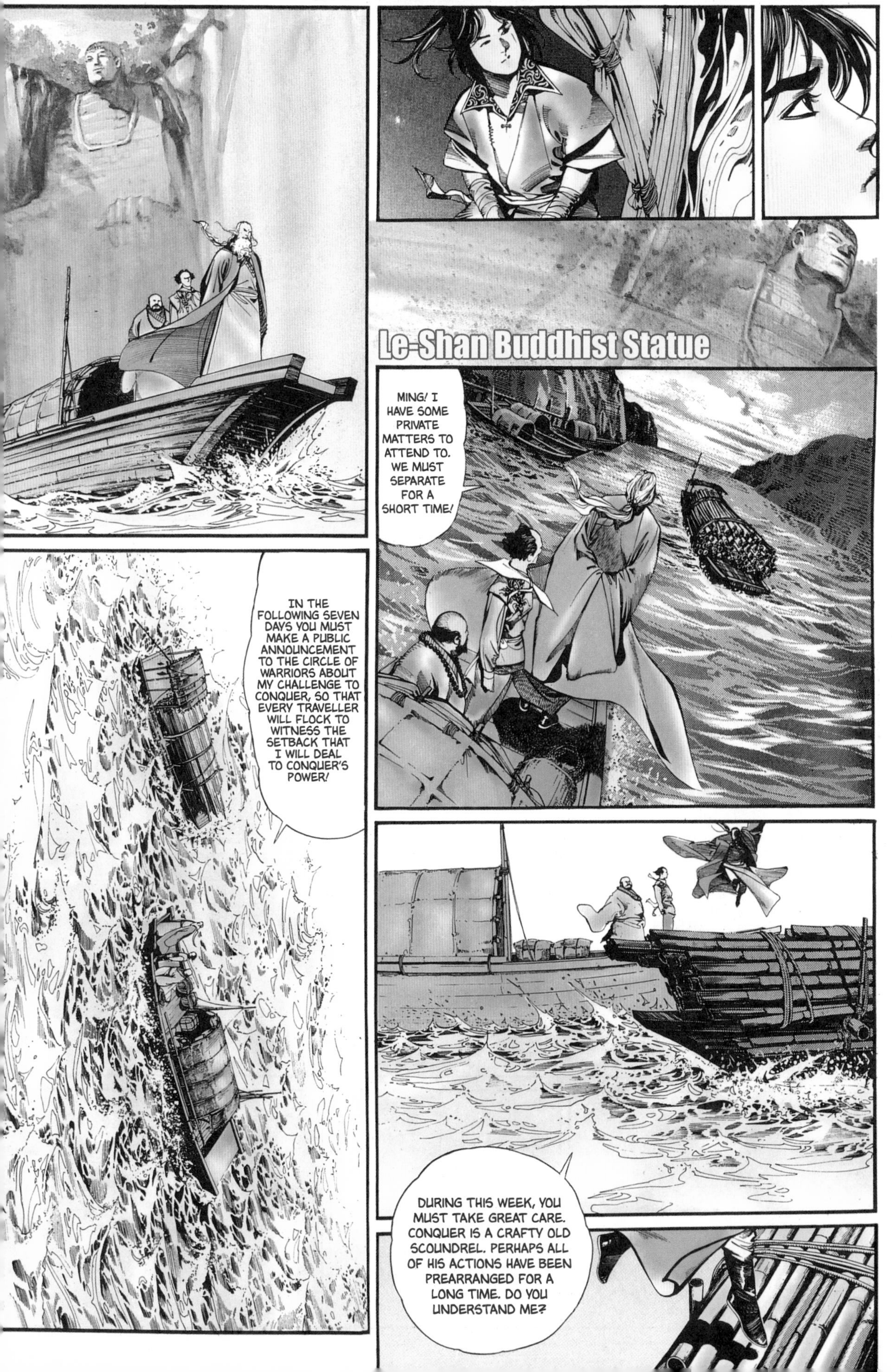
Le-Shan Buddhist Statue
MING! I HAVE SOME PRIVATE MATTERS TO ATTEND TO. WE MUST SEPARATE FOR A SHORT TIME!
IN THE FOLLOWING SEVEN DAYS YOU MUST MAKE A PUBLIC ANNOUNCEMENT TO THE CIRCLE OF WARRIORS ABOUT MY CHALLENGE TO CONQUER, SO THAT EVERY TRAVELLER WILL FLOCK TO WITNESS THE SETBACK THAT I WILL DEAL TO CONQUER'S POWER!
DURING THIS WEEK, YOU MUST TAKE GREAT CARE. CONQUER IS A CRAFTY OLD SCOUNDREL. PERHAPS ALL OF HIS ACTIONS HAVE BEEN PREARRANGED FOR A LONG TIME. DO YOU UNDERSTAND ME?

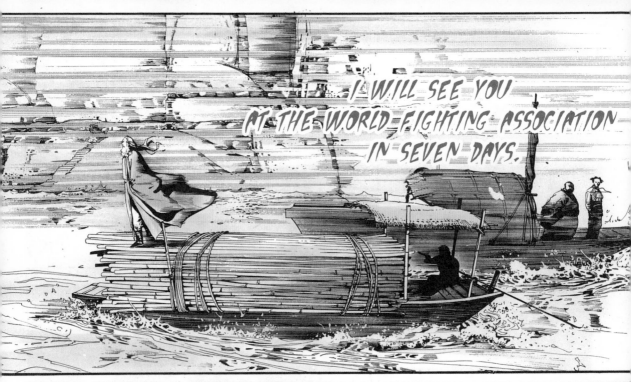

I WILL SEE YOU AT THE WORLD FIGHTING ASSOCIATION IN SEVEN DAYS.

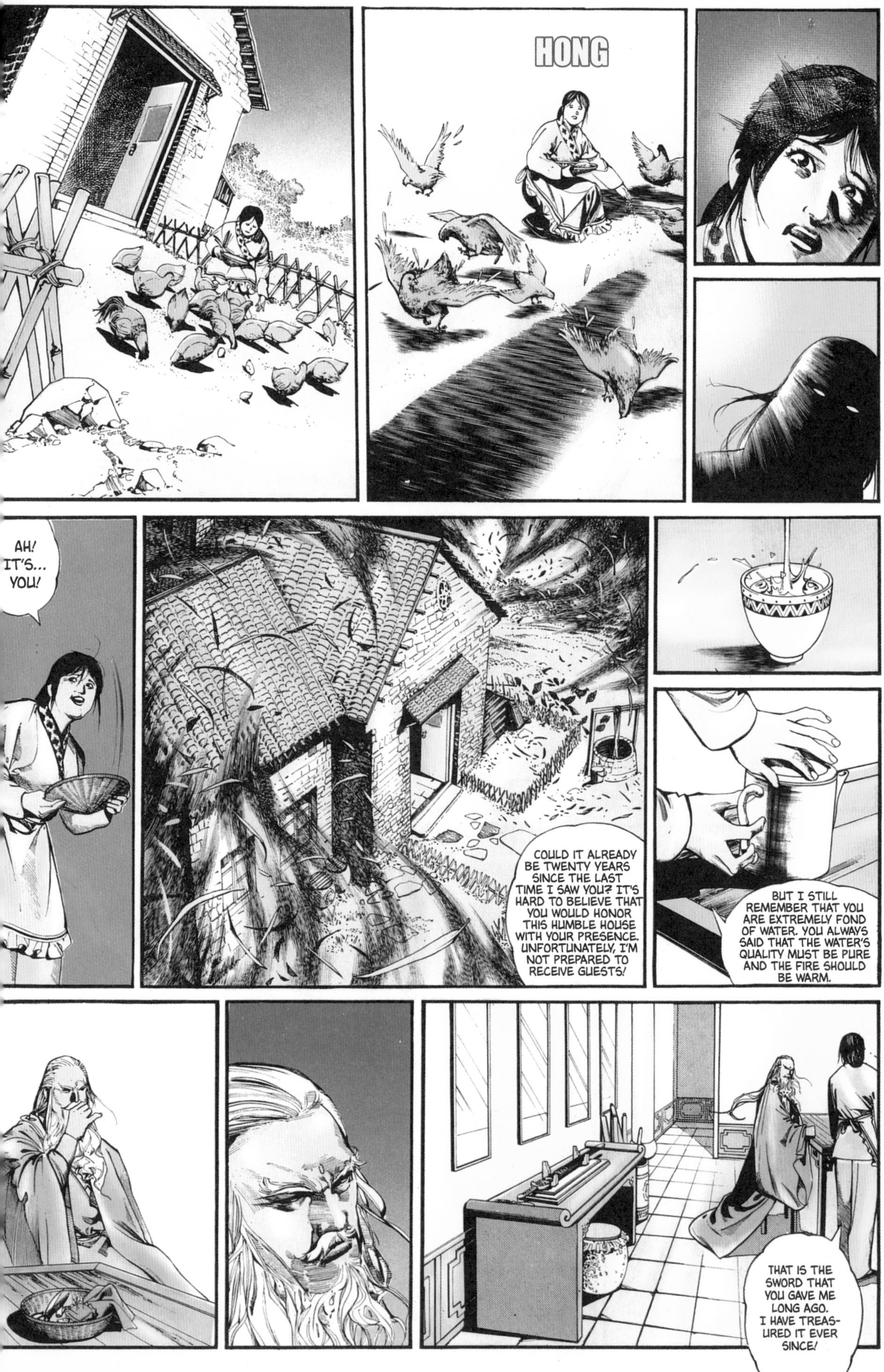
HONG
AH! IT'S... YOU!
COULD IT ALREADY BE TWENTY YEARS SINCE THE LAST TIME I SAW YOU? IT'S HARD TO BELIEVE THAT YOU WOULD HONOR THIS HUMBLE HOUSE WITH YOUR PRESENCE. UNFORTUNATELY, I'M NOT PREPARED TO RECEIVE GUESTS!
BUT I STILL REMEMBER THAT YOU ARE EXTREMELY FOND OF WATER. YOU ALWAYS SAID THAT THE WATER'S QUALITY MUST BE PURE AND THE FIRE SHOULD BE WARM.
THAT IS THE SWORD THAT YOU GAVE ME LONG AGO. I HAVE TREAS-URED IT EVER SINCE!

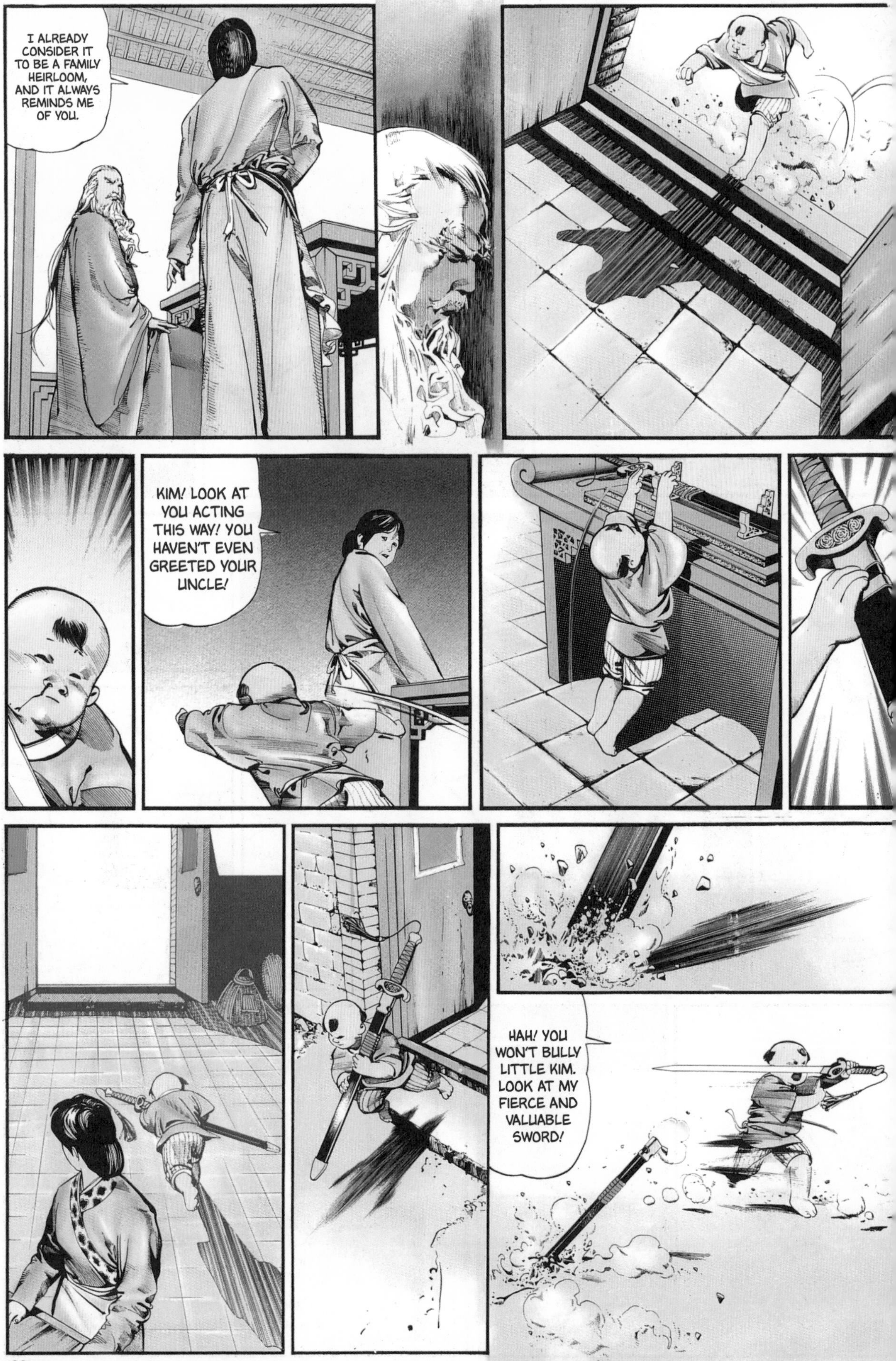

I ALREADY CONSIDER IT TO BE A FAMILY HEIRLOOM, AND IT ALWAYS REMINDS ME OF YOU.
KIM! LOOK AT YOU ACTING THIS WAY! YOU HAVEN'T EVEN GREETED YOUR UNCLE!
HAH! YOU WON'T BULLY LITTLE KIM. LOOK AT MY FIERCE AND VALUABLE SWORD!

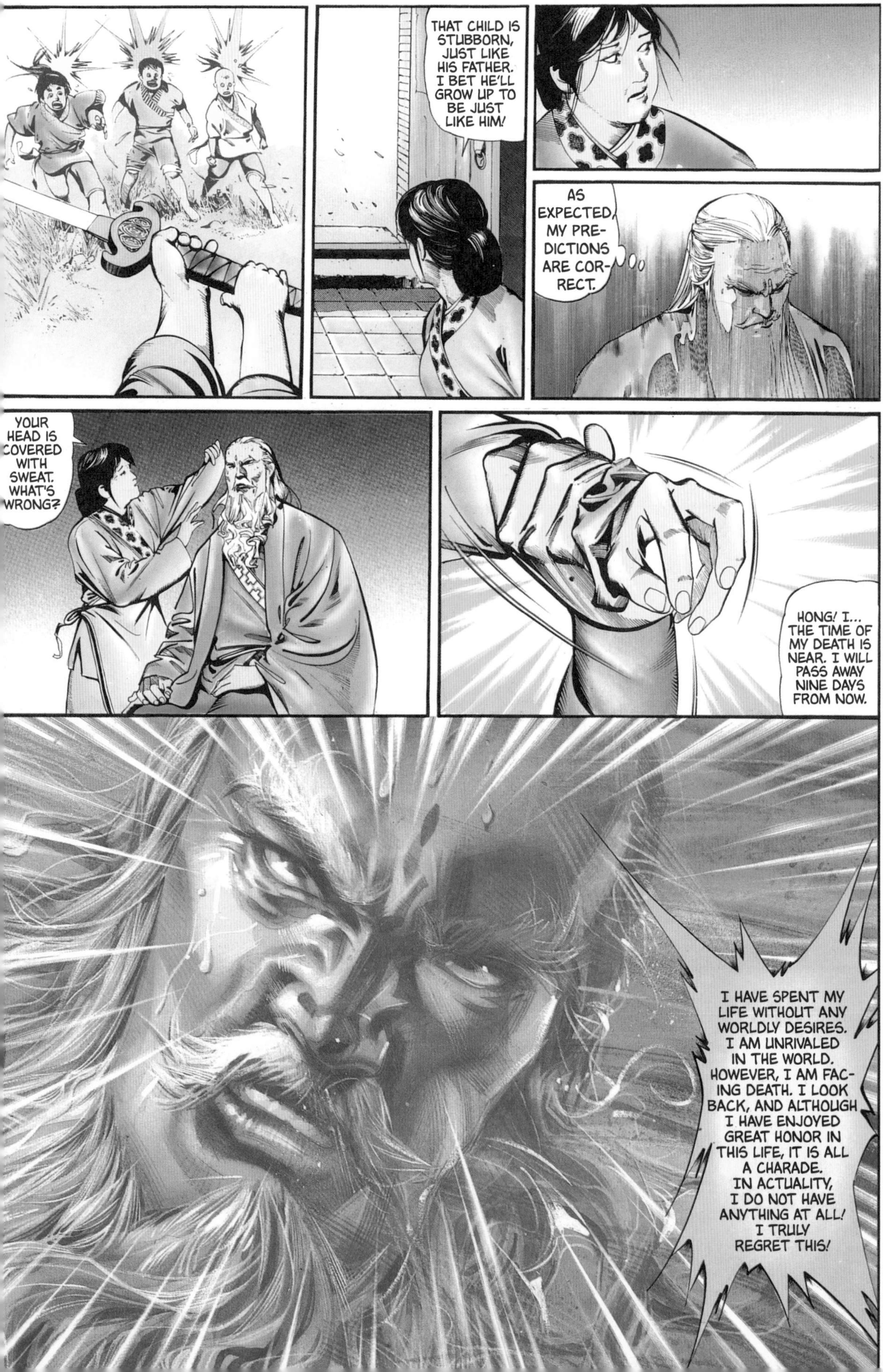
THAT CHILD IS STUBBORN, JUST LIKE HIS FATHER. I BET HE'LL GROW UP TO BE JUST LIKE HIM!
AS EXPECTED, MY PREDICTIONS ARE CORRECT.
YOUR HEAD IS COVERED WITH SWEAT. WHAT'S WRONG?
HONG! I... THE TIME OF MY DEATH IS NEAR. I WILL PASS AWAY NINE DAYS FROM NOW.
I HAVE SPENT MY LIFE WITHOUT ANY WORLDLY DESIRES. I AM UNRIVALED IN THE WORLD. HOWEVER, I AM FACING DEATH. I LOOK BACK, AND ALTHOUGH I HAVE ENJOYED GREAT HONOR IN THIS LIFE, IT IS ALL A CHARADE. IN ACTUALITY, I DO NOT HAVE ANYTHING AT ALL! I TRULY REGRET THIS!

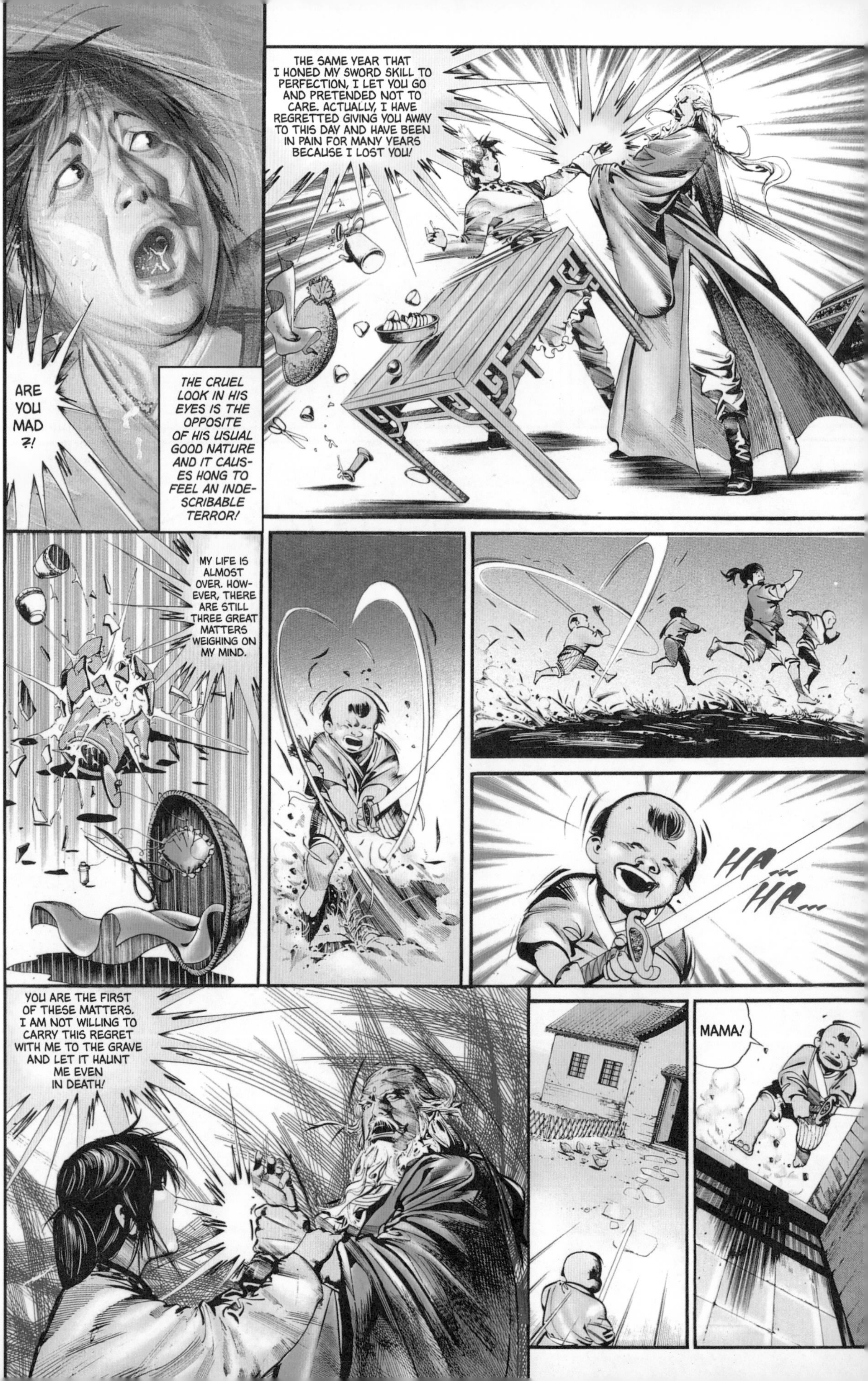
THE SAME YEAR THAT I HONED MY SWORD SKILL TO PERFECTION, I LET YOU GO AND PRETENDED NOT TO CARE. ACTUALLY, I HAVE REGRETTED GIVING YOU AWAY TO THIS DAY AND HAVE BEEN IN PAIN FOR MANY YEARS BECAUSE I LOST YOU!
ARE YOU MAD ?!
THE CRUEL LOOK IN HIS EYES IS THE OPPOSITE OF HIS USUAL GOOD NATURE AND IT CAUSES HONG TO FEEL AN INDESCRIBABLE TERROR!
MY LIFE IS ALMOST OVER. HOWEVER, THERE ARE STILL THREE GREAT MATTERS WEIGHING ON MY MIND.
HA... HA...
YOU ARE THE FIRST OF THESE MATTERS. I AM NOT WILLING TO CARRY THIS REGRET WITH ME TO THE GRAVE AND LET IT HAUNT ME EVEN IN DEATH!
MAMA!

KIM, RUN AWAY!

HYAH!

WPHH!

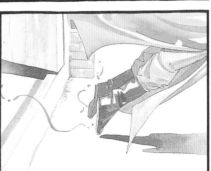

IN ORDER TO KEEP ALL MY STRENGTH FOR THE NEXT TWO MATTERS, I MUST HAVE NOTHING ELSE WEIGHING ON MY MIND.

HONG... PLEASE EXCUSE ME FOR HAVING SUCH AN IRON HEART!

MOTHER!

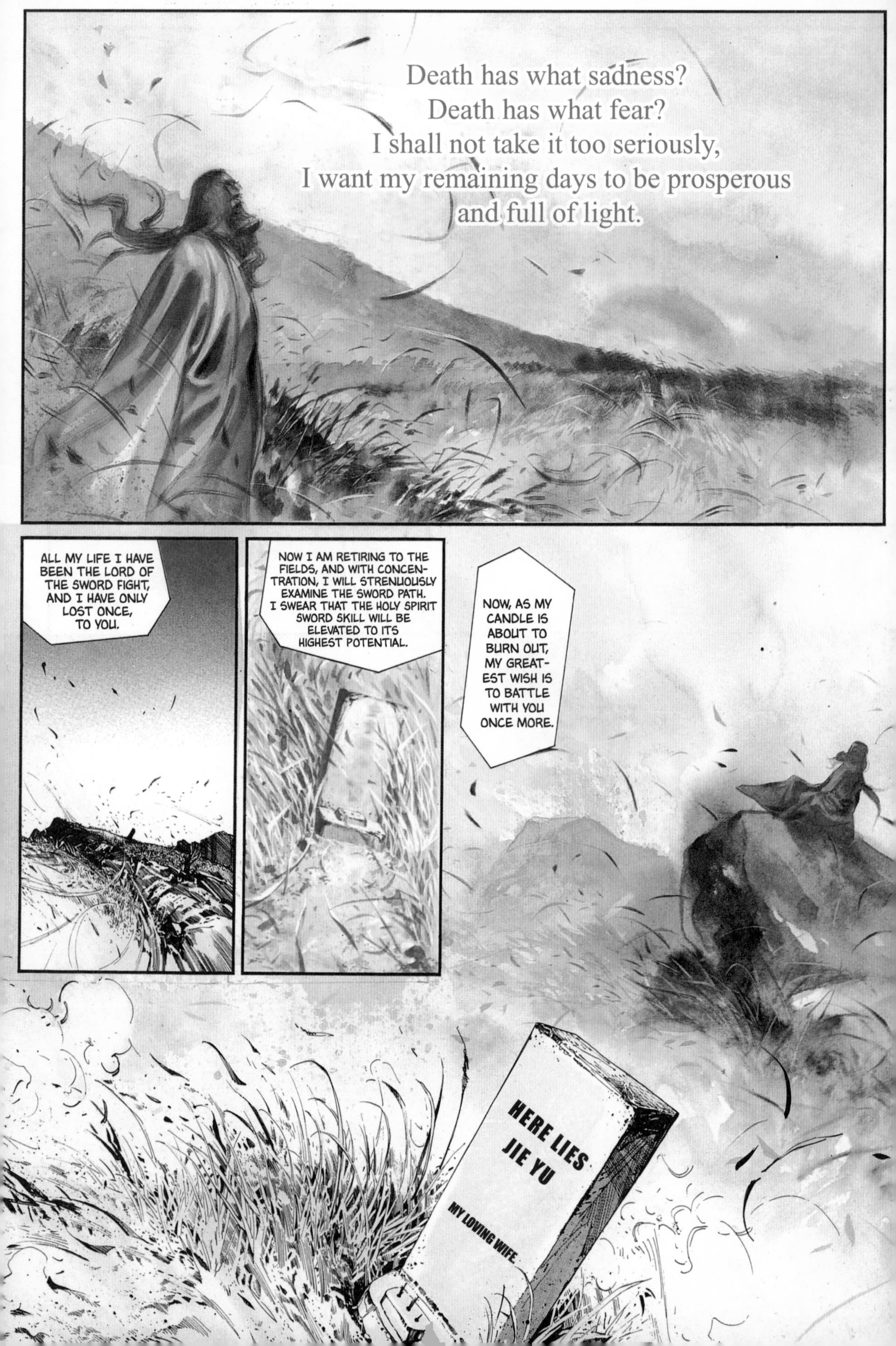
Death has what sadness?
Death has what fear?
I shall not take it too seriously,
I want my remaining days to be prosperous
and full of light.
ALL MY LIFE I HAVE BEEN THE LORD OF THE SWORD FIGHT, AND I HAVE ONLY LOST ONCE, TO YOU.
NOW I AM RETIRING TO THE FIELDS, AND WITH CONCENTRATION, I WILL STRENUOUSLY EXAMINE THE SWORD PATH. I SWEAR THAT THE HOLY SPIRIT SWORD SKILL WILL BE ELEVATED TO ITS HIGHEST POTENTIAL.
NOW, AS MY CANDLE IS ABOUT TO BURN OUT, MY GREATEST WISH IS TO BATTLE WITH YOU ONCE MORE.
HERE LIES JIE YU
MY LOVING WIFE

THE HERO SWORD REFLECTS THE WORLD. ITS PROUD BLADE HATES TO BE IGNORED.

NAMELESS...

YOU COULD NOT HAVE DIED SO EASILY!

HERE LIES JIE YU

MY LOVING WIFE.

THIS DAY IS THE ANNIVERSARY OF YOUR WIFE'S DEATH. IF YOU ARE NOT DEAD, THEN YOU WILL CERTAINLY COME TO PAY YOUR RESPECTS... I WILL WAIT FOR YOU HERE!

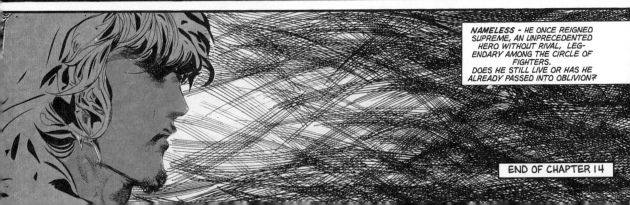

NAMELESS - HE ONCE REIGNED SUPREME, AN UNPRECEDENTED HERO WITHOUT RIVAL, LEGENDARY AMONG THE CIRCLE OF FIGHTERS. DOES HE STILL LIVE OR HAS HE ALREADY PASSED INTO OBLIVION?

END OF CHAPTER 14

Chapter 15: Nameless Hero

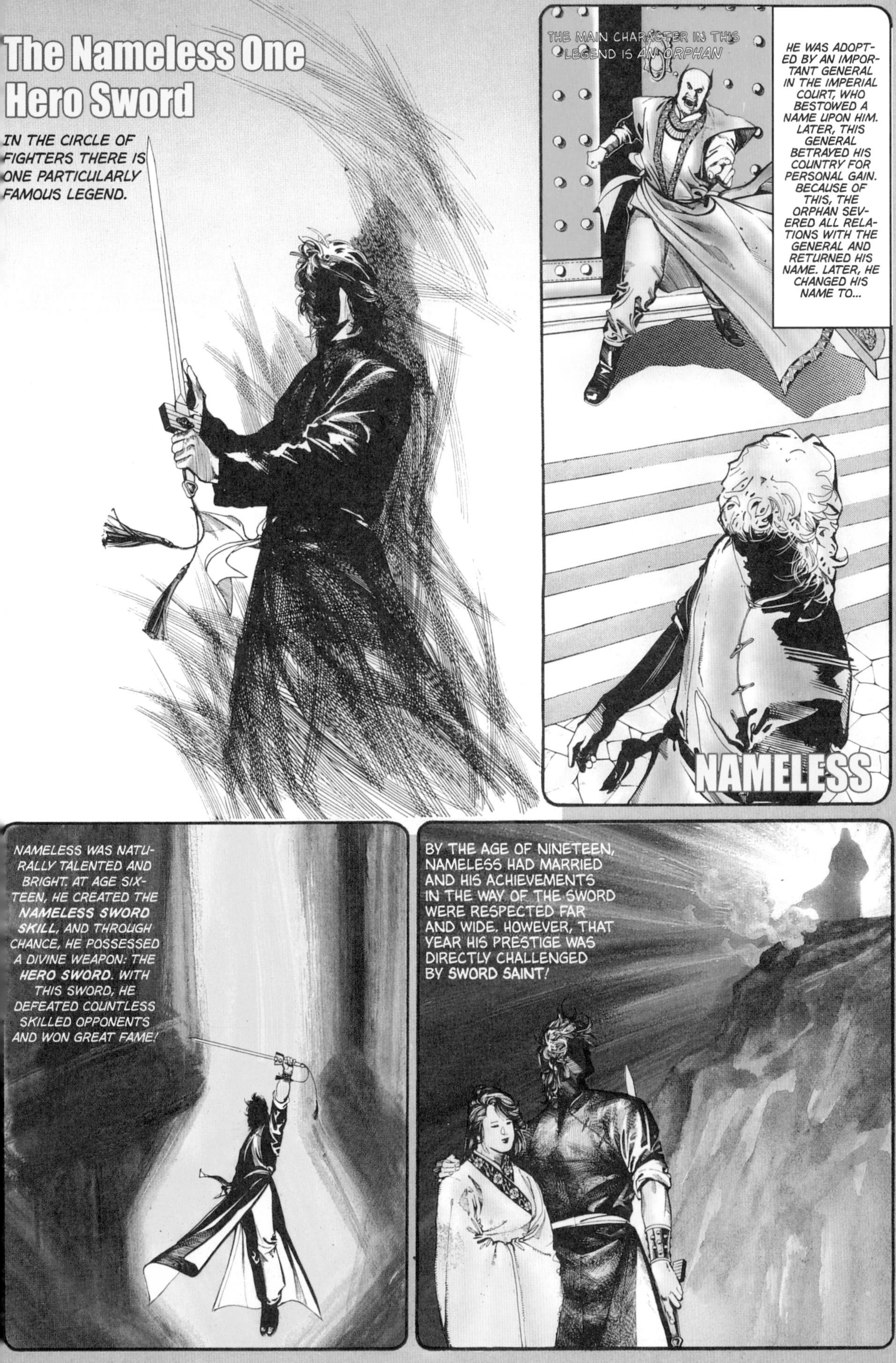

The Nameless One Hero Sword
IN THE CIRCLE OF FIGHTERS THERE IS ONE PARTICULARLY FAMOUS LEGEND.
THE MAIN CHARACTER IN THIS LEGEND IS AN ORPHAN
HE WAS ADOPTED BY AN IMPORTANT GENERAL IN THE IMPERIAL COURT, WHO BESTOWED A NAME UPON HIM. LATER, THIS GENERAL BETRAYED HIS COUNTRY FOR PERSONAL GAIN. BECAUSE OF THIS, THE ORPHAN SEVERED ALL RELATIONS WITH THE GENERAL AND RETURNED HIS NAME. LATER, HE CHANGED HIS NAME TO...
NAMELESS
NAMELESS WAS NATURALLY TALENTED AND BRIGHT. AT AGE SIXTEEN, HE CREATED THE NAMELESS SWORD SKILL, AND THROUGH CHANCE, HE POSSESSED A DIVINE WEAPON: THE HERO SWORD. WITH THIS SWORD, HE DEFEATED COUNTLESS SKILLED OPPONENTS AND WON GREAT FAME!
BY THE AGE OF NINETEEN, NAMELESS HAD MARRIED AND HIS ACHIEVEMENTS IN THE WAY OF THE SWORD WERE RESPECTED FAR AND WIDE. HOWEVER, THAT YEAR HIS PRESTIGE WAS DIRECTLY CHALLENGED BY SWORD SAINT!

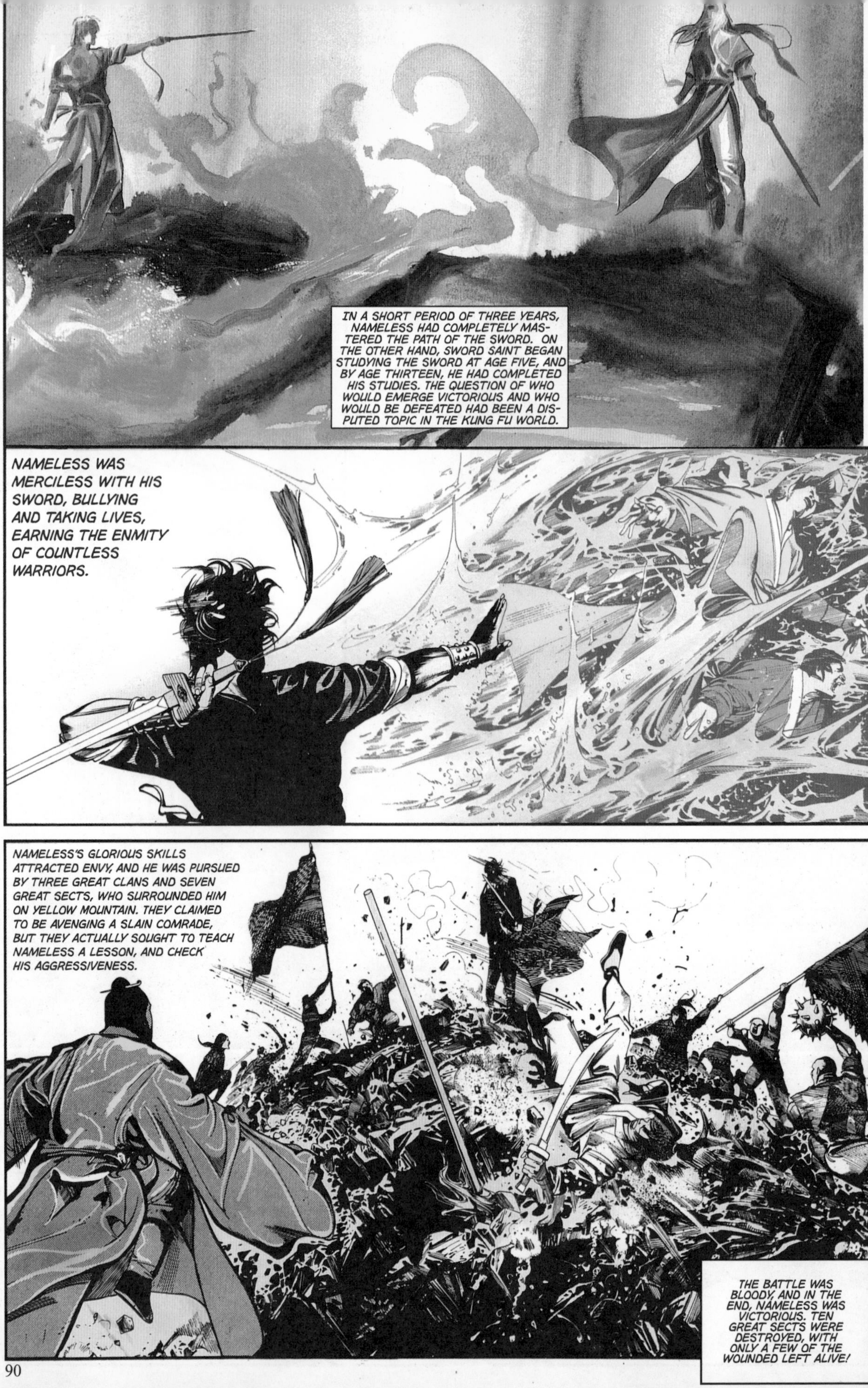
IN A SHORT PERIOD OF THREE YEARS, NAMELESS HAD COMPLETELY MASTERED THE PATH OF THE SWORD. ON THE OTHER HAND, SWORD SAINT BEGAN STUDYING THE SWORD AT AGE FIVE, AND BY AGE THIRTEEN, HE HAD COMPLETED HIS STUDIES. THE QUESTION OF WHO WOULD EMERGE VICTORIOUS AND WHO WOULD BE DEFEATED HAD BEEN A DISPUTED TOPIC IN THE KUNG FU WORLD.
NAMELESS WAS MERCILESS WITH HIS SWORD, BULLYING AND TAKING LIVES, EARNING THE ENMITY OF COUNTLESS WARRIORS.
NAMELESS'S GLORIOUS SKILLS ATTRACTED ENVY, AND HE WAS PURSUED BY THREE GREAT CLANS AND SEVEN GREAT SECTS, WHO SURROUNDED HIM ON YELLOW MOUNTAIN. THEY CLAIMED TO BE AVENGING A SLAIN COMRADE, BUT THEY ACTUALLY SOUGHT TO TEACH NAMELESS A LESSON, AND CHECK HIS AGGRESSIVENESS.
THE BATTLE WAS BLOODY, AND IN THE END, NAMELESS WAS VICTORIOUS. TEN GREAT SECTS WERE DESTROYED, WITH ONLY A FEW OF THE WOUNDED LEFT ALIVE!

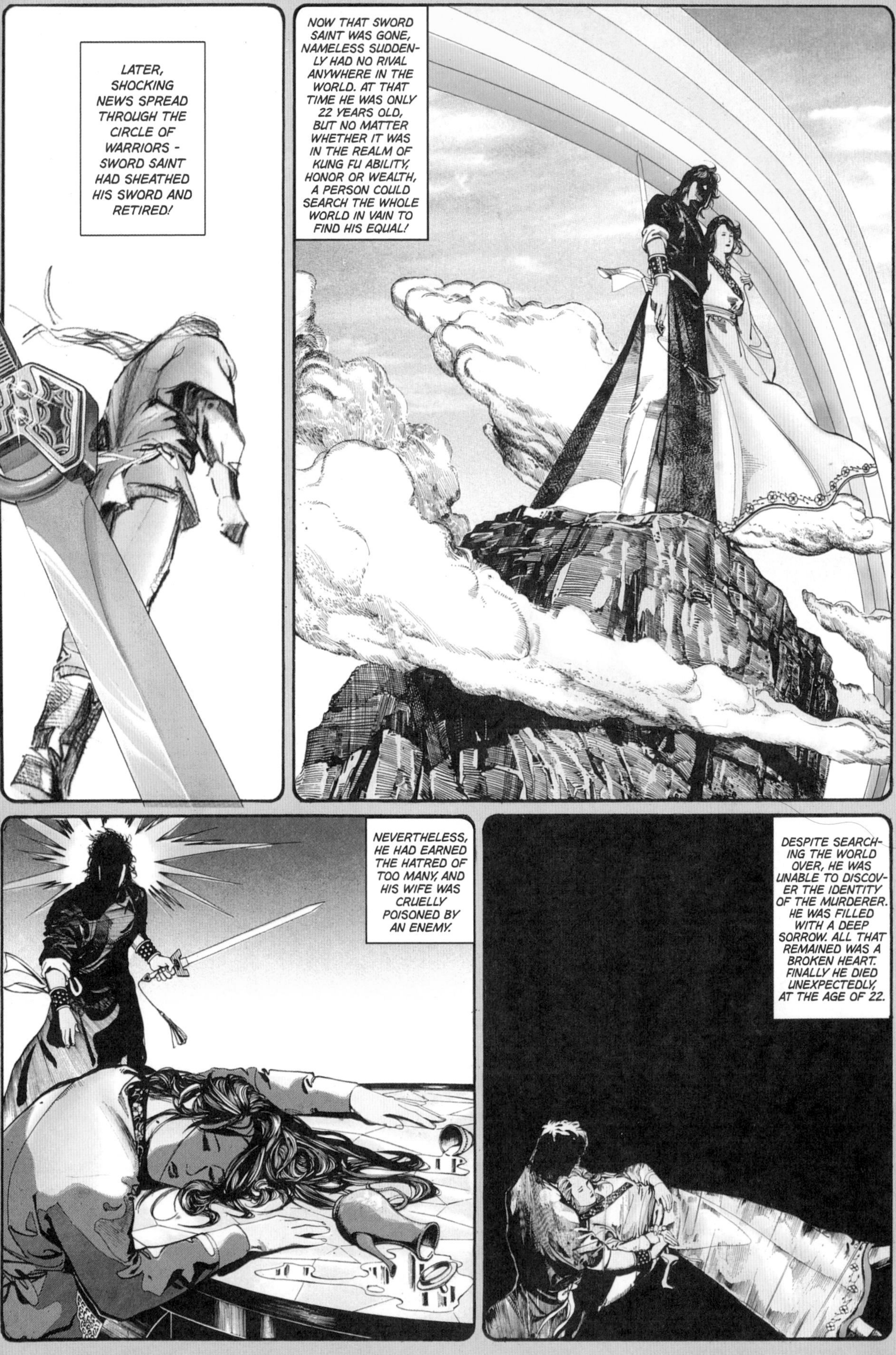
LATER, SHOCKING NEWS SPREAD THROUGH THE CIRCLE OF WARRIORS - SWORD SAINT HAD SHEATHED HIS SWORD AND RETIRED!
NOW THAT SWORD SAINT WAS GONE, NAMELESS SUDDENLY HAD NO RIVAL ANYWHERE IN THE WORLD. AT THAT TIME HE WAS ONLY 22 YEARS OLD, BUT NO MATTER WHETHER IT WAS IN THE REALM OF KUNG FU ABILITY, HONOR OR WEALTH, A PERSON COULD SEARCH THE WHOLE WORLD IN VAIN TO FIND HIS EQUAL!
NEVERTHELESS, HE HAD EARNED THE HATRED OF TOO MANY, AND HIS WIFE WAS CRUELLY POISONED BY AN ENEMY.
DESPITE SEARCHING THE WORLD OVER, HE WAS UNABLE TO DISCOVER THE IDENTITY OF THE MURDERER. HE WAS FILLED WITH A DEEP SORROW. ALL THAT REMAINED WAS A BROKEN HEART. FINALLY HE DIED UNEXPECTEDLY, AT THE AGE OF 22.

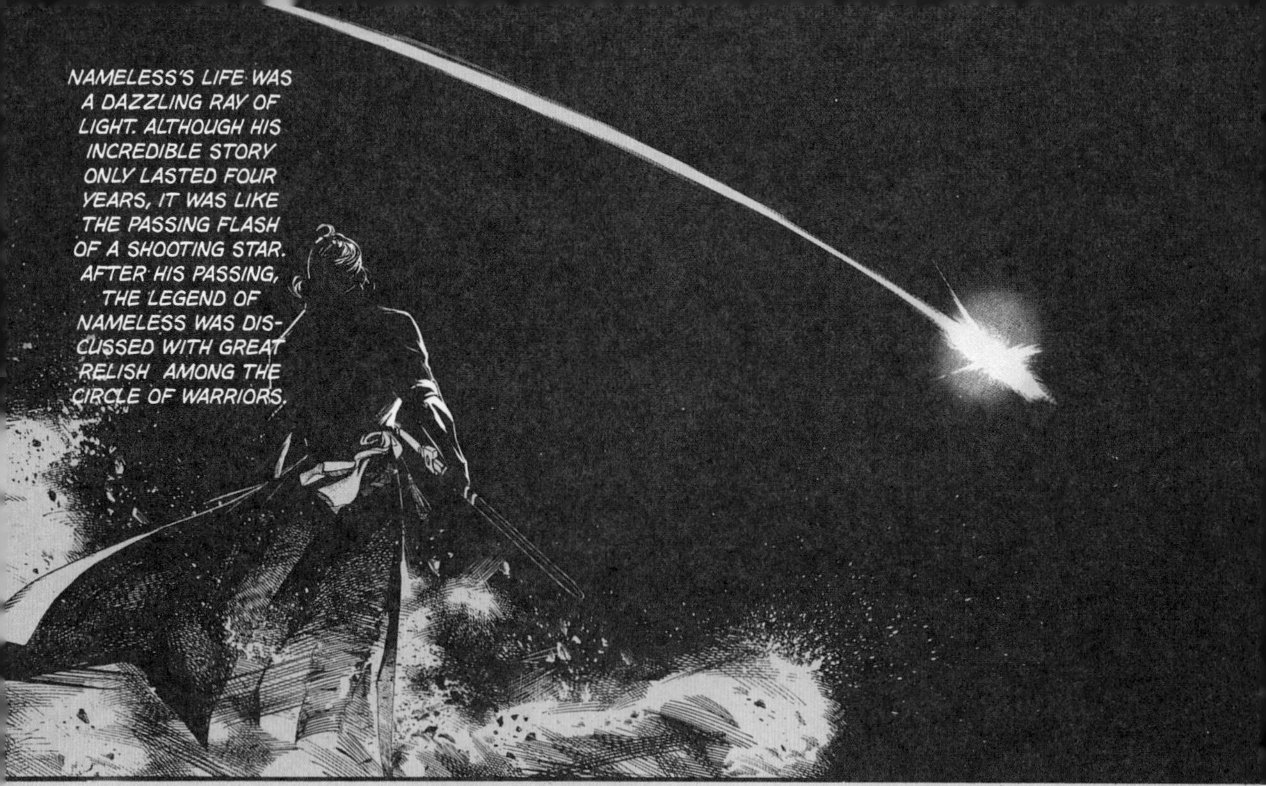
NAMELESS'S LIFE WAS A DAZZLING RAY OF LIGHT. ALTHOUGH HIS INCREDIBLE STORY ONLY LASTED FOUR YEARS, IT WAS LIKE THE PASSING FLASH OF A SHOOTING STAR. AFTER HIS PASSING, THE LEGEND OF NAMELESS WAS DISCUSSED WITH GREAT RELISH AMONG THE CIRCLE OF WARRIORS.

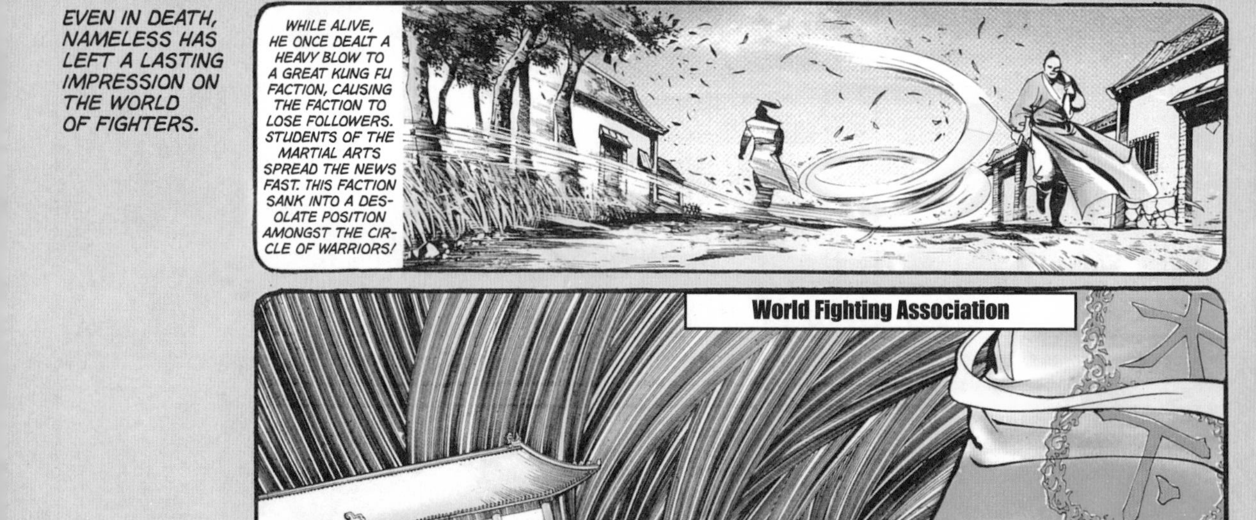
EVEN IN DEATH, NAMELESS HAS LEFT A LASTING IMPRESSION ON THE WORLD OF FIGHTERS.
WHILE ALIVE, HE ONCE DEALT A HEAVY BLOW TO A GREAT KUNG FU FACTION, CAUSING THE FACTION TO LOSE FOLLOWERS. STUDENTS OF THE MARTIAL ARTS SPREAD THE NEWS FAST. THIS FACTION SANK INTO A DESOLATE POSITION AMONGST THE CIRCLE OF WARRIORS!

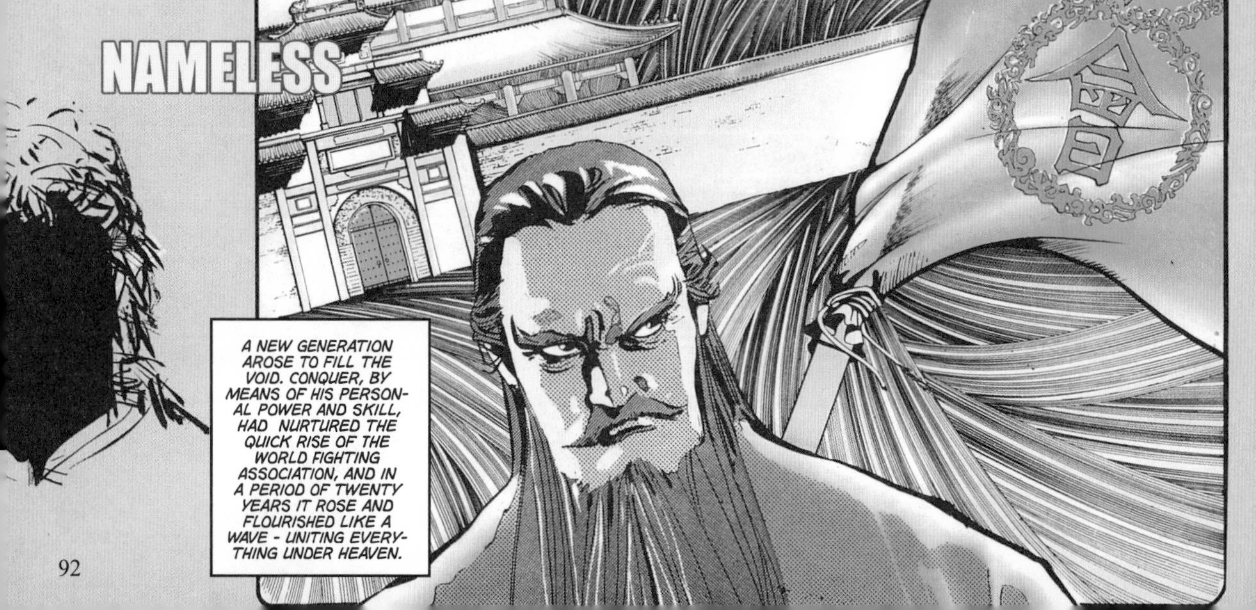
World Fighting Association
NAMELESS
A NEW GENERATION AROSE TO FILL THE VOID. CONQUER, BY MEANS OF HIS PERSONAL POWER AND SKILL, HAD NURTURED THE QUICK RISE OF THE WORLD FIGHTING ASSOCIATION, AND IN A PERIOD OF TWENTY YEARS IT ROSE AND FLOURISHED LIKE A WAVE - UNITING EVERYTHING UNDER HEAVEN.

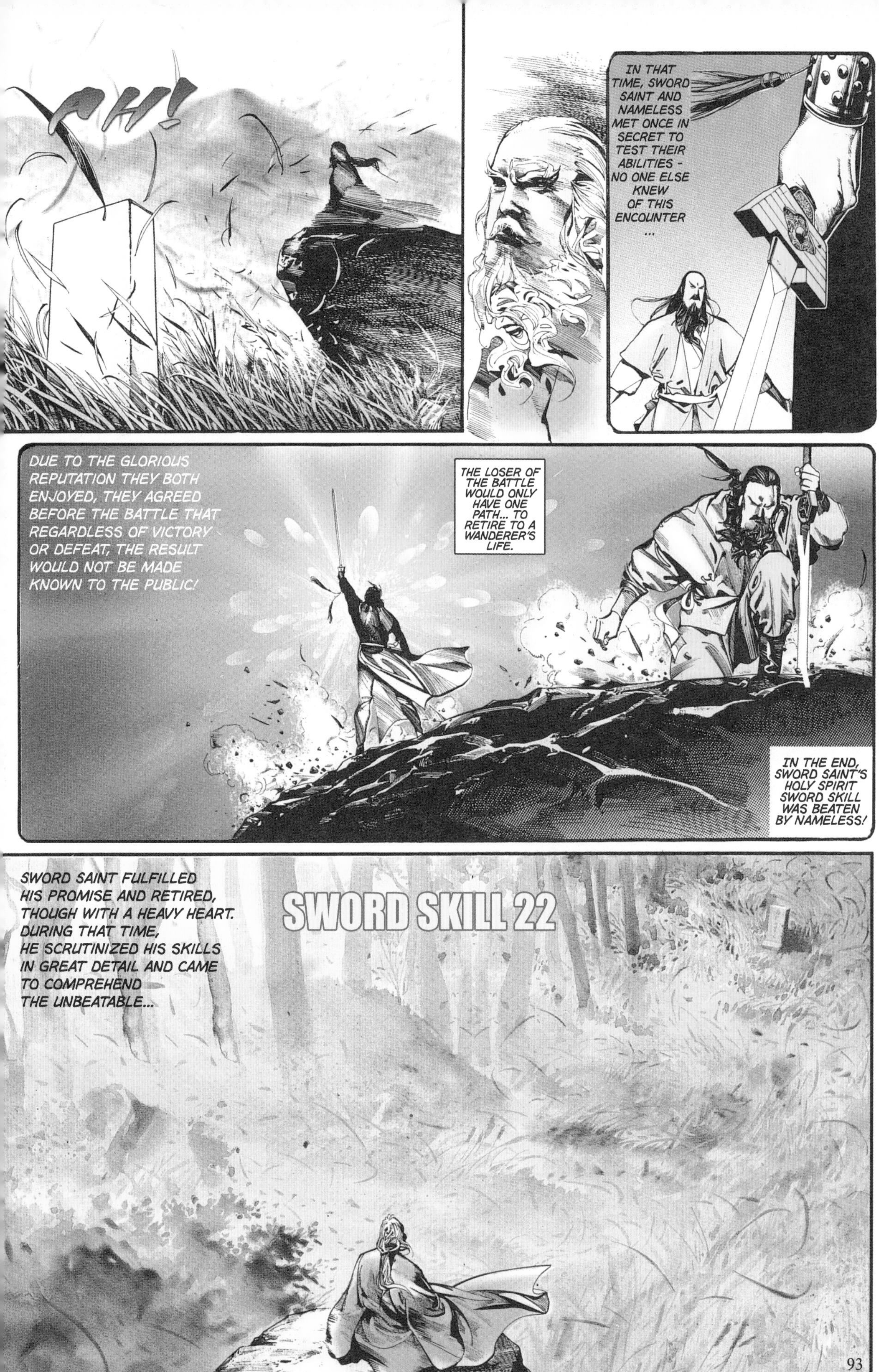
PH!
IN THAT TIME, SWORD SAINT AND NAMELESS MET ONCE IN SECRET TO TEST THEIR ABILITIES - NO ONE ELSE KNEW OF THIS ENCOUNTER ...
DUE TO THE GLORIOUS REPUTATION THEY BOTH ENJOYED, THEY AGREED BEFORE THE BATTLE THAT REGARDLESS OF VICTORY OR DEFEAT, THE RESULT WOULD NOT BE MADE KNOWN TO THE PUBLIC!
THE LOSER OF THE BATTLE WOULD ONLY HAVE ONE PATH... TO RETIRE TO A WANDERER'S LIFE.
IN THE END, SWORD SAINT'S HOLY SPIRIT SWORD SKILL WAS BEATEN BY NAMELESS!
SWORD SAINT FULFILLED HIS PROMISE AND RETIRED, THOUGH WITH A HEAVY HEART. DURING THAT TIME, HE SCRUTINIZED HIS SKILLS IN GREAT DETAIL AND CAME TO COMPREHEND THE UNBEATABLE...
SWORD SKILL 22

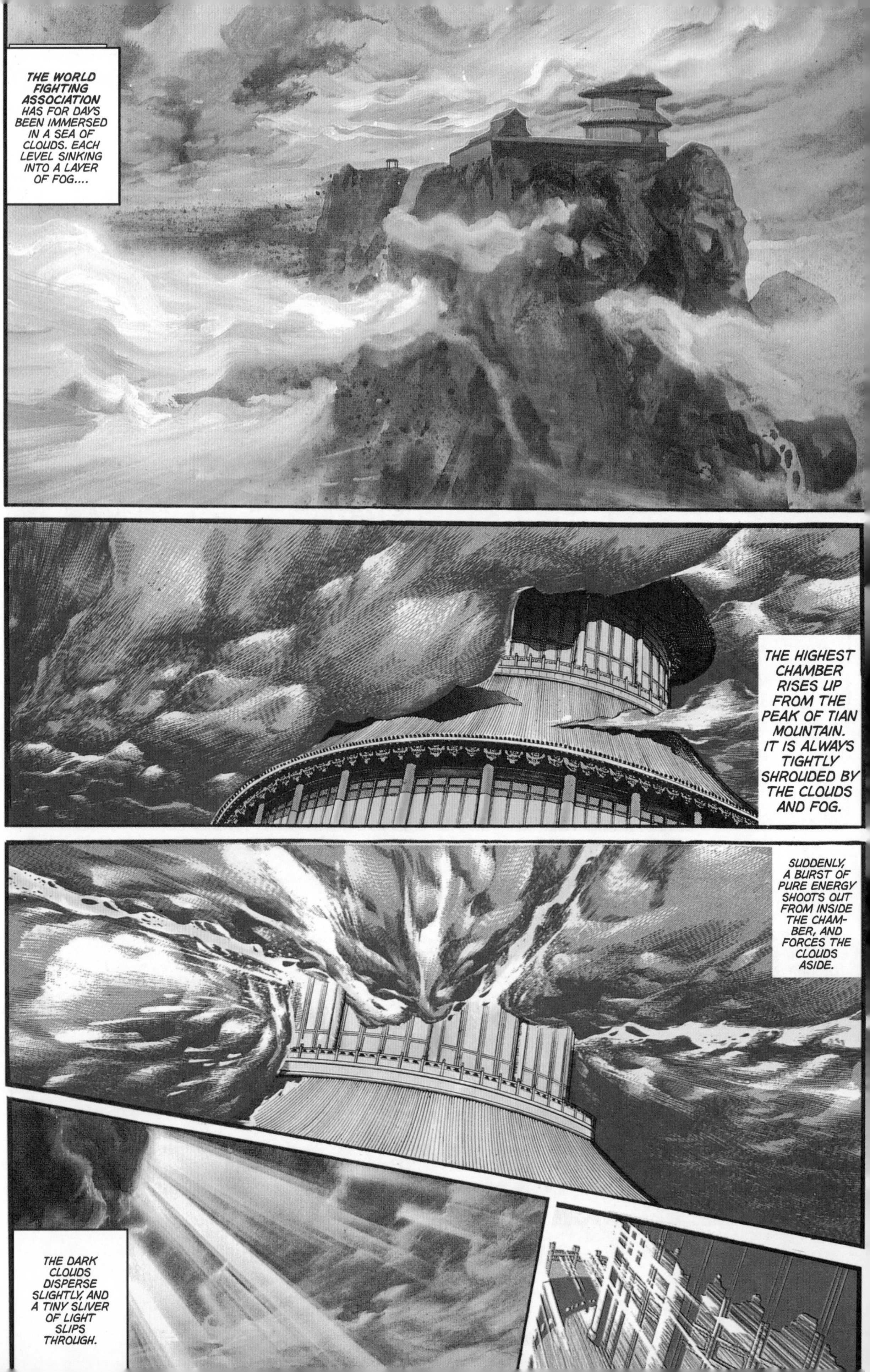
THE WORLD FIGHTING ASSOCIATION HAS FOR DAYS BEEN IMMERSED IN A SEA OF CLOUDS. EACH LEVEL SINKING INTO A LAYER OF FOG....
THE HIGHEST CHAMBER RISES UP FROM THE PEAK OF TIAN MOUNTAIN. IT IS ALWAYS TIGHTLY SHROUDED BY THE CLOUDS AND FOG.
SUDDENLY, A BURST OF PURE ENERGY SHOOTS OUT FROM INSIDE THE CHAMBER, AND FORCES THE CLOUDS ASIDE.
THE DARK CLOUDS DISPERSE SLIGHTLY, AND A TINY SLIVER OF LIGHT SLIPS THROUGH.

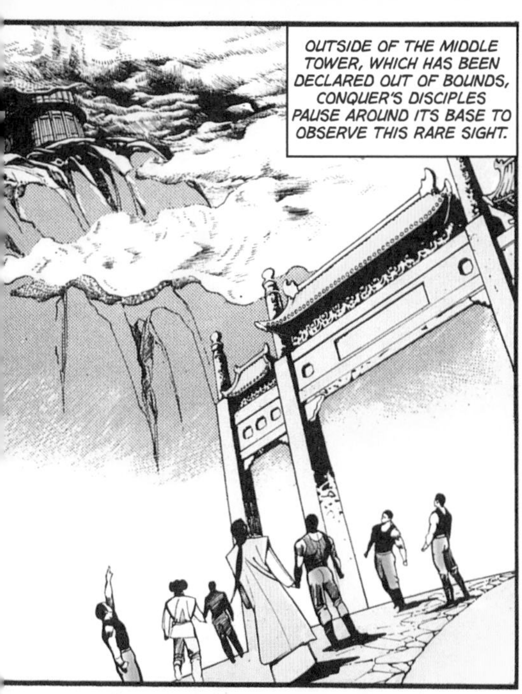
OUTSIDE OF THE MIDDLE TOWER, WHICH HAS BEEN DECLARED OUT OF BOUNDS, CONQUER'S DISCIPLES PAUSE AROUND ITS BASE TO OBSERVE THIS RARE SIGHT.

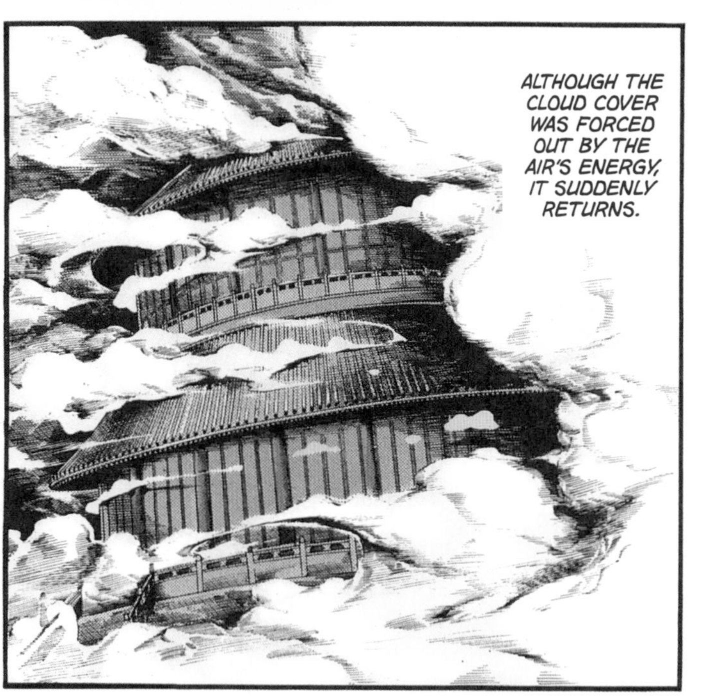
ALTHOUGH THE CLOUD COVER WAS FORCED OUT BY THE AIR'S ENERGY, IT SUDDENLY RETURNS.

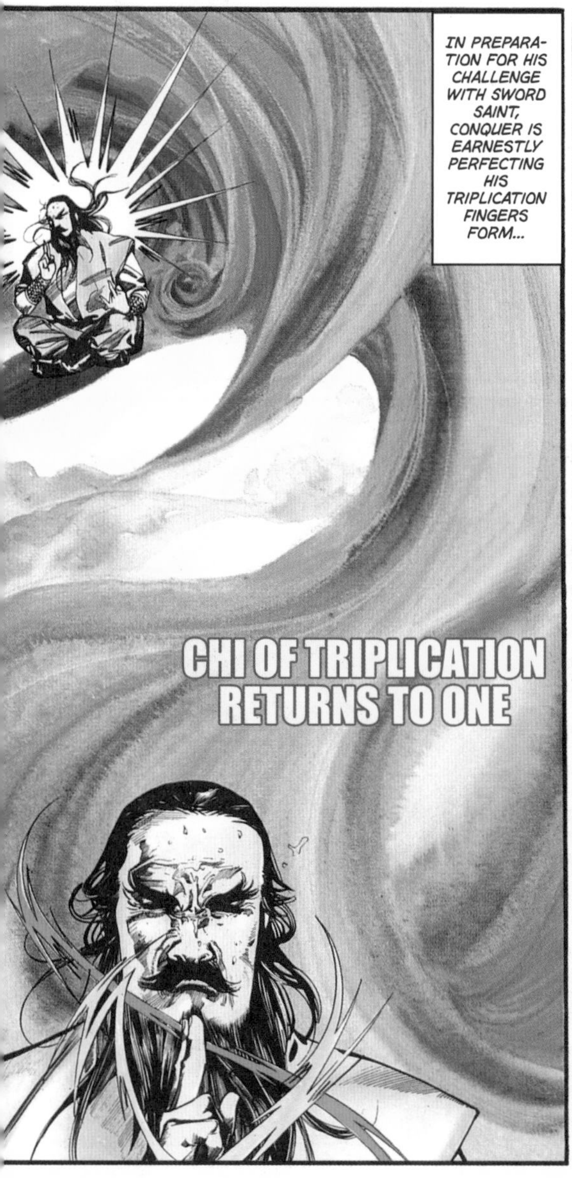
IN PREPARATION FOR HIS CHALLENGE WITH SWORD SAINT, CONQUER IS EARNESTLY PERFECTING HIS TRIPLICATION FINGERS FORM...
CHI OF TRIPLICATION RETURNS TO ONE

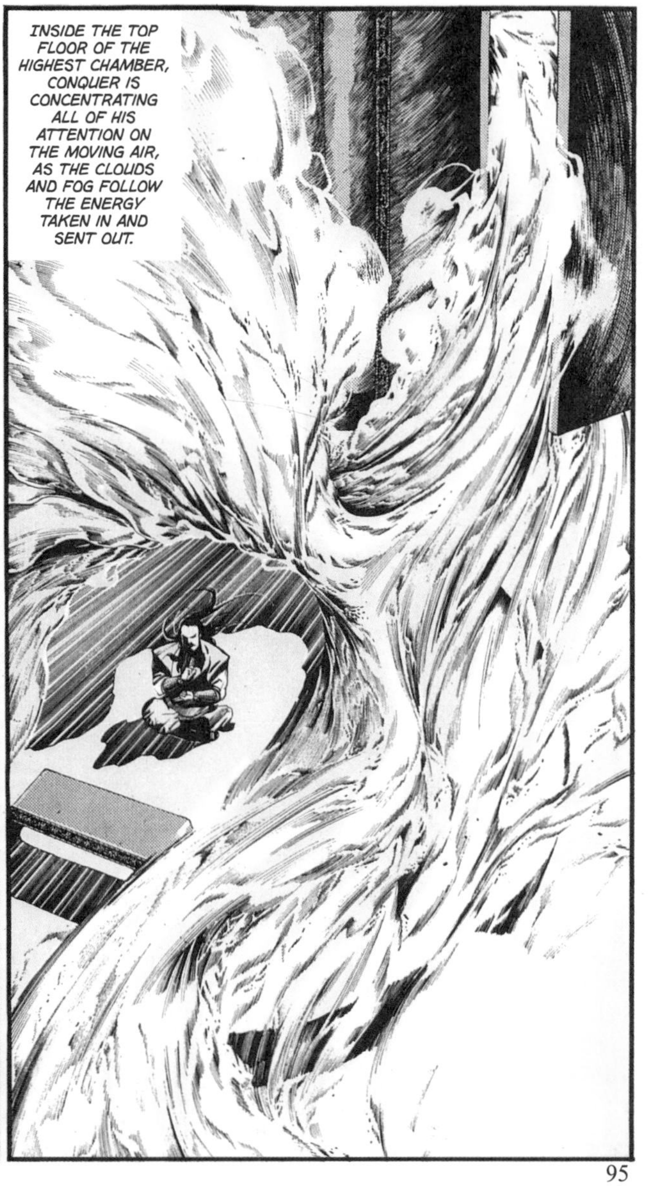
INSIDE THE TOP FLOOR OF THE HIGHEST CHAMBER, CONQUER IS CONCENTRATING ALL OF HIS ATTENTION ON THE MOVING AIR, AS THE CLOUDS AND FOG FOLLOW THE ENERGY TAKEN IN AND SENT OUT.

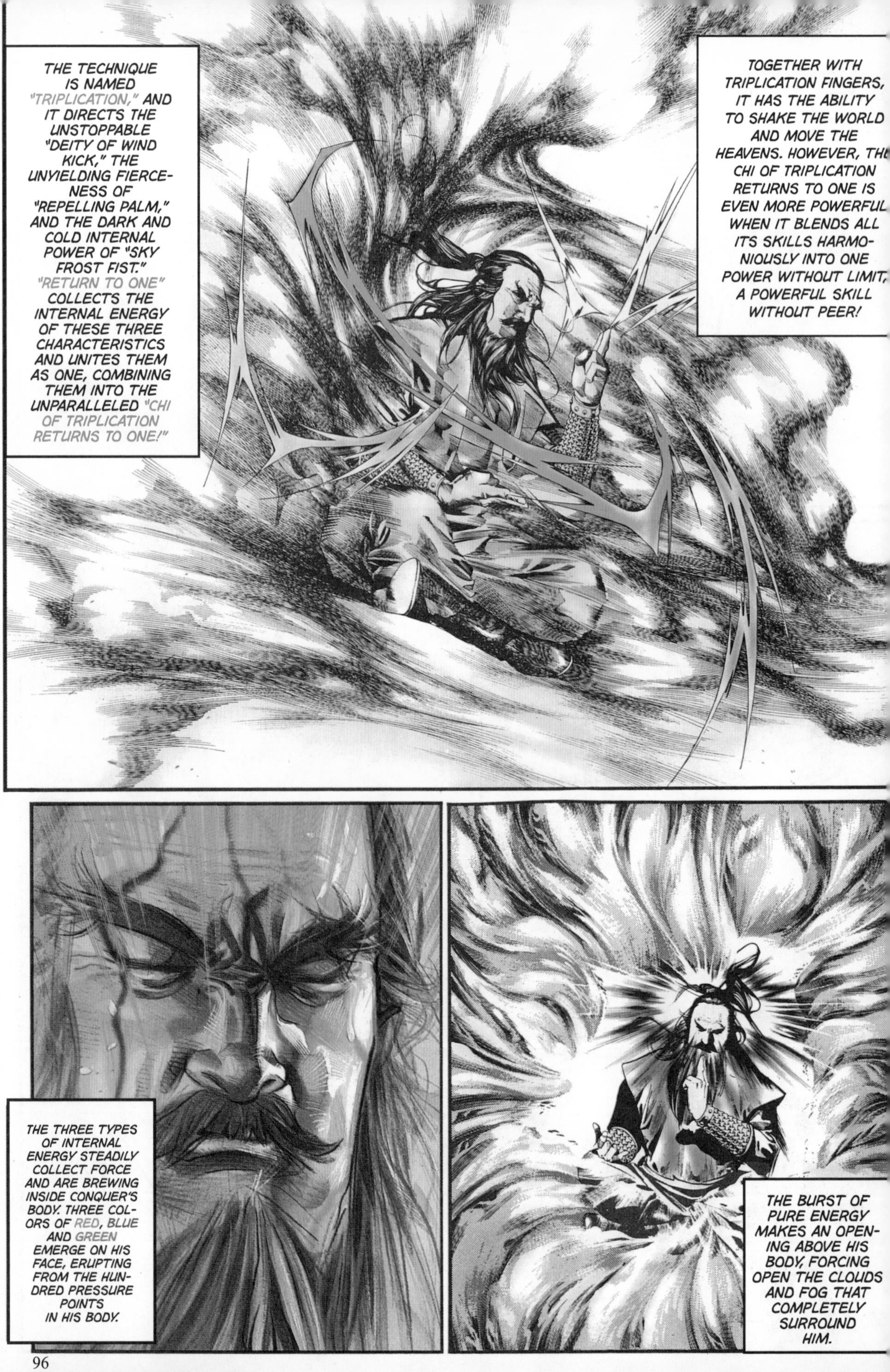
THE TECHNIQUE IS NAMED "TRIPLICATION," AND IT DIRECTS THE UNSTOPPABLE "DEITY OF WIND KICK," THE UNYIELDING FIERCENESS OF "REPELLING PALM," AND THE DARK AND COLD INTERNAL POWER OF "SKY FROST FIST." "RETURN TO ONE" COLLECTS THE INTERNAL ENERGY OF THESE THREE CHARACTERISTICS AND UNITES THEM AS ONE, COMBINING THEM INTO THE UNPARALLELED "CHI OF TRIPLICATION RETURNS TO ONE!"
TOGETHER WITH TRIPLICATION FINGERS, IT HAS THE ABILITY TO SHAKE THE WORLD AND MOVE THE HEAVENS. HOWEVER, THE CHI OF TRIPLICATION RETURNS TO ONE IS EVEN MORE POWERFUL WHEN IT BLENDS ALL ITS SKILLS HARMONIOUSLY INTO ONE POWER WITHOUT LIMIT, A POWERFUL SKILL WITHOUT PEER!
THE THREE TYPES OF INTERNAL ENERGY STEADILY COLLECT FORCE AND ARE BREWING INSIDE CONQUER'S BODY. THREE COLORS OF RED, BLUE AND GREEN EMERGE ON HIS FACE, ERUPTING FROM THE HUNDRED PRESSURE POINTS IN HIS BODY.
THE BURST OF PURE ENERGY MAKES AN OPENING ABOVE HIS BODY, FORCING OPEN THE CLOUDS AND FOG THAT COMPLETELY SURROUND HIM.

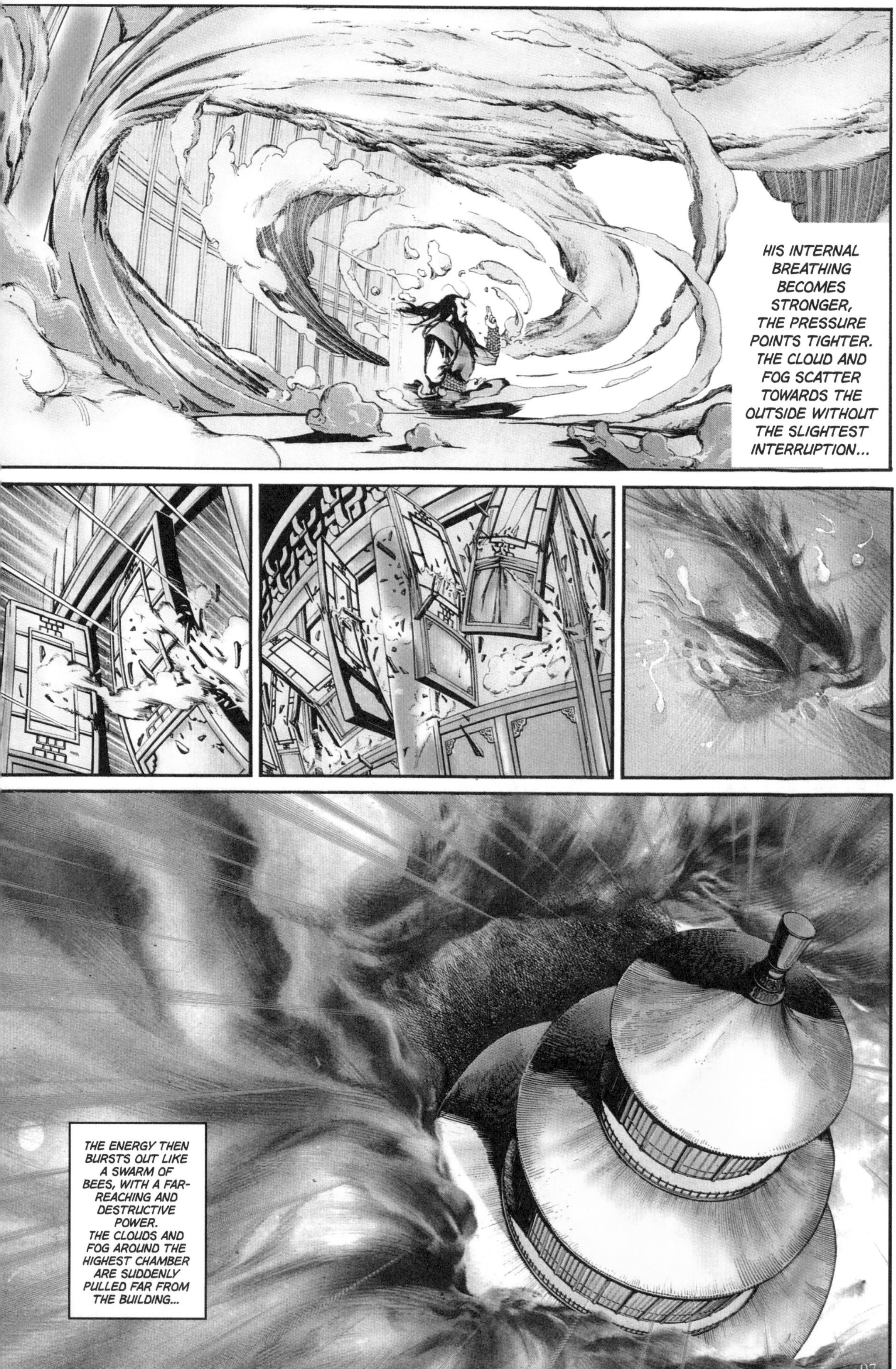
HIS INTERNAL BREATHING BECOMES STRONGER, THE PRESSURE POINTS TIGHTER. THE CLOUD AND FOG SCATTER TOWARDS THE OUTSIDE WITHOUT THE SLIGHTEST INTERRUPTION...
THE ENERGY THEN BURSTS OUT LIKE A SWARM OF BEES, WITH A FAR-REACHING AND DESTRUCTIVE POWER. THE CLOUDS AND FOG AROUND THE HIGHEST CHAMBER ARE SUDDENLY PULLED FAR FROM THE BUILDING...

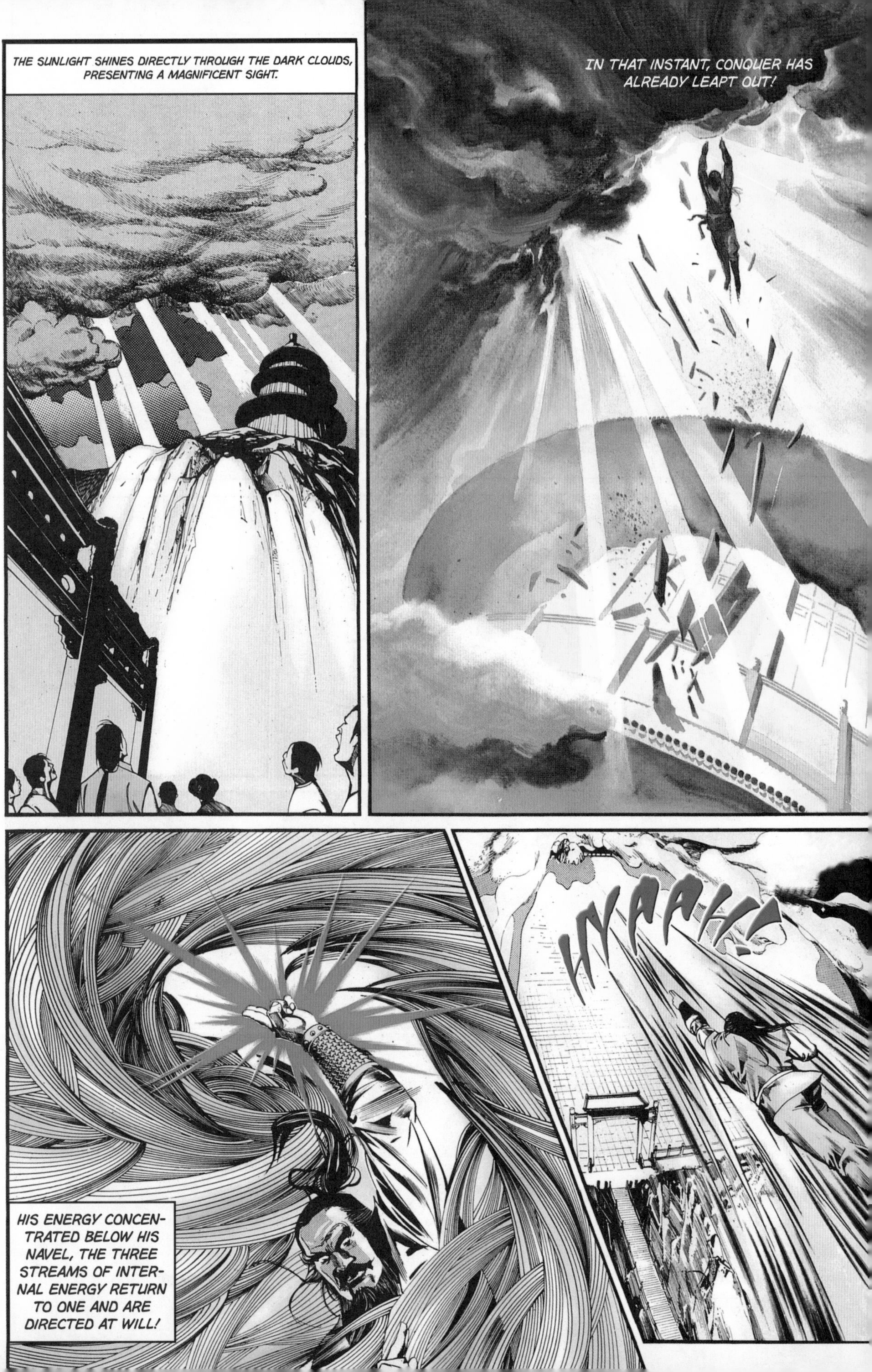
THE SUNLIGHT SHINES DIRECTLY THROUGH THE DARK CLOUDS, PRESENTING A MAGNIFICENT SIGHT.
IN THAT INSTANT, CONQUER HAS ALREADY LEAPT OUT!
HIS ENERGY CONCENTRATED BELOW HIS NAVEL, THE THREE STREAMS OF INTERNAL ENERGY RETURN TO ONE AND ARE DIRECTED AT WILL!
HYAAH!!

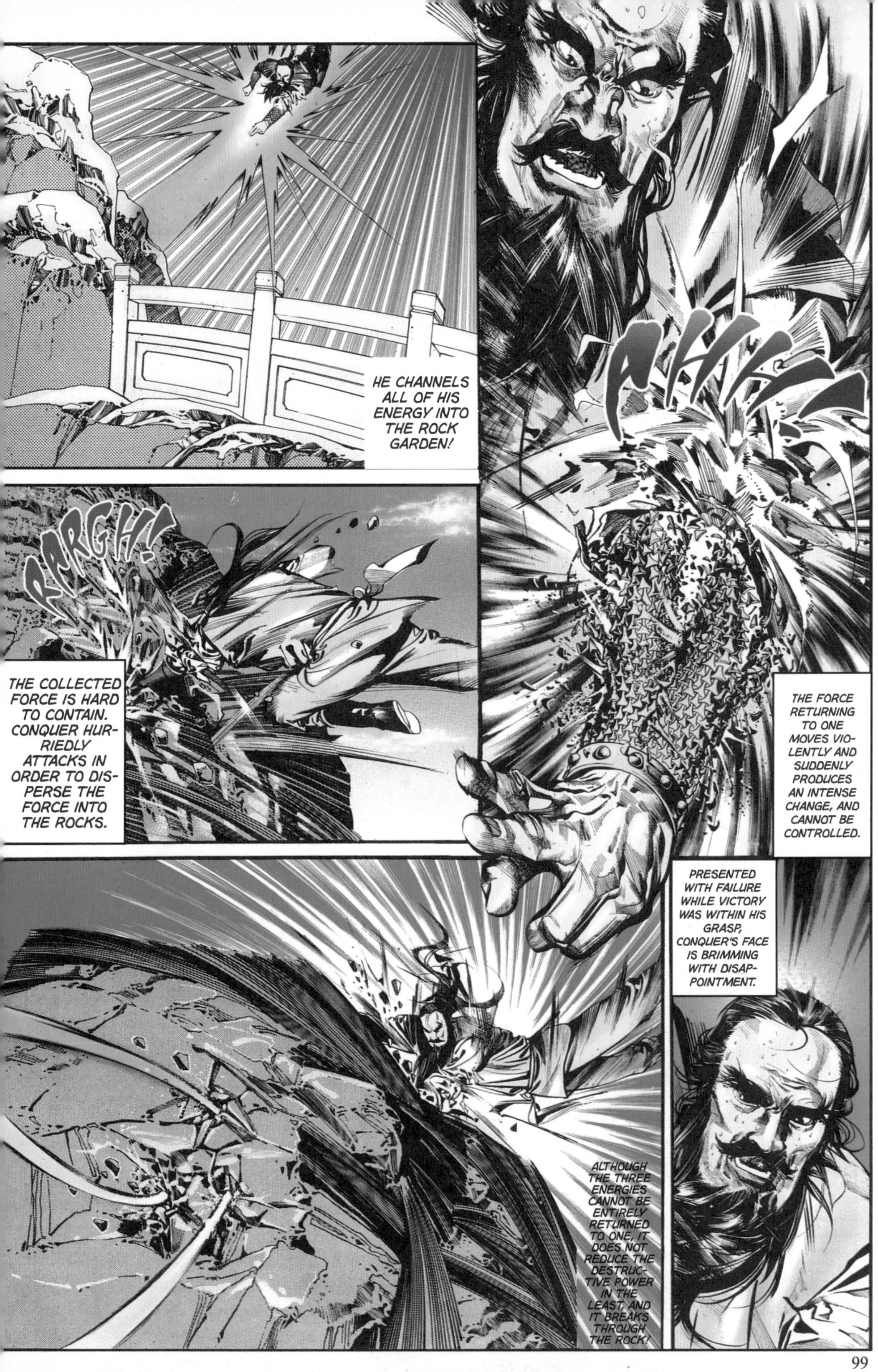
HE CHANNELS ALL OF HIS ENERGY INTO THE ROCK GARDEN!
AHH--!
RARGH!
THE COLLECTED FORCE IS HARD TO CONTAIN. CONQUER HURRIEDLY ATTACKS IN ORDER TO DISPERSE THE FORCE INTO THE ROCKS.
THE FORCE RETURNING TO ONE MOVES VIOLENTLY AND SUDDENLY PRODUCES AN INTENSE CHANGE, AND CANNOT BE CONTROLLED.
PRESENTED WITH FAILURE WHILE VICTORY WAS WITHIN HIS GRASP, CONQUER'S FACE IS BRIMMING WITH DISAPPOINTMENT.
ALTHOUGH THE THREE ENERGIES CANNOT BE ENTIRELY RETURNED TO ONE, IT DOES NOT REDUCE THE DESTRUCTIVE POWER IN THE LEAST, AND IT BREAKS THROUGH THE ROCK!

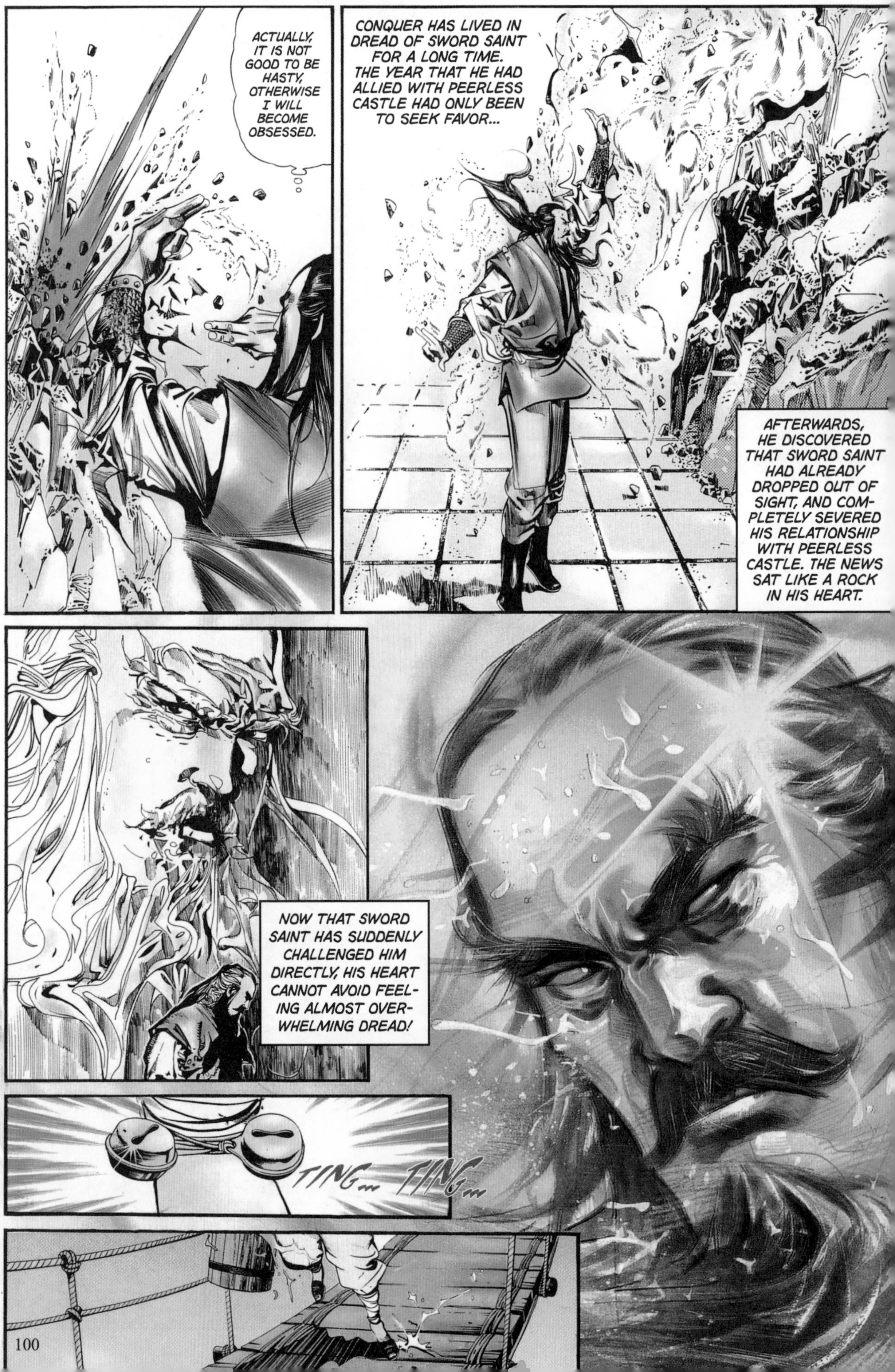
ACTUALLY, IT IS NOT GOOD TO BE HASTY, OTHERWISE I WILL BECOME OBSESSED.
CONQUER HAS LIVED IN DREAD OF SWORD SAINT FOR A LONG TIME. THE YEAR THAT HE HAD ALLIED WITH PEERLESS CASTLE HAD ONLY BEEN TO SEEK FAVOR...
AFTERWARDS, HE DISCOVERED THAT SWORD SAINT HAD ALREADY DROPPED OUT OF SIGHT, AND COMPLETELY SEVERED HIS RELATIONSHIP WITH PEERLESS CASTLE. THE NEWS SAT LIKE A ROCK IN HIS HEART.
NOW THAT SWORD SAINT HAS SUDDENLY CHALLENGED HIM DIRECTLY, HIS HEART CANNOT AVOID FEELING ALMOST OVERWHELMING DREAD!
TING... TING...

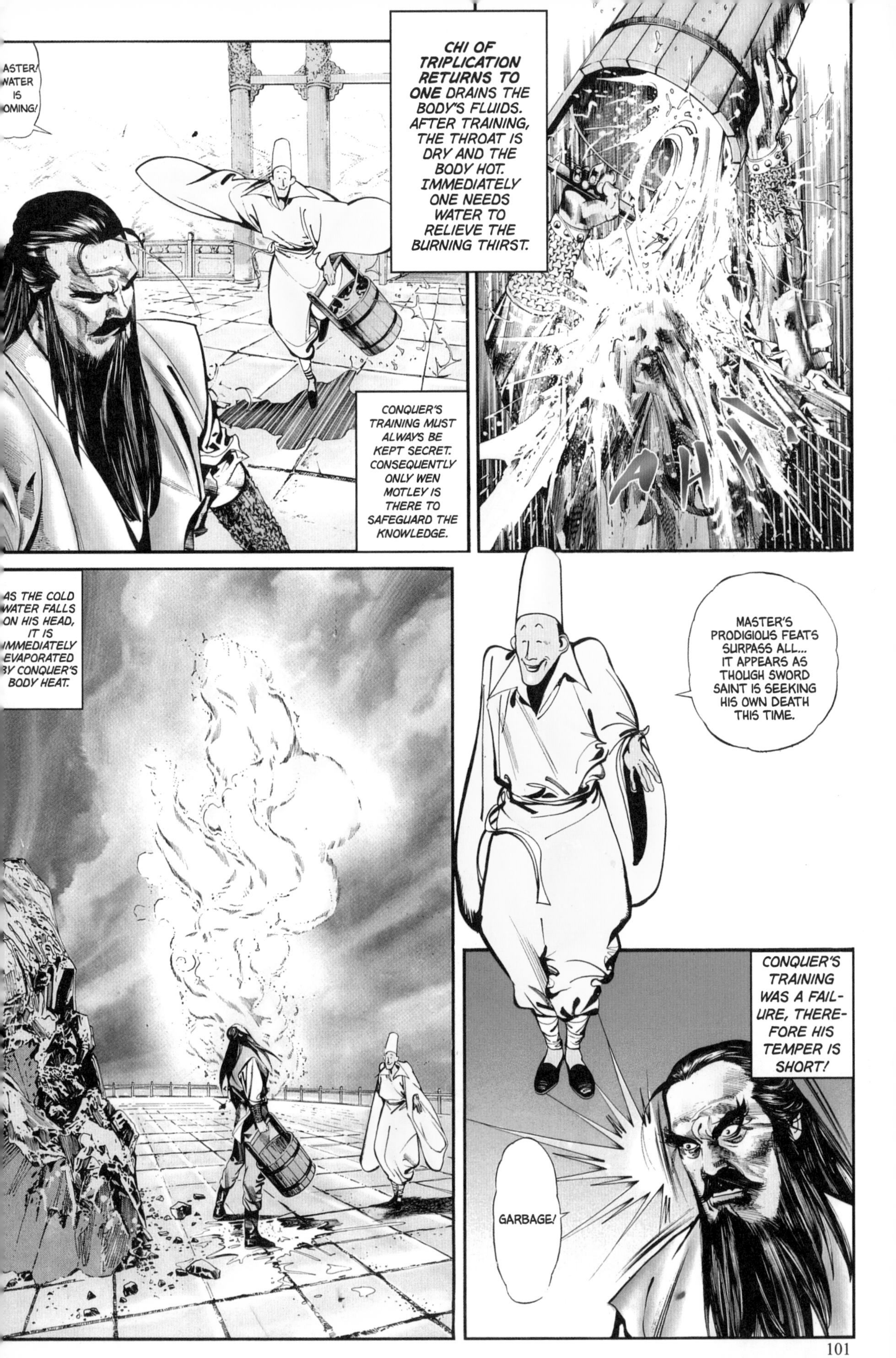

ASTER! WATER IS OMING!
CHI OF TRIPLICATION RETURNS TO ONE DRAINS THE BODY'S FLUIDS. AFTER TRAINING, THE THROAT IS DRY AND THE BODY HOT. IMMEDIATELY ONE NEEDS WATER TO RELIEVE THE BURNING THIRST.
CONQUER'S TRAINING MUST ALWAYS BE KEPT SECRET. CONSEQUENTLY ONLY WEN MOTLEY IS THERE TO SAFEGUARD THE KNOWLEDGE.
AHH!
AS THE COLD WATER FALLS ON HIS HEAD, IT IS IMMEDIATELY EVAPORATED BY CONQUER'S BODY HEAT.
MASTER'S PRODIGIOUS FEATS SURPASS ALL... IT APPEARS AS THOUGH SWORD SAINT IS SEEKING HIS OWN DEATH THIS TIME.
CONQUER'S TRAINING WAS A FAIL- URE, THERE- FORE HIS TEMPER IS SHORT!
GARBAGE!

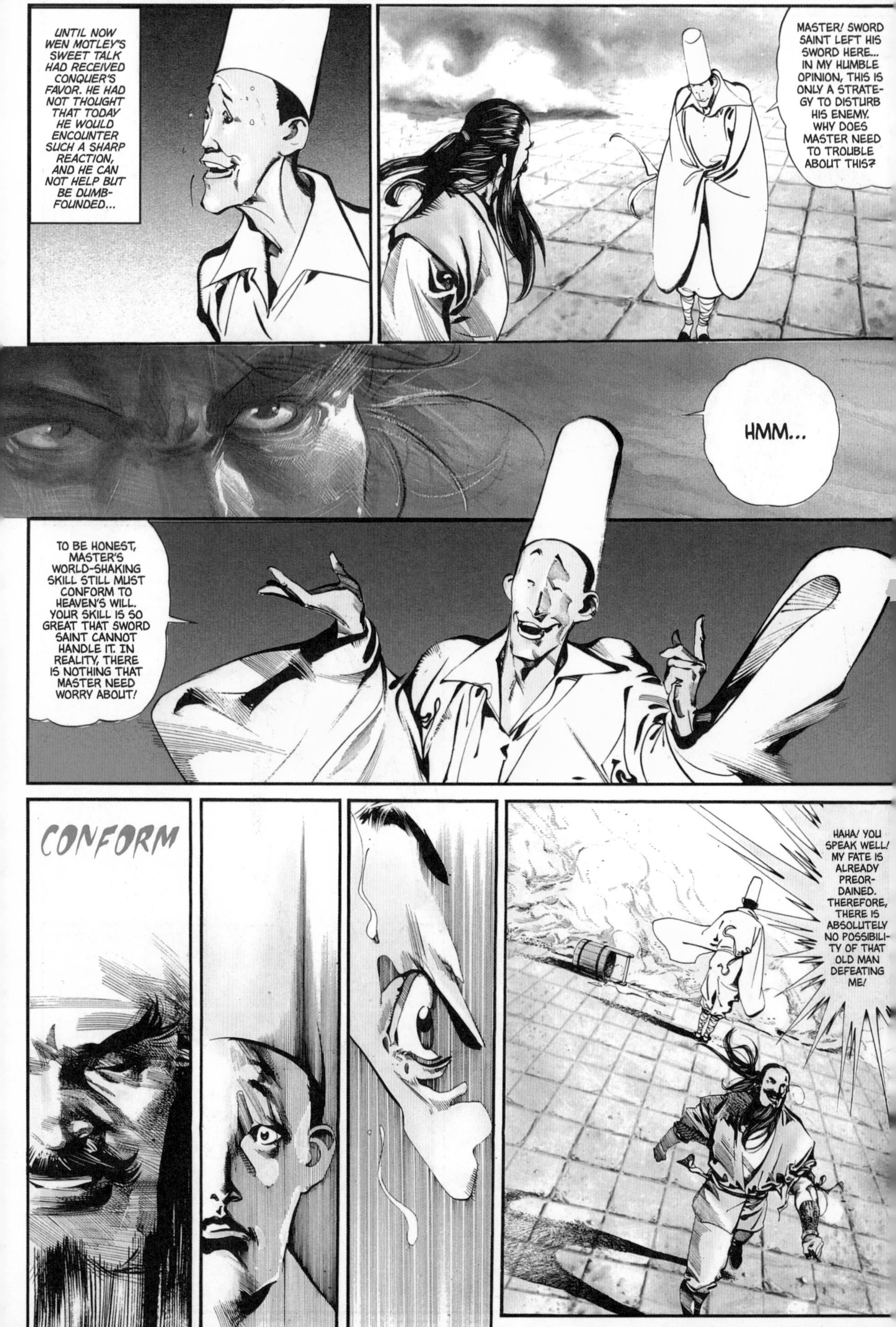
UNTIL NOW WEN MOTLEY'S SWEET TALK HAD RECEIVED CONQUER'S FAVOR. HE HAD NOT THOUGHT THAT TODAY HE WOULD ENCOUNTER SUCH A SHARP REACTION, AND HE CAN NOT HELP BUT BE DUMB-FOUNDED...
MASTER! SWORD SAINT LEFT HIS SWORD HERE... IN MY HUMBLE OPINION, THIS IS ONLY A STRATE-GY TO DISTURB HIS ENEMY. WHY DOES MASTER NEED TO TROUBLE ABOUT THIS?
HMM...
TO BE HONEST, MASTER'S WORLD-SHAKING SKILL STILL MUST CONFORM TO HEAVEN'S WILL. YOUR SKILL IS SO GREAT THAT SWORD SAINT CANNOT HANDLE IT. IN REALITY, THERE IS NOTHING THAT MASTER NEED WORRY ABOUT!
CONFORM
HAHA! YOU SPEAK WELL! MY FATE IS ALREADY PREOR-DAINED. THEREFORE, THERE IS ABSOLUTELY NO POSSIBILI-TY OF THAT OLD MAN DEFEATING ME!

WEN MOTLEY'S HEART SUDDENLY TURNS TO ICE, BECAUSE HE KNOWS THAT HE HAS SAID THE WRONG THING.

HP...HP......

HE WOULD PAY ANY PRICE TO TAKE THAT SENTENCE BACK... GIVE ANYTHING THAT HE HAS, EVEN TURN INTO A DEAF-MUTE...

TODAY I AM IN A GOOD MOOD. COME HAVE A FEW ROUNDS OF DRINKS WITH ME. THE JOY OF DRINK WILL BE THE SOLUTION.

BOOM

START YOUR SEARCH, BROTH-ERS!

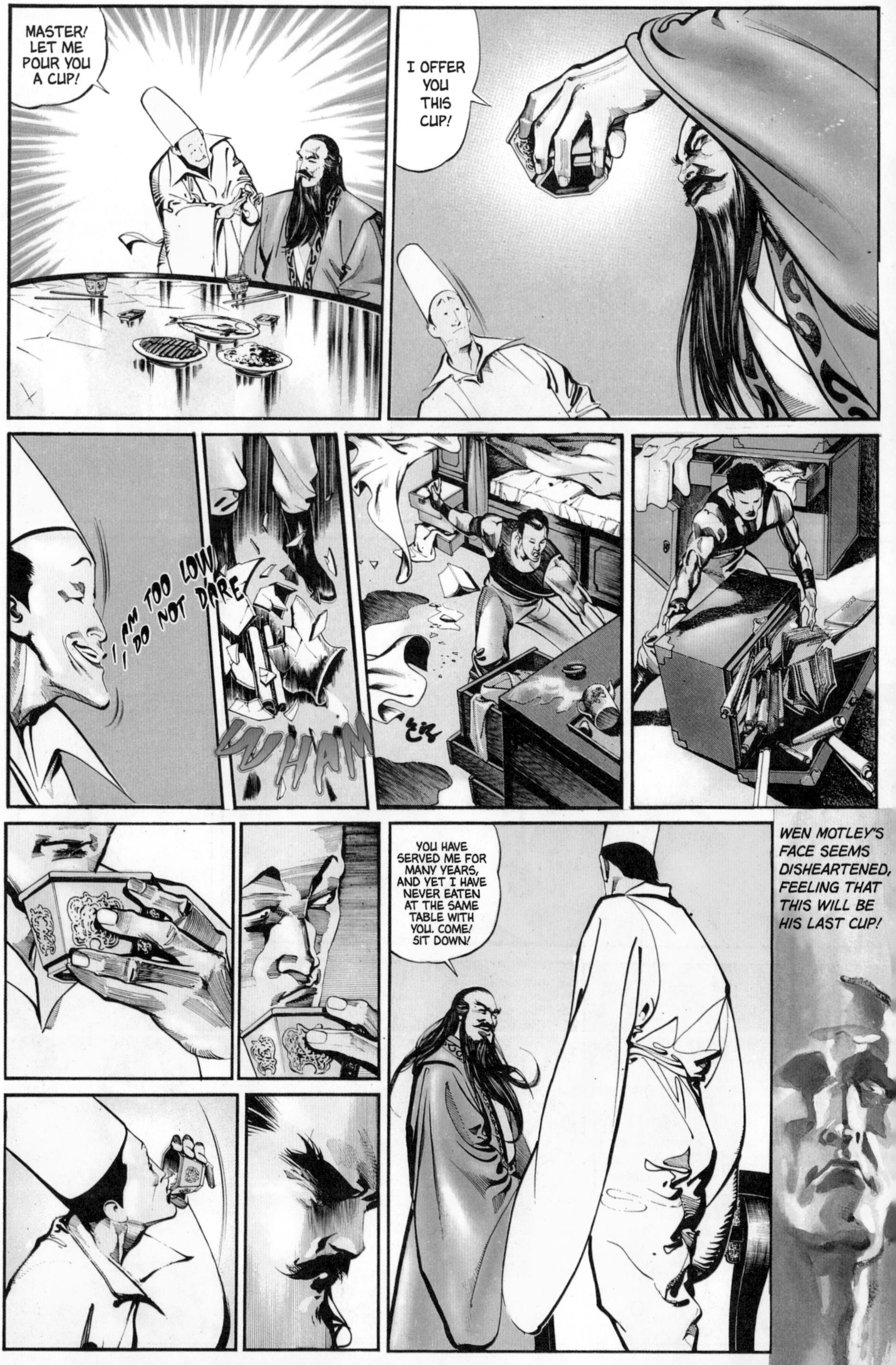
MASTER! LET ME POUR YOU A CUP!
I OFFER YOU THIS CUP!
I AM TOO LOW! I DO NOT DARE
WHAM
YOU HAVE SERVED ME FOR MANY YEARS, AND YET I HAVE NEVER EATEN AT THE SAME TABLE WITH YOU. COME! SIT DOWN!
WEN MOTLEY'S FACE SEEMS DISHEARTENED, FEELING THAT THIS WILL BE HIS LAST CUP!

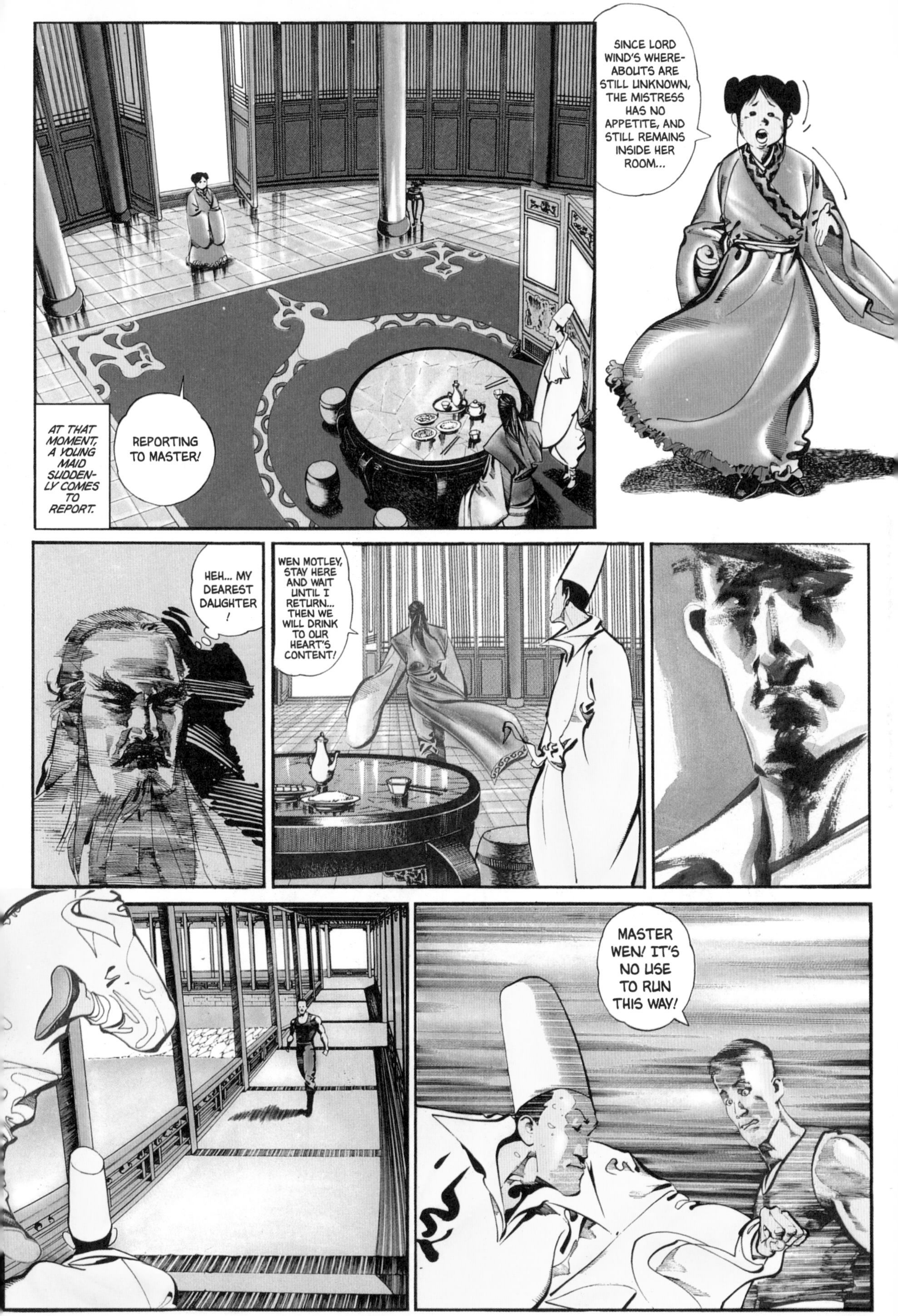
AT THAT MOMENT, A YOUNG MAID SUDDEN-LY COMES TO REPORT.
REPORTING TO MASTER!
SINCE LORD WIND'S WHERE-ABOUTS ARE STILL UNKNOWN, THE MISTRESS HAS NO APPETITE, AND STILL REMAINS INSIDE HER ROOM...
HEH... MY DEAREST DAUGHTER!
WEN MOTLEY, STAY HERE AND WAIT UNTIL I RETURN... THEN WE WILL DRINK TO OUR HEART'S CONTENT!
MASTER WEN! IT'S NO USE TO RUN THIS WAY!

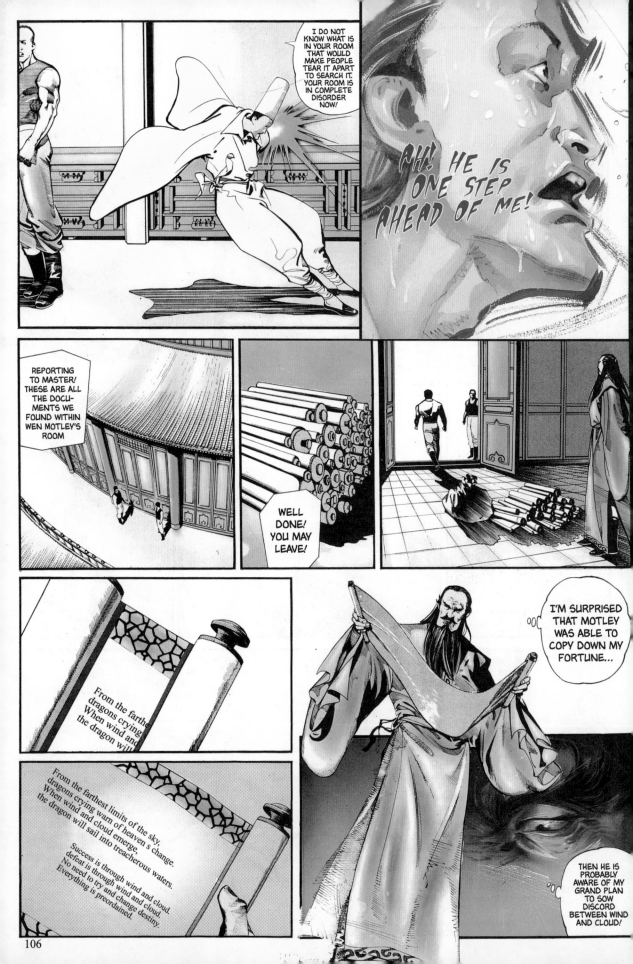

I DO NOT KNOW WHAT IS IN YOUR ROOM THAT WOULD MAKE PEOPLE TEAR IT APART TO SEARCH IT. YOUR ROOM IS IN COMPLETE DISORDER NOW!

AH! HE IS ONE STEP AHEAD OF ME!

REPORTING TO MASTER! THESE ARE ALL THE DOCUMENTS WE FOUND WITHIN WEN MOTLEY'S ROOM

WELL DONE! YOU MAY LEAVE!

I'M SURPRISED THAT MOTLEY WAS ABLE TO COPY DOWN MY FORTUNE...

From the farthest dragons crying When wind and the dragon will

From the farthest limits of the sky, dragons crying warn of heaven's change. When wind and cloud emerge, the dragon will sail into treacherous waters.

Success is through wind and cloud. defeat is through wind and cloud. No need to try and change destiny. Everything is preordained.

THEN HE IS PROBABLY AWARE OF MY GRAND PLAN TO SOW DISCORD BETWEEN WIND AND CLOUD!

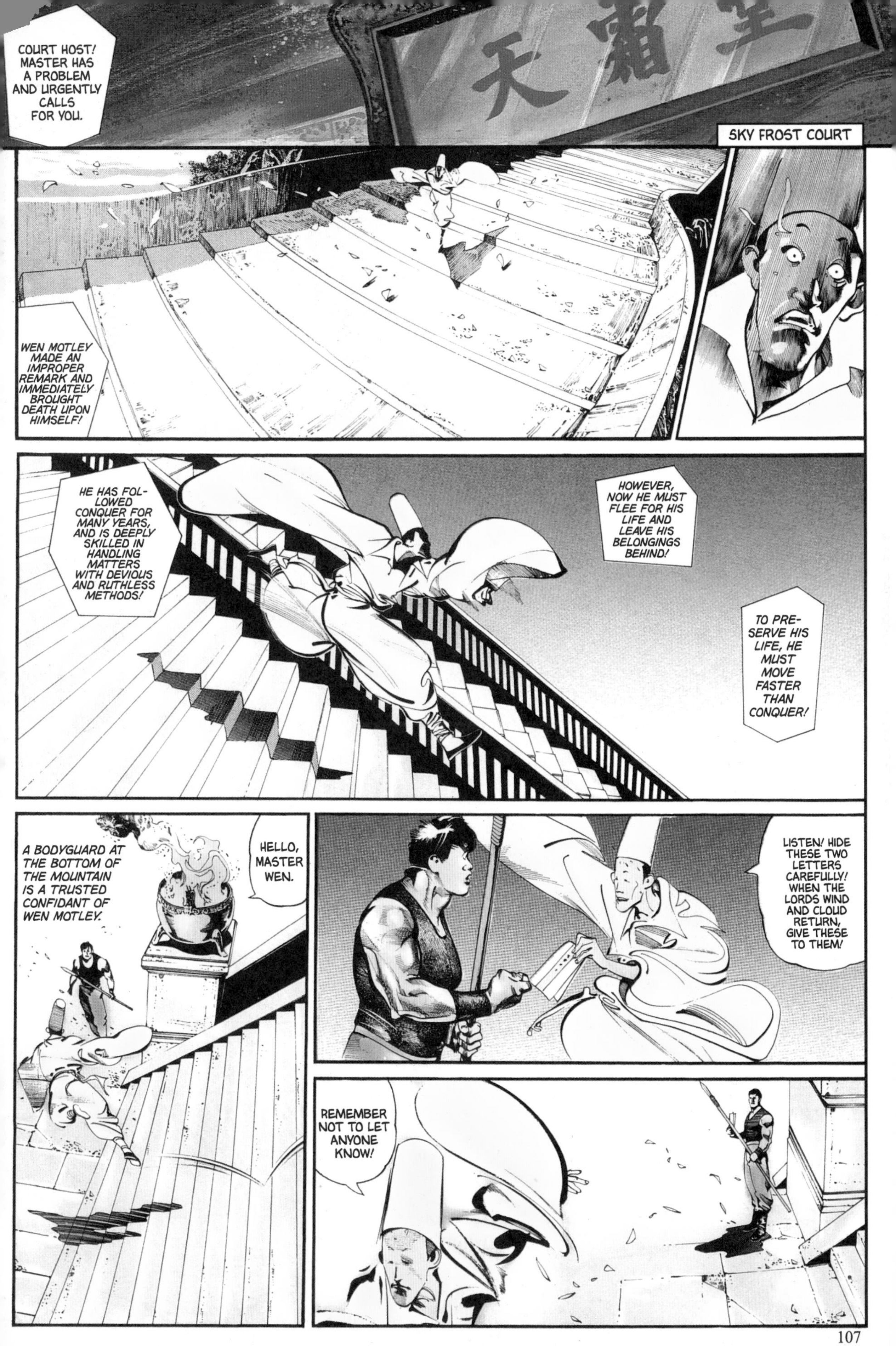
COURT HOST! MASTER HAS A PROBLEM AND URGENTLY CALLS FOR YOU.
天霜堂
SKY FROST COURT
WEN MOTLEY MADE AN IMPROPER REMARK AND IMMEDIATELY BROUGHT DEATH UPON HIMSELF!
HE HAS FOL-LOWED CONQUER FOR MANY YEARS, AND IS DEEPLY SKILLED IN HANDLING MATTERS WITH DEVIOUS AND RUTHLESS METHODS!
HOWEVER, NOW HE MUST FLEE FOR HIS LIFE AND LEAVE HIS BELONGINGS BEHIND!
TO PRE-SERVE HIS LIFE, HE MUST MOVE FASTER THAN CONQUER!
A BODYGUARD AT THE BOTTOM OF THE MOUNTAIN IS A TRUSTED CONFIDANT OF WEN MOTLEY.
HELLO, MASTER WEN.
LISTEN! HIDE THESE TWO LETTERS CAREFULLY! WHEN THE LORDS WIND AND CLOUD RETURN, GIVE THESE TO THEM!
REMEMBER NOT TO LET ANYONE KNOW!

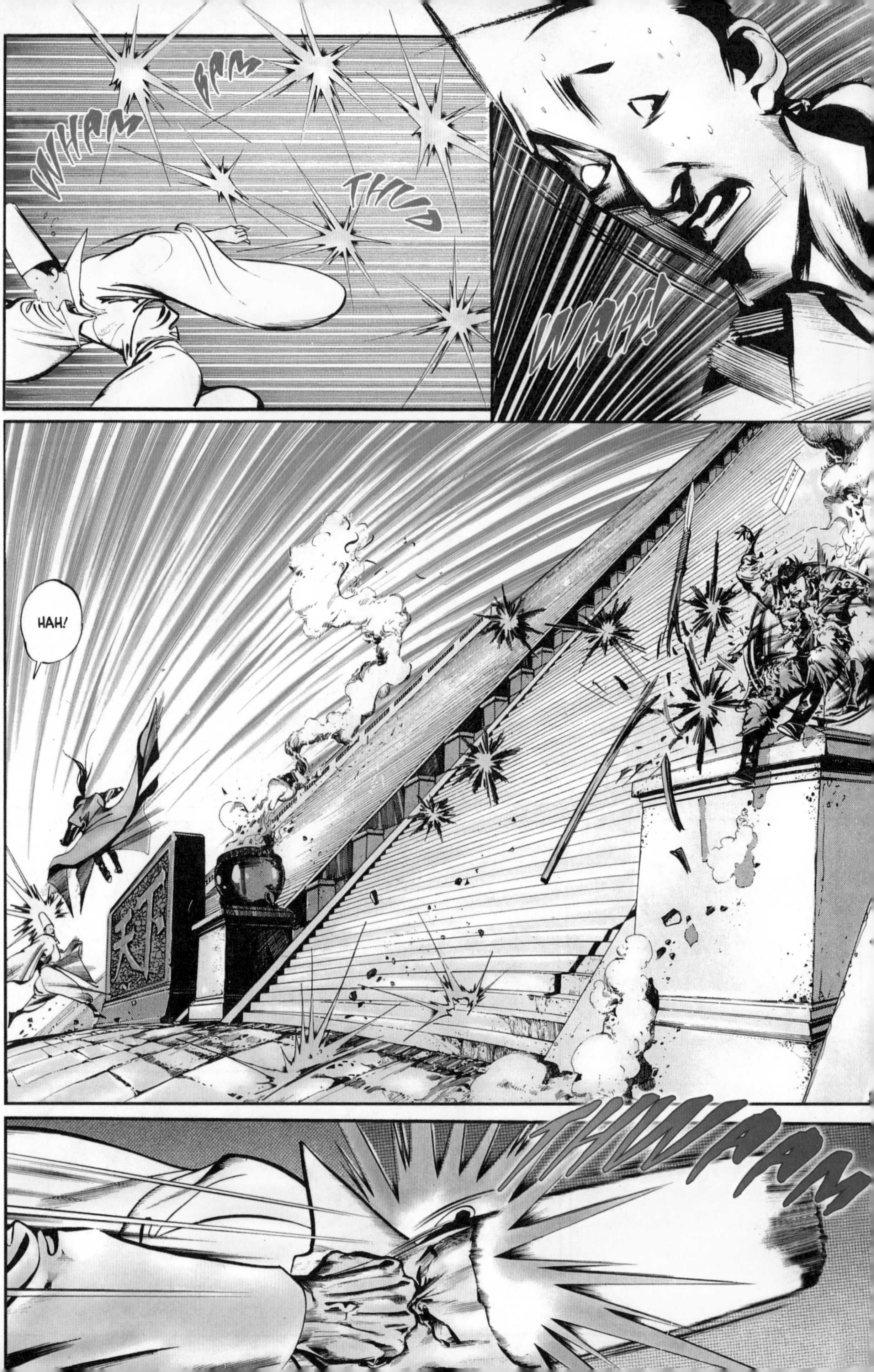

WHAM
BAM
THUD
WAH!
HAH!
THWAAM

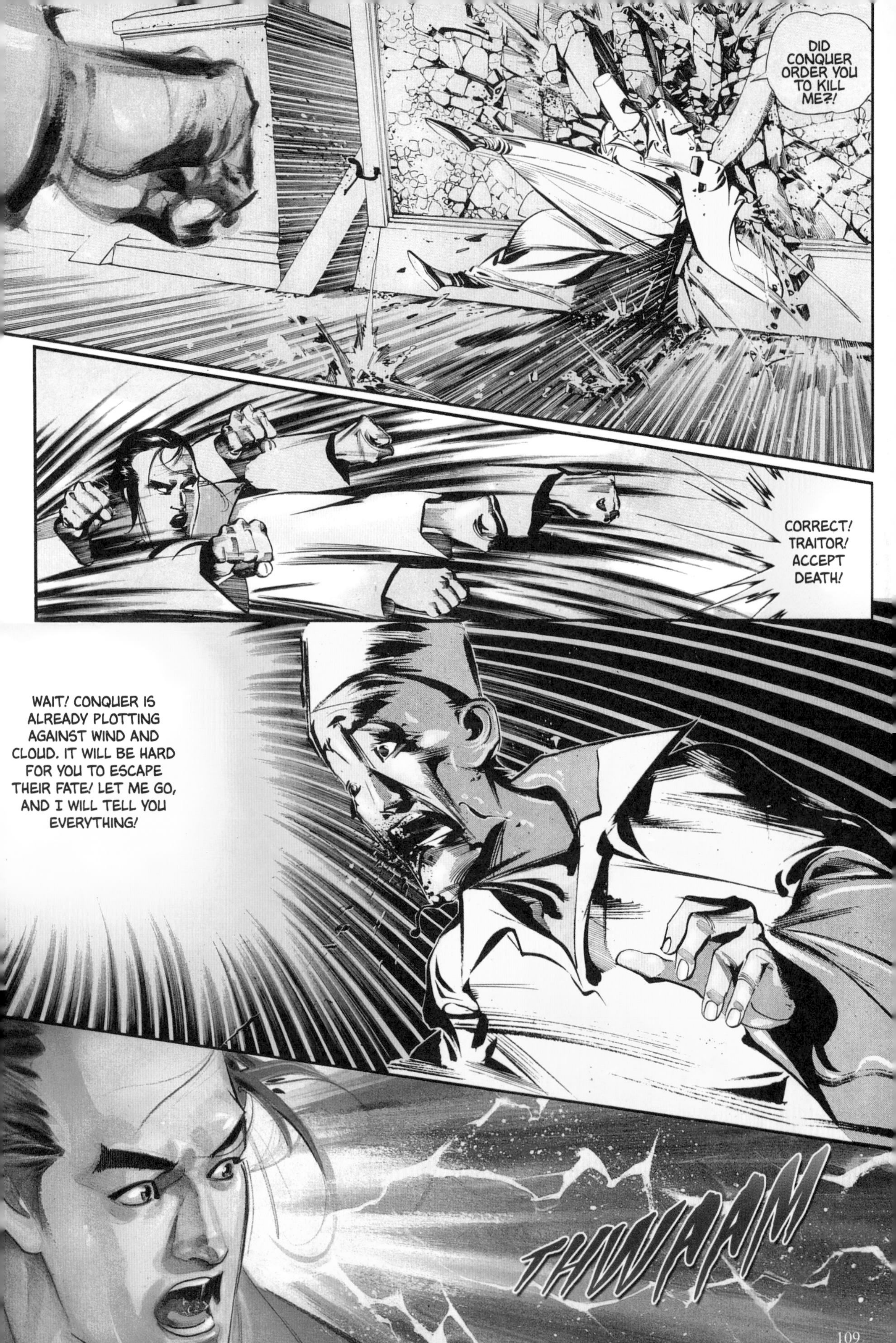
DID CONQUER ORDER YOU TO KILL ME?!
CORRECT! TRAITOR! ACCEPT DEATH!
WAIT! CONQUER IS ALREADY PLOTTING AGAINST WIND AND CLOUD. IT WILL BE HARD FOR YOU TO ESCAPE THEIR FATE! LET ME GO, AND I WILL TELL YOU EVERYTHING!
THWAAM

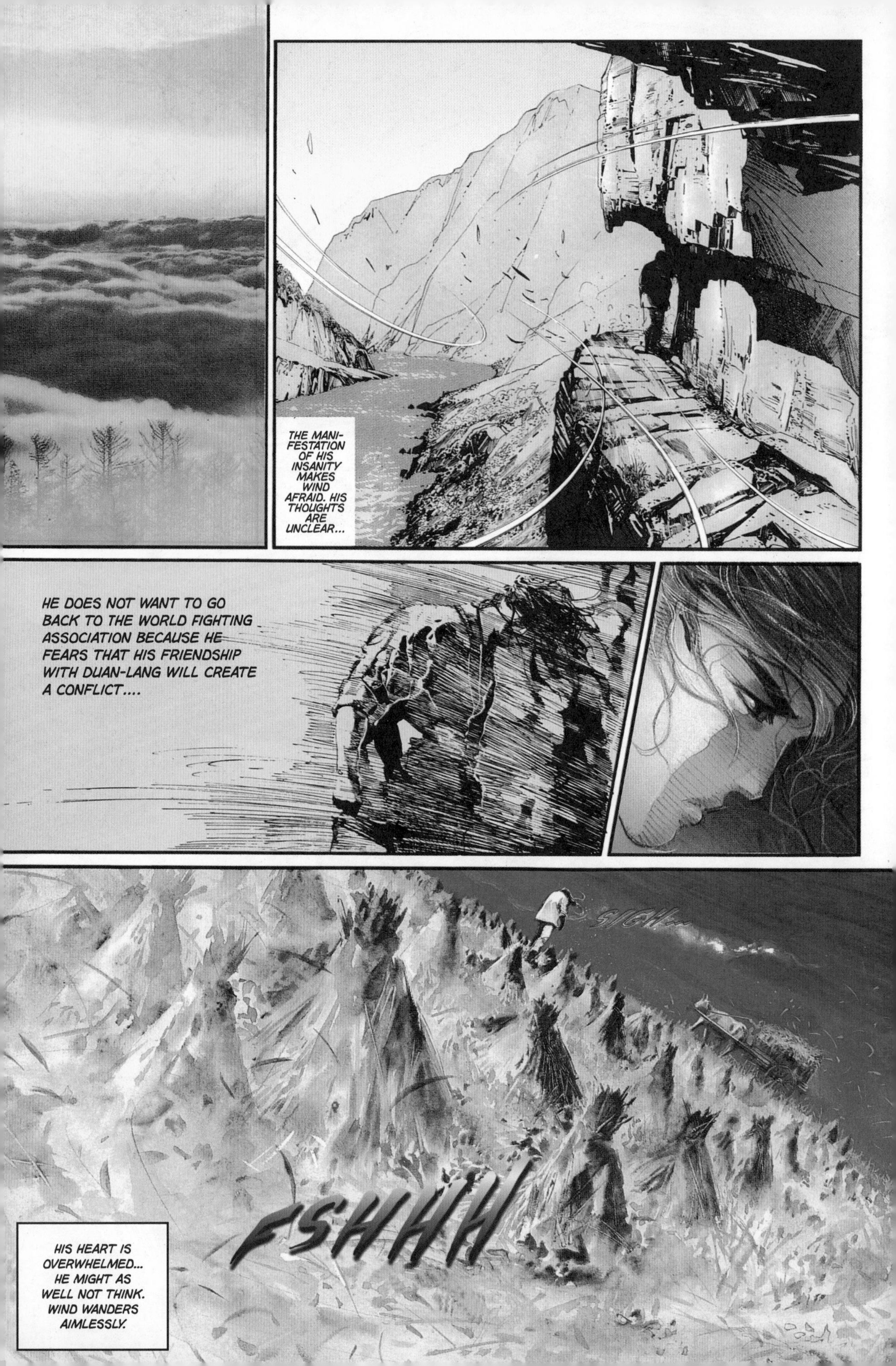

THE MANI-FESTATION OF HIS INSANITY MAKES WIND AFRAID. HIS THOUGHTS ARE UNCLEAR...
HE DOES NOT WANT TO GO BACK TO THE WORLD FIGHTING ASSOCIATION BECAUSE HE FEARS THAT HIS FRIENDSHIP WITH DUAN-LANG WILL CREATE A CONFLICT....
SIGH...
FSHHH
HIS HEART IS OVERWHELMED... HE MIGHT AS WELL NOT THINK. WIND WANDERS AIMLESSLY.

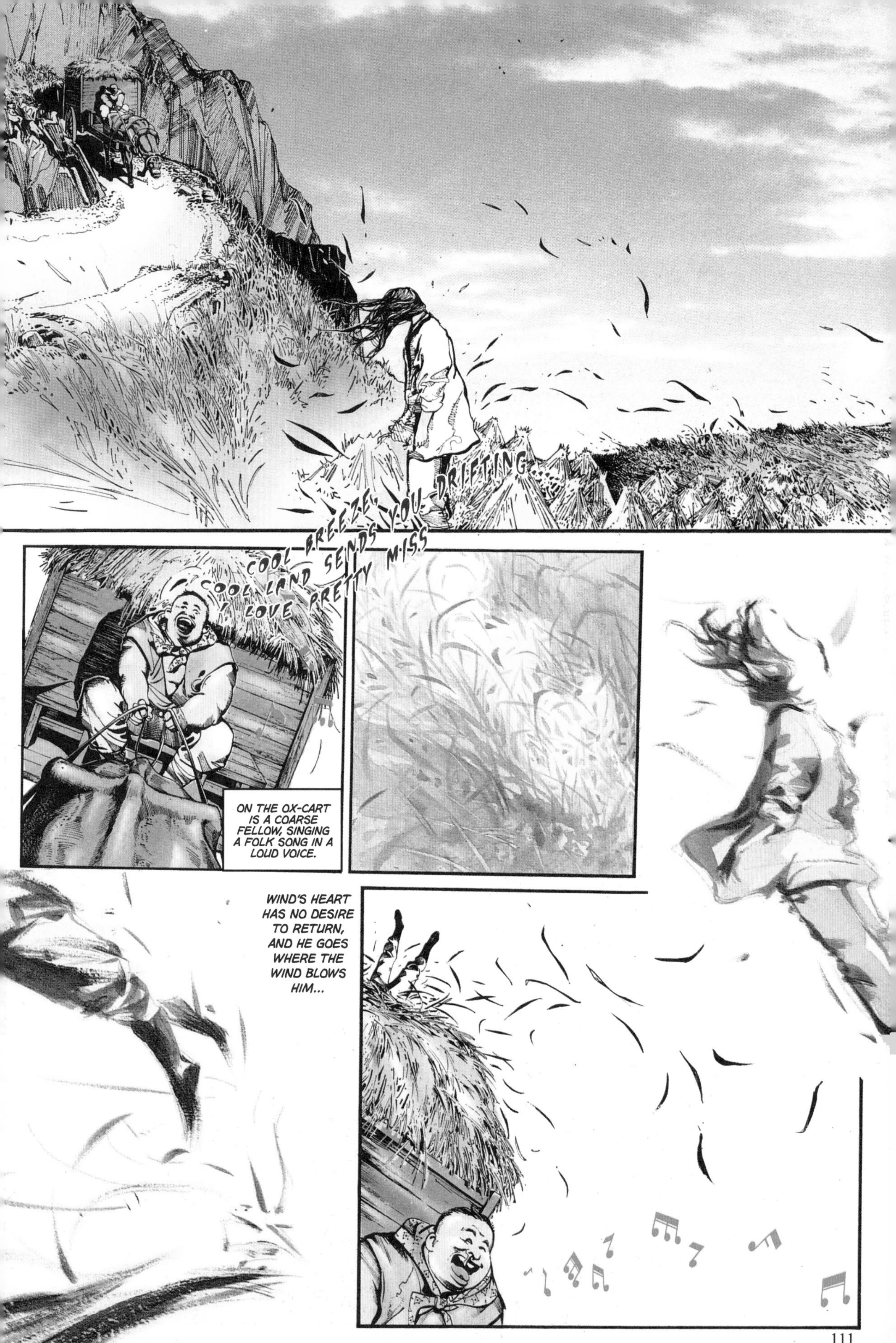
COOL BREEZE, YOU DRIFTING...
COOL LAND SENDS YOU PRETTY MISS
I LOVE
ON THE OX-CART IS A COARSE FELLOW, SINGING A FOLK SONG IN A LOUD VOICE.
WIND'S HEART HAS NO DESIRE TO RETURN, AND HE GOES WHERE THE WIND BLOWS HIM...

♪ MOUNTAIN MAIDEN BEAUTIFUL AND SWEET

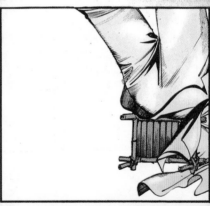

LARGE MOUTH, DELICATE EYES BORN TO BE MINE

112

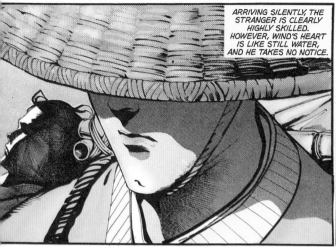

ARRIVING SILENTLY, THE STRANGER IS CLEARLY HIGHLY SKILLED. HOWEVER, WIND'S HEART IS LIKE STILL WATER, AND HE TAKES NO NOTICE.

AH!

YOU NOISY BUFFOON, IF YOU WANT TO LIVE, SHUT YOUR MOUTH RIGHT NOW!

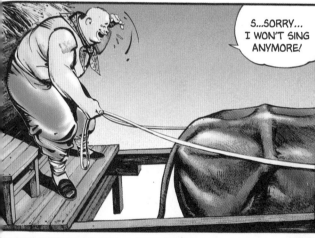

S...SORRY... I WON'T SING ANYMORE!

GET OUT OF MY WAY!

SURE! I WILL IMMEDIATELY GO BY ANOTHER ROUTE!

HOLD IT!

113

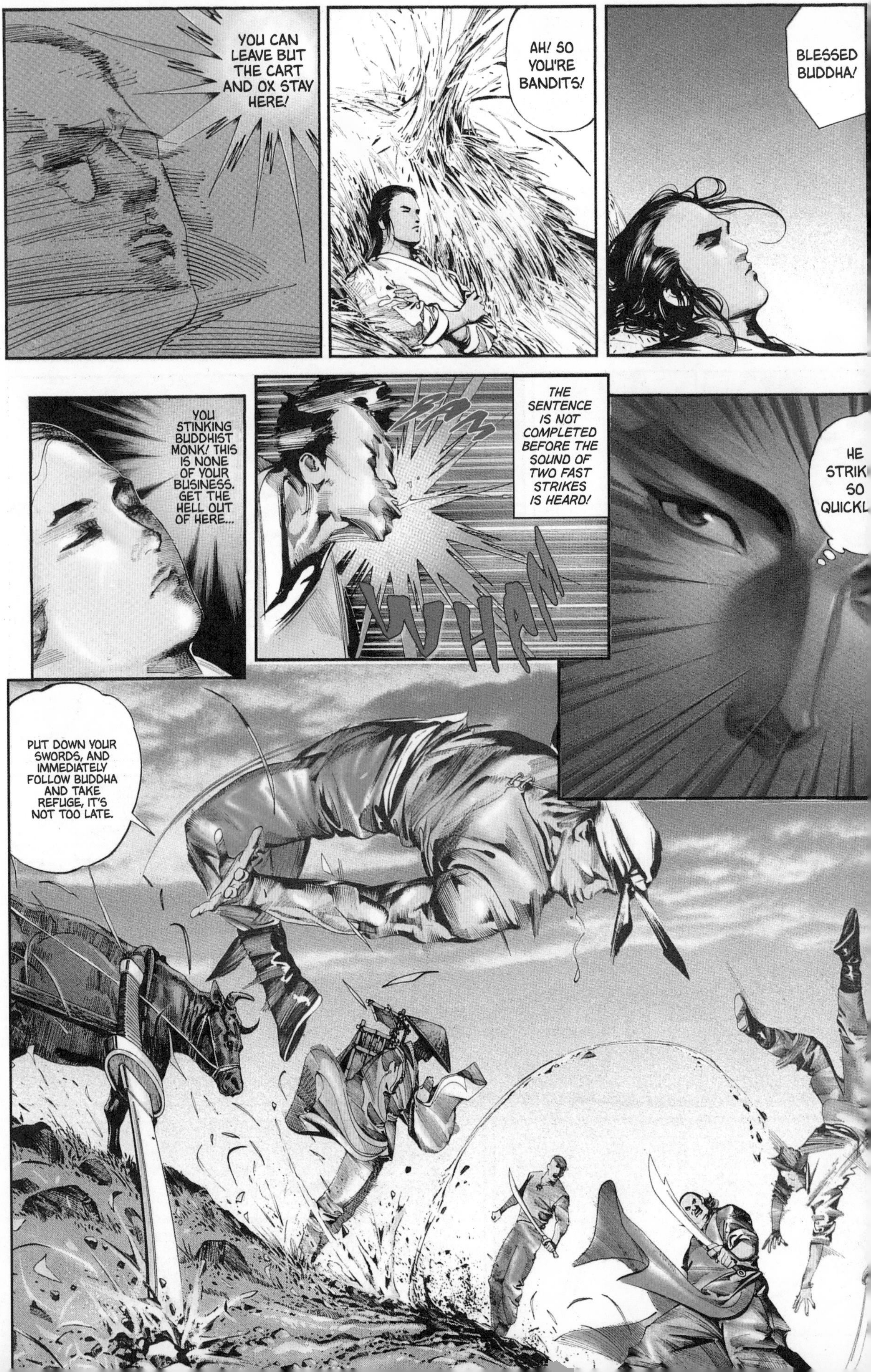
YOU CAN LEAVE BUT THE CART AND OX STAY HERE!
AH! SO YOU'RE BANDITS!
BLESSED BUDDHA!
YOU STINKING BUDDHIST MONK! THIS IS NONE OF YOUR BUSINESS. GET THE HELL OUT OF HERE...
THE SENTENCE IS NOT COMPLETED BEFORE THE SOUND OF TWO FAST STRIKES IS HEARD!
WHAM
PUT DOWN YOUR SWORDS, AND IMMEDIATELY FOLLOW BUDDHA AND TAKE REFUGE, IT'S NOT TOO LATE.

HAH! NONSENSE! THIS MONK MUST BE GET-TING TIRED OF LIVING. LET US HELP YOU GET TO HEAVEN!
HMM! THERE IS NOT A SINGLE DAY WITHOUT A DISPUTE AMONG THE CIRCLE OF FIGHTERS. WHEN WILL THESE CON-FLICTS COME TO AN END AT LAST?
TRANSFORMATION KNACK
'S THE YCLE OF AUSE AND FECT...
WHACK
FROM YOUR EVIL CAUSE, YOU RECEIVE ITS EVIL EFFECTS!

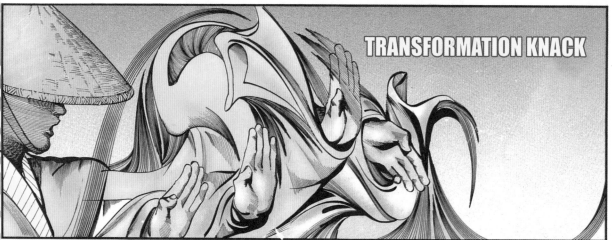

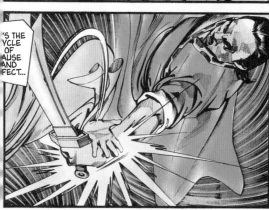

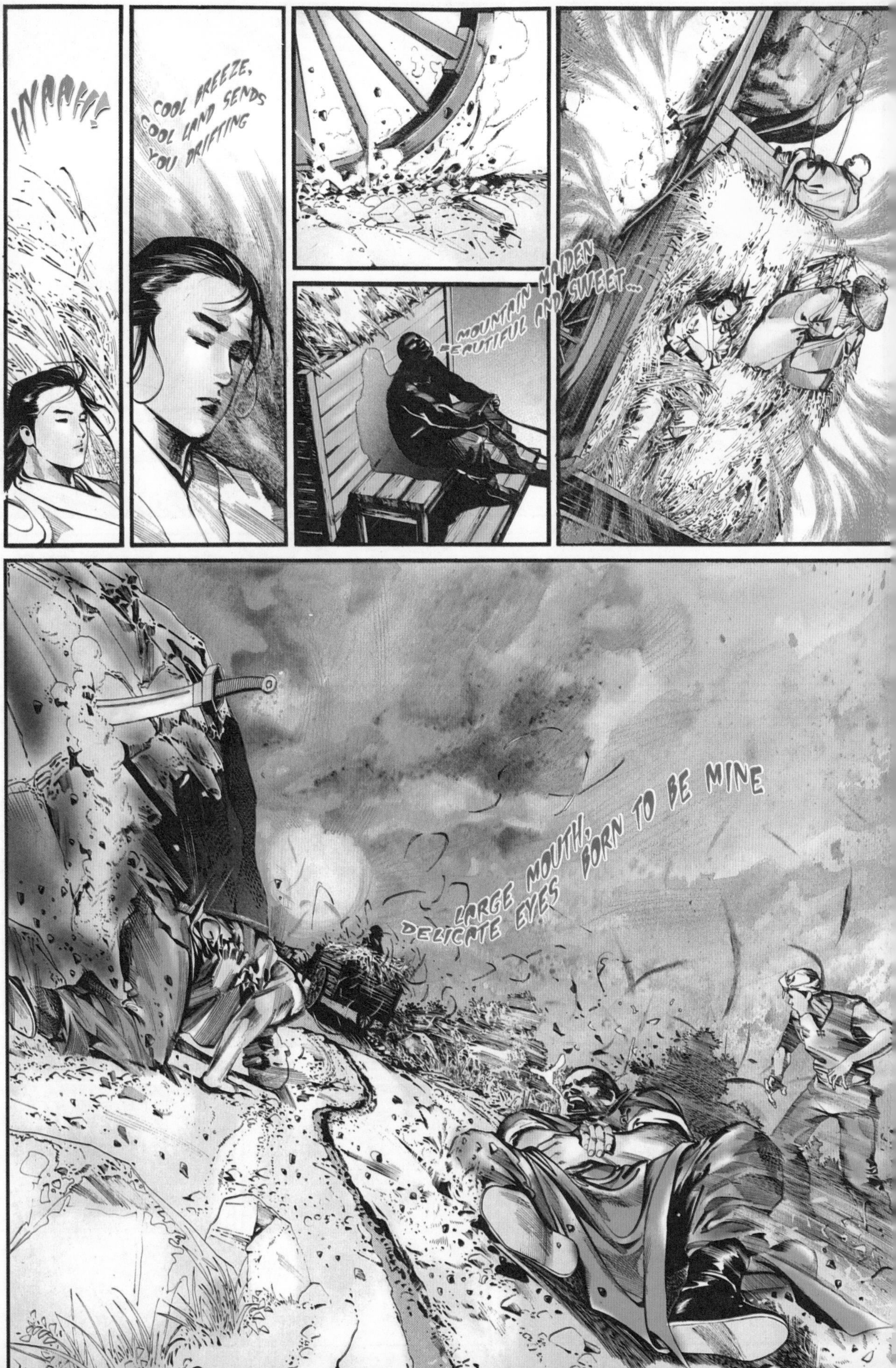
HYAAH!
COOL BREEZE, COOL LAND SENDS YOU DRIFTING
MOUNTAIN MAIDEN BEAUTIFUL AND SWEET...
LARGE MOUTH, DELICATE EYES BORN TO BE MINE

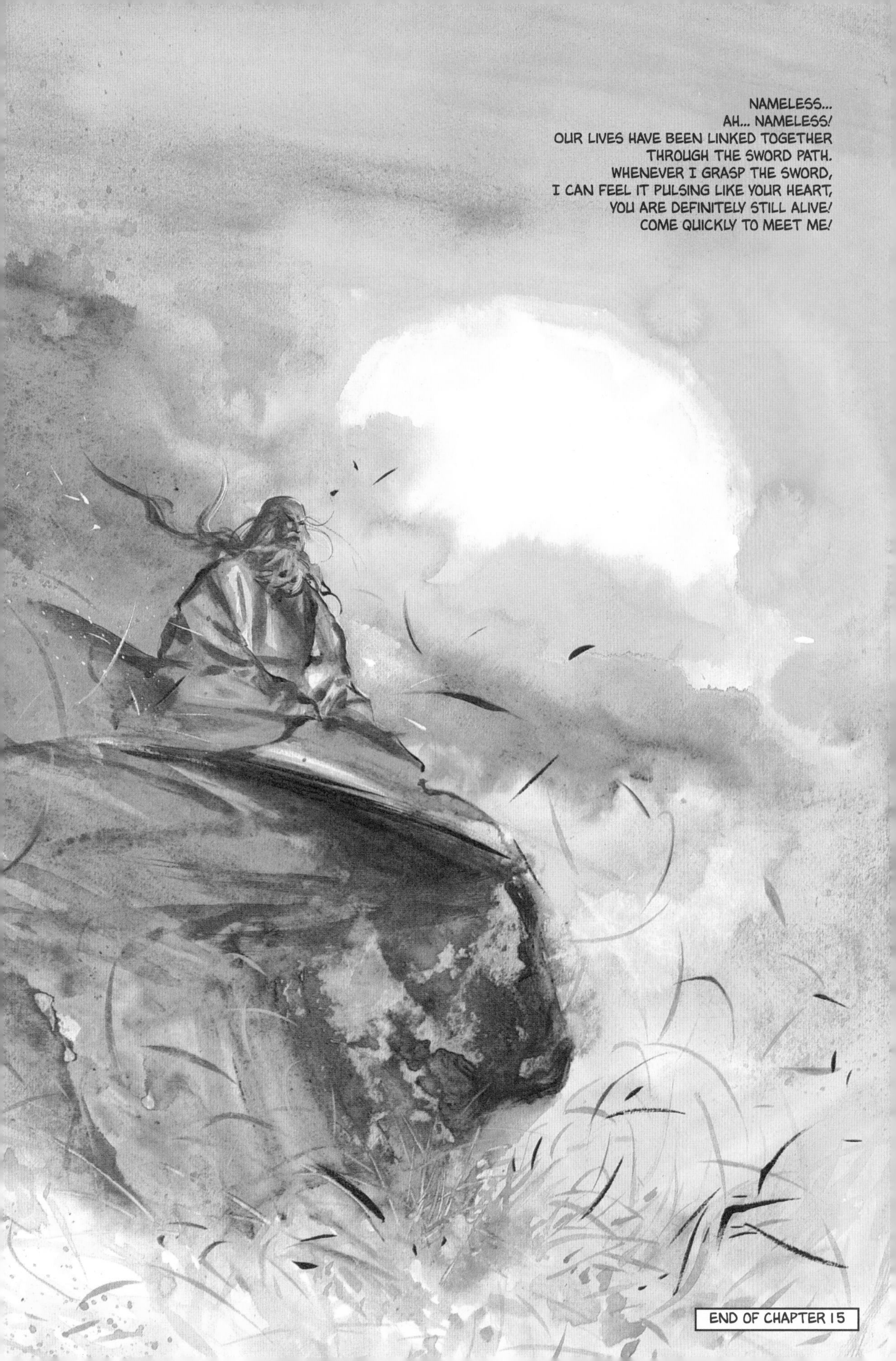
NAMELESS...
AH... NAMELESS!
OUR LIVES HAVE BEEN LINKED TOGETHER
THROUGH THE SWORD PATH.
WHENEVER I GRASP THE SWORD,
I CAN FEEL IT PULSING LIKE YOUR HEART,
YOU ARE DEFINITELY STILL ALIVE!
COME QUICKLY TO MEET ME!
END OF CHAPTER 15

Author's Notes

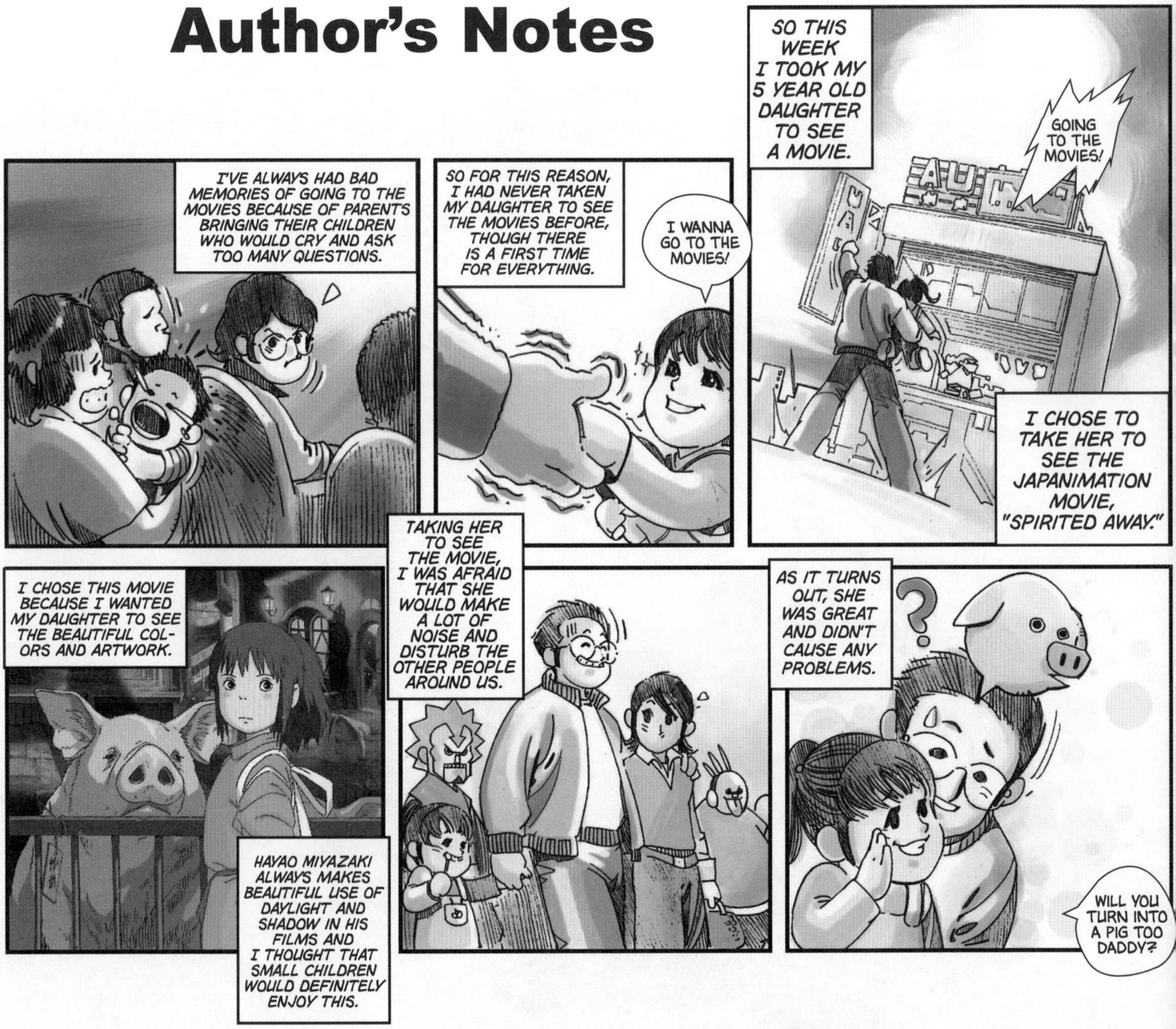

I'VE ALWAYS HAD BAD MEMORIES OF GOING TO THE MOVIES BECAUSE OF PARENTS BRINGING THEIR CHILDREN WHO WOULD CRY AND ASK TOO MANY QUESTIONS.
SO FOR THIS REASON, I HAD NEVER TAKEN MY DAUGHTER TO SEE THE MOVIES BEFORE, THOUGH THERE IS A FIRST TIME FOR EVERYTHING.
I WANNA GO TO THE MOVIES!
SO THIS WEEK I TOOK MY 5 YEAR OLD DAUGHTER TO SEE A MOVIE.
GOING TO THE MOVIES!
I CHOSE TO TAKE HER TO SEE THE JAPANIMATION MOVIE, "SPIRITED AWAY."
I CHOSE THIS MOVIE BECAUSE I WANTED MY DAUGHTER TO SEE THE BEAUTIFUL COLORS AND ARTWORK.
HAYAO MIYAZAKI ALWAYS MAKES BEAUTIFUL USE OF DAYLIGHT AND SHADOW IN HIS FILMS AND I THOUGHT THAT SMALL CHILDREN WOULD DEFINITELY ENJOY THIS.
TAKING HER TO SEE THE MOVIE, I WAS AFRAID THAT SHE WOULD MAKE A LOT OF NOISE AND DISTURB THE OTHER PEOPLE AROUND US.
AS IT TURNS OUT, SHE WAS GREAT AND DIDN'T CAUSE ANY PROBLEMS.
?
WILL YOU TURN INTO A PIG TOO DADDY?

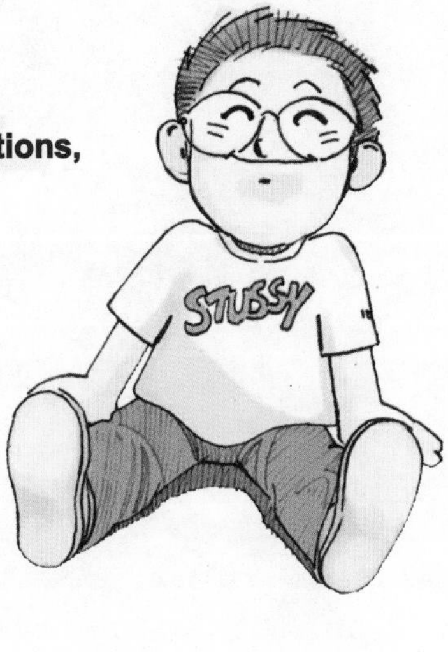

STUSSY

If you have any comments or suggestions, we'd really like to hear from you.

Jonesky Limited
Room 1205-1208, 12F,
Westlands Centre, 20 Westlands Road,
Quarry Bay, Hong Kong
WWW.COMICSWORLD.COM

STORM RIDERS 風雲

Storm Riders volume 5 Coming out in June!

Vind goes to Lin-Yin Cave to visit the scene of his ather's death. To his surprise, Cloud is being held aptive within the cave. Cloud reveals that the killer of Vind's father was the Flame Kylin Beast. After Wind ees him, Cloud is unable to repress his urges and ontinues his affair with Kong-Chi (Frost's wife). When Vind discovers their tryst, he offers this ultimatum: bandon Kong-Chi or abandon the World Fighting ssociation. Unable to choose between the two, Cloud ecides his only alternative is to kill Wind. Wind and loud launch into battle, eaving Kong-Chi caught in ne middle.

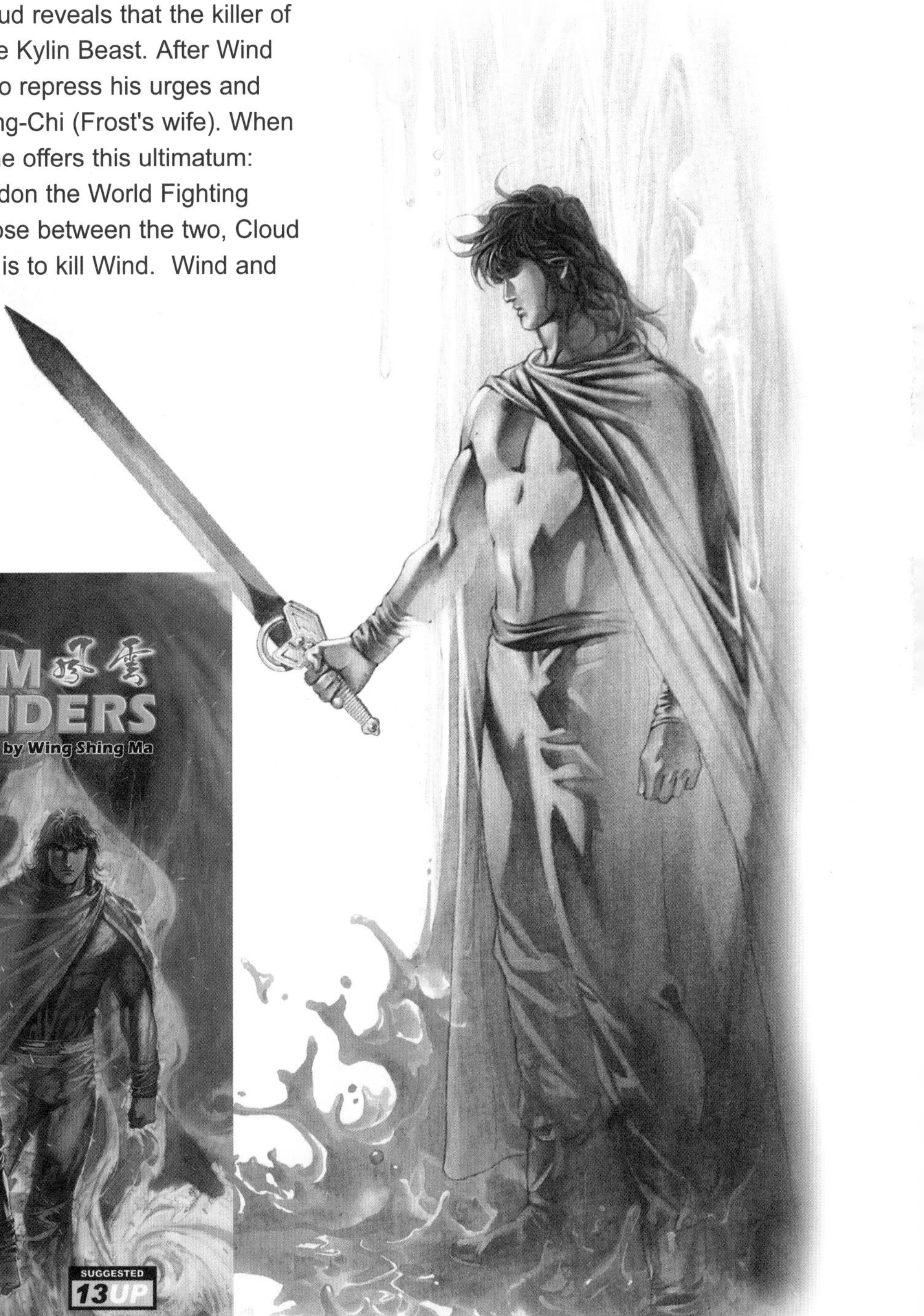

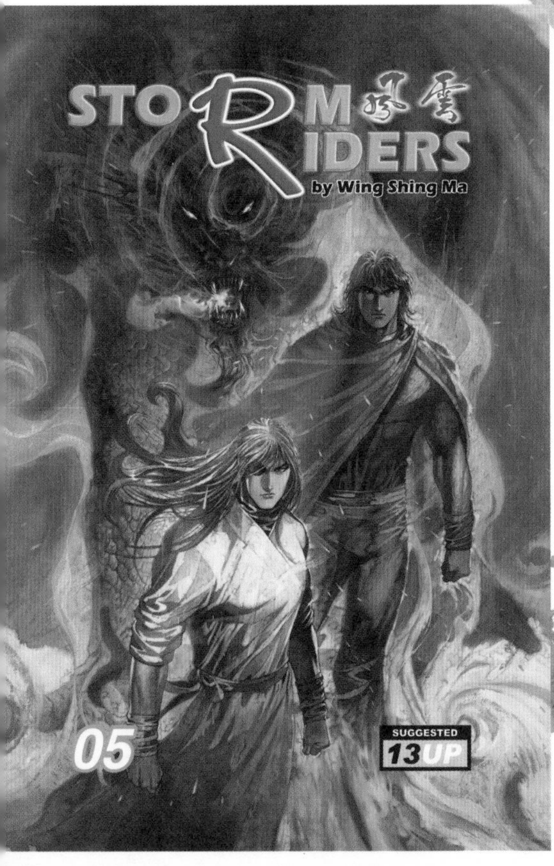

STORM RIDERS 風雲
by Wing Shing Ma
05
SUGGESTED
13UP

STORM 風雲 RIDERS
Merchandise

Snowy Saber: 9 inch Letter Opener (box included)

Flame Kylin Sword: 5.5 inch Letter Opener

Hero Sword: 9 inch Letter
Opener (box included)

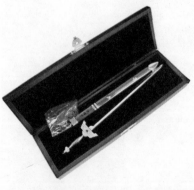

**Please visit our website for
order and weapon information
at www.comicsone.com or
www.comicsworld.com**

STORM RIDERS

by Wing Shing Ma

WHO'S YOUR FAVORITE MEMBER OF WILD 7?

Welcome to Wild 7, a wild tale about a group of bandits commissioned by the Japanese government to eradicat[e] any and all potential threats to the status quo. Read as Hiba, an incarcerated felon, gathers a group of outlaw[s] to form and lead the group known as Wild 7. See as this bunch of ruffians try to overthrow a corrupt politicia[n]. Using crooks to fight crooks, you say? Fighting fire with fire is a good thing? Finding the good in the bad an[d] the bad in the good is possible? Let's see what happens…

50+ vols - 200+ pages B&W
Hardcopy: US $9.95 each

Mikiya Mochizuki
WILD 7

JOAN

Yoshikazu Yasuhiko

Set in Medieval France during the Hundred Years War, Joan is the story of Emil, a young woman raised as a man by Baudricourt, the same man who took Joan of Arc under his wing. Guided by visions of La Pucelle (the name given to Joan by followers), Emil seeks to unite France under the divine rule of the King. In her quest, Emil travels through many of the same landmark battlefields as Joan, and gains her own followers in the process.

Joan is a beautiful full color manga from Yoshikazu Yasuhiko, one of the original character designers of *Mobile Suit Gundam*.

3 vols - 200+ pages Color
Hardcopy: US $14.95 each
eBook: US $4.95 each

JOAN
BOOK I
Yoshikazu Yasuhiko

JOAN
BOOK II
Yoshikazu Yasuhiko

JOAN
BOOK III
Yoshikazu Yasuhiko

FULL COLOR

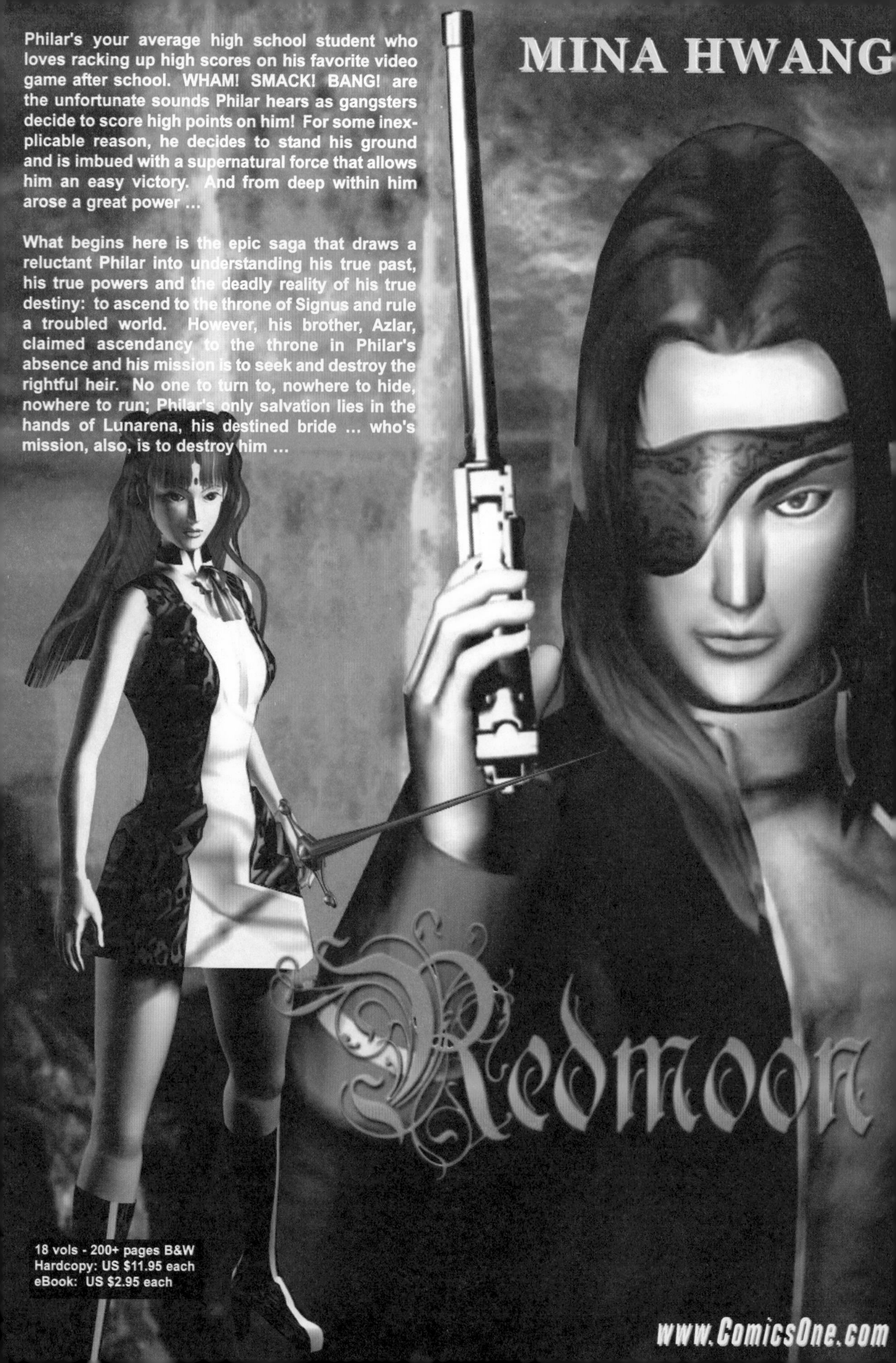
MINA HWANG
Philar's your average high school student who loves racking up high scores on his favorite video game after school. WHAM! SMACK! BANG! are the unfortunate sounds Philar hears as gangsters decide to score high points on him! For some inexplicable reason, he decides to stand his ground and is imbued with a supernatural force that allows him an easy victory. And from deep within him arose a great power ...
What begins here is the epic saga that draws a reluctant Philar into understanding his true past, his true powers and the deadly reality of his true destiny: to ascend to the throne of Signus and rule a troubled world. However, his brother, Azlar, claimed ascendancy to the throne in Philar's absence and his mission is to seek and destroy the rightful heir. No one to turn to, nowhere to hide, nowhere to run; Philar's only salvation lies in the hands of Lunarena, his destined bride ... who's mission, also, is to destroy him ...
Redmoon
18 vols - 200+ pages B&W
Hardcopy: US $11.95 each
eBook: US $2.95 each
www.ComicsOne.com

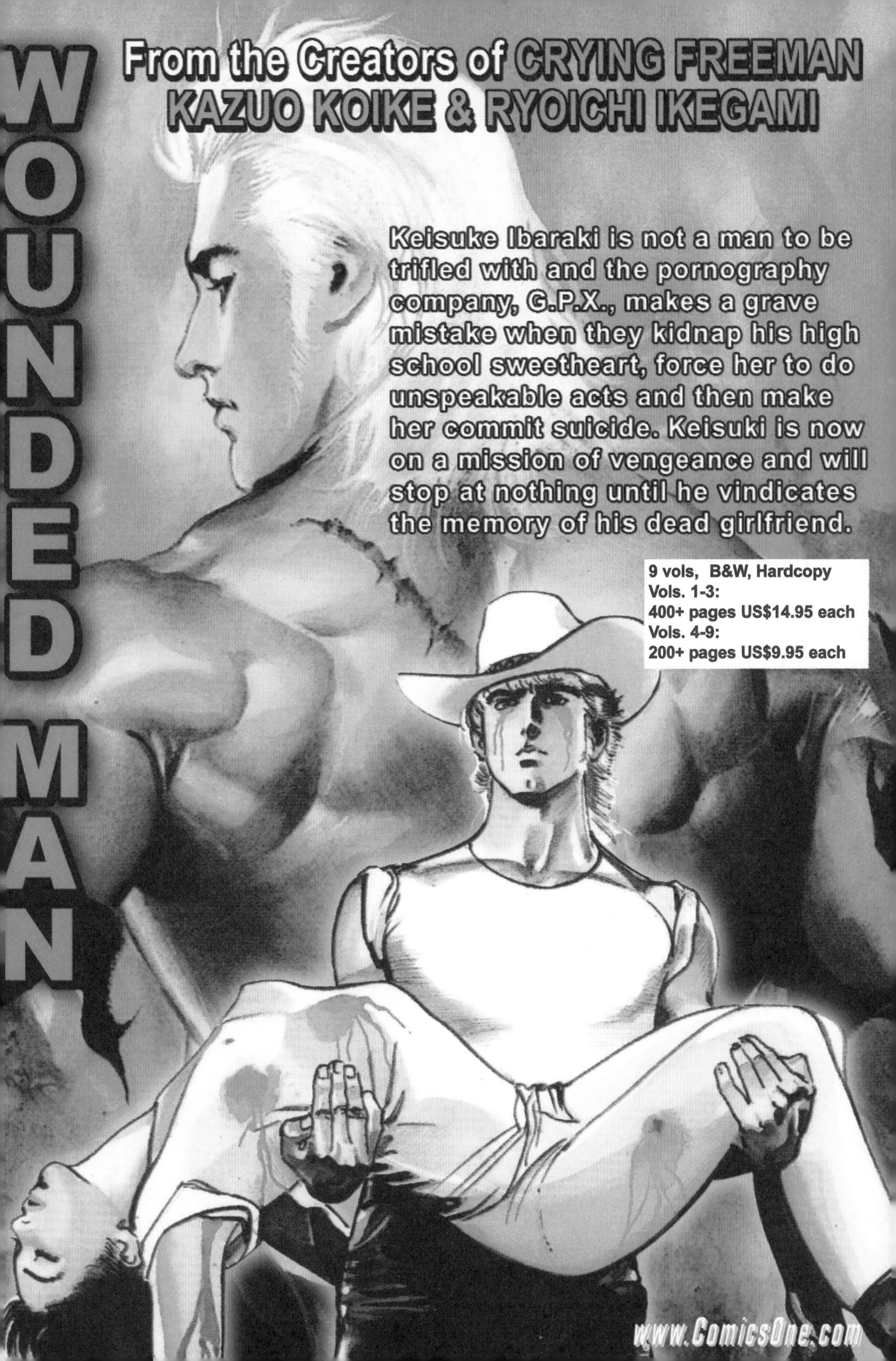
WOUNDED MAN
From the Creators of CRYING FREEMAN
KAZUO KOIKE & RYOICHI IKEGAMI
Keisuke Ibaraki is not a man to be trifled with and the pornography company, G.P.X., makes a grave mistake when they kidnap his high school sweetheart, force her to do unspeakable acts and then make her commit suicide. Keisuki is now on a mission of vengeance and will stop at nothing until he vindicates the memory of his dead girlfriend.
9 vols, B&W, Hardcopy
Vols. 1-3:
400+ pages US$14.95 each
Vols. 4-9:
200+ pages US$9.95 each
www.ComicsOne.com

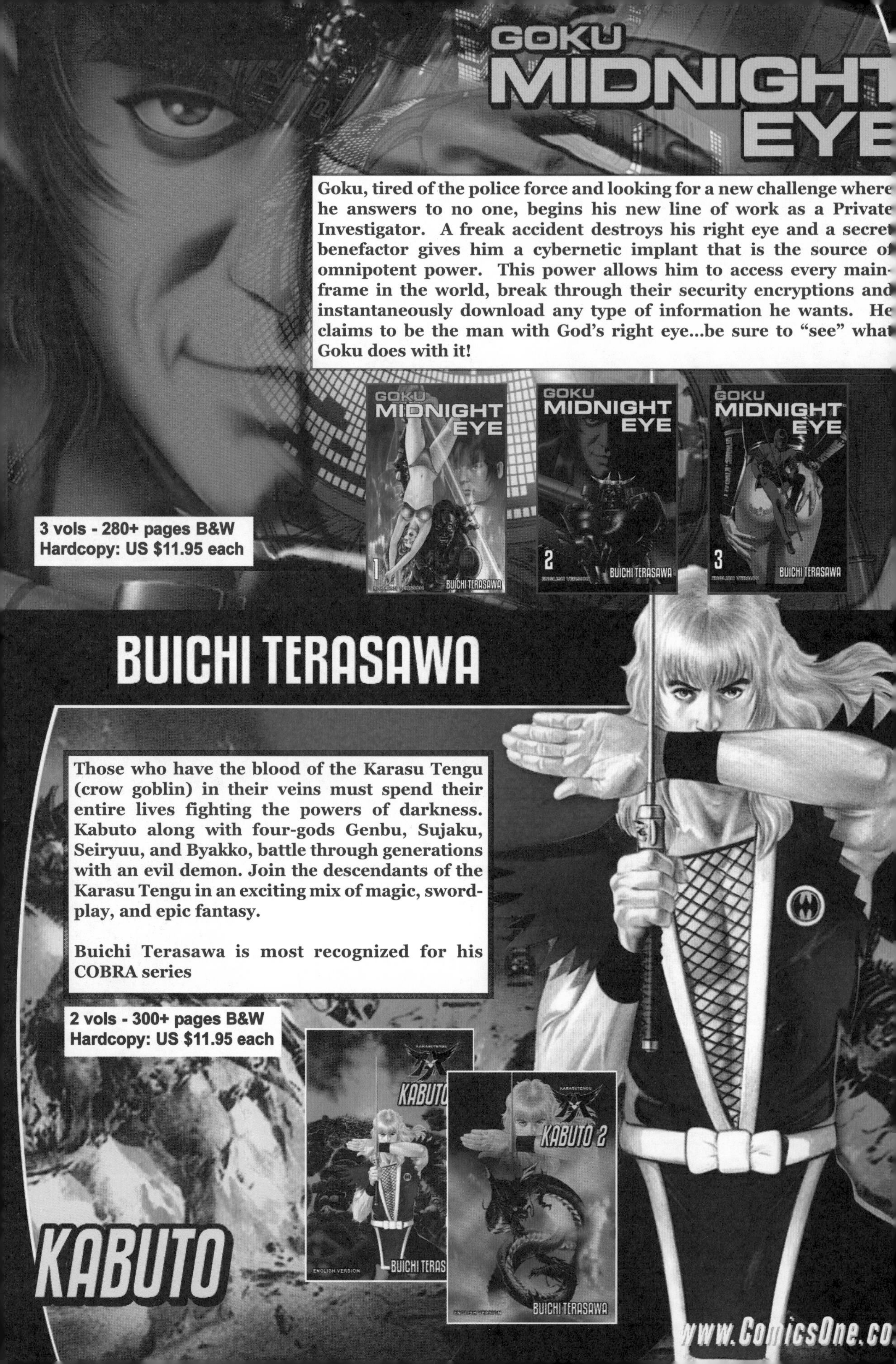
GOKU MIDNIGHT EYE
Goku, tired of the police force and looking for a new challenge where he answers to no one, begins his new line of work as a Private Investigator. A freak accident destroys his right eye and a secret benefactor gives him a cybernetic implant that is the source of omnipotent power. This power allows him to access every mainframe in the world, break through their security encryptions and instantaneously download any type of information he wants. He claims to be the man with God's right eye...be sure to "see" what Goku does with it!
3 vols - 280+ pages B&W
Hardcopy: US $11.95 each
GOKU MIDNIGHT EYE 1 BUICHI TERASAWA
GOKU MIDNIGHT EYE 2 BUICHI TERASAWA
GOKU MIDNIGHT EYE 3 BUICHI TERASAWA
BUICHI TERASAWA
Those who have the blood of the Karasu Tengu (crow goblin) in their veins must spend their entire lives fighting the powers of darkness. Kabuto along with four-gods Genbu, Sujaku, Seiryuu, and Byakko, battle through generations with an evil demon. Join the descendants of the Karasu Tengu in an exciting mix of magic, swordplay, and epic fantasy.
Buichi Terasawa is most recognized for his COBRA series
2 vols - 300+ pages B&W
Hardcopy: US $11.95 each
KABUTO ENGLISH VERSION BUICHI TERAS
KABUTO 2 BUICHI TERASAWA
KABUTO
www.ComicsOne.co